FROM FIGHTING NAPOLEON TO THE SCOTTISH MILITARY ACADEMY

To my lovely granddaughters Hannah and Zara

FROM FIGHTING NAPOLEON TO THE SCOTTISH MILITARY ACADEMY

THE LIFE OF CAPTAIN JOHN ORR

ROSSLYN MACPHAIL

Pen & Sword
MILITARY

First published in Great Britain in 2024 by
PEN AND SWORD MILITARY
An imprint of
Pen & Sword Books Limited
Yorkshire – Philadelphia

ISBN 978 1 39903 444 9

A CIP catalogue record for this book is available from the British Library.

Typeset in Times New Roman 11.5/14.5 by
SJmagic DESIGN SERVICES, India.
Printed and bound in the UK by CPI Group (UK) Ltd.

Pen & Sword Books Limited incorporates the imprints of Atlas, Archaeology, Aviation, Discovery, Family History, Fiction, History, Maritime, Military, Military Classics, Politics, Select, Transport, True Crime, Air World, Frontline Publishing, Leo Cooper, Remember When, Seaforth Publishing, The Praetorian Press, Wharncliffe Local History, Wharncliffe Transport, Wharncliffe True Crime and White Owl.

For a complete list of Pen & Sword titles please contact
PEN & SWORD BOOKS LIMITED
George House, Units 12 & 13, Beevor Street, Off Pontefract Road,
Barnsley, South Yorkshire, S71 1HN, England
E-mail: enquiries@pen-and-sword.co.uk
Website: www.pen-and-sword.co.uk

or

PEN AND SWORD BOOKS
1950 Lawrence Rd, Havertown, PA 19083, USA
E-mail: uspen-and-sword@casematepublishers.com
Website: www.penandswordbooks.com

MIX
Paper | Supporting responsible forestry
FSC® C013604

Contents

List of Appendices

Glossary of Terms

CS	Company Service. Civil Service of the East India Company
EIC	East India Company
FRSE	Fellow of the Royal Society of Edinburgh
NLS	National Library of Scotland
OUP	Oxford University Press
PP	Parliamentary Papers
RMA	Royal Military Academy, Woolwich
RMAS	Royal Military Academy, Sandhurst
RMC	Royal Military College, Sandhurst
RSA	Royal Scottish Academy
SNMA	Scottish Naval & Military Academy (Called the Scottish Military & Naval Academy from 1825 to 1830.)
TNA	The National Archive
WS	Writer to the Signet

Author's note regarding the use of currency conversions

Many history books do not use currency conversions. I consider, however, that they are useful for the reader even though they may at times be misleading and inaccurate. I have chosen Measuring Worth because it enables single years to be selected rather than the National Archive Converter which only allows ten-year ranges. According to their website, Measuring Worth 'was created in the 1990s by Samuel H. Williamson (with the help of a grant from NSF International) to be a source of useful tools for economic historians'. Their Real Price adjustment measures the relative cost of a bundle of goods and services (food, shelter, clothing) that an average household could buy. It must be remembered that these conversion figures are rough approximations.

Copyright approval

Introduction

In the corner of my hall, I have a large wooden cabin trunk which contains an archive which has belonged to my family for over 150 years **(Illustration 01 colour)**.

Sometimes, when I was young, on a cold winter's evening, my mother and I would open the lid and look at the papers. It was fun for a brief period. It is, however, tiring trying to read old manuscripts and letters. After a while the papers were put back. It was only after my husband died in 2009 that I began to look at the archive in a systematic way.

I realised that apart from family documents and letters there were papers to relating the Scottish Naval & Military Academy (SNMA) which I knew had been run by my great great-grandfather Captain John Orr. An engraved copy of a painting of him in the Academy uniform hung in our hall. I started to research the SNMA but found few references to it in history books. I knew John Orr had fought in the Peninsular War and had been wounded at the Battle of Waterloo. My curiosity was roused. What was John like as a person? Who had started the Military Academy? Why did it no longer exist?

The family archive is wide ranging. As far as John is concerned, one of the most precious things is his Peninsular War Diary kept during the eighteen months when he was a foot soldier in Portugal and Spain. I was excited to unfold such documents as his commissions and his post-nuptial wedding contract, all on parchment. There were, sadly, only a few letters, but at the bottom of the trunk, I found some of the valentine cards to his children when they were little and bundles of his and his daughter Maggie's death papers. In the cellar, I discovered a long heavy metal box which was painted black with odd dents and scratches. There I found a few items of John's uniform including his scarlet militia jacket, a pair of epaulettes, two pairs of shoulder crescents, a red sash, and his militia sword.

The most valuable item in the archive relating to the SNMA is the student register which was started by John when he became superintendent in October 1831. It is headed *Roll of Students entered into the Scottish Naval & Military Academy.* I call it the Roll Book. It is a large ledger giving personal information about each pupil. There are over 2,000 enrolments which I have entered into a spreadsheet.

This book is the story of my research journey as I try to piece together John's life. I start by describing John's early days when he was a foot soldier in the Peninsular War and then fought in the Battles of Quatre Bras and Waterloo. In 1821, he was placed on the retired list and there followed ten difficult years when four of his children died and he was not recalled for service.

I try to find out more about the Scottish Naval & Military Academy and why John became its superintendent, six years after it opened. Under John's superintendency it became a successful military college, reaching its peak in the mid-1840s. I build up a picture of the Academy and how it functioned and give biographies of some of the directors, masters and alumni. The thread running through the book is John and how he ran the Academy, handled any problems and supported the boys. The last chapter is about John's old age and death.

I hope you will enjoy meeting Captain John Orr and reading about his varied life and all the other characters who appear throughout the book. A part of Edinburgh and Scotland's forgotten history has been uncovered.

Chapter 1

John Orr's Early Life and the Peninsular War

> 'The great thing was simply to summon up for a moment a living breathing shape, to make the dead walk again, to make the reader *see* a figure and *hear* a voice.'[1]
>
> Richard Holmes. *Sidetracks.*

John was born in Greenock, Inverclyde, on 3 April 1790 and his birth was registered in the parish of Mid Kirk, a recently completed church in the town. His father, also John Orr (a genealogist's nightmare) is variously called a goldsmith, a silversmith and a jeweller in the birth registers of young John and his siblings.

In the late sixteenth century, Greenock was a small fishing village; at that time the Firth of Clyde was full of herring. In the seventeenth century, a breakwater was created, and ships started to be built. By the early eighteenth century, particularly after the Act of Union in 1707, it became a busy port with ships coming from the Caribbean bringing sugar to be refined. The islands of the West Indies were producing large amounts of sugar cane grown by enslaved workers from Africa; a significant amount of the sugar was landed at different towns in Scotland. Greenock port was extended, and a major shipbuilding industry was established. By 1791, a year after John was born, a new pier had been built to accommodate the importation of sugar, cotton, wine from Spain and fish from North America. The population in 1700 was about 2,000 but by 1801 it was over 23,000. The Orr family were growing up in a busy prosperous Georgian town.

I have found no record of where John's parents lived nor what school he attended, but it would probably have been Greenock Grammar

School. This was the only school in the town at the time and was in an old tenement block in 'Wee Kirk Street'. John may have spent his last three years at a new school, Greenock Academy, which opened in 1806. (The school no longer has its early records.) John's well-written Peninsular War campaign diary, started when he was only 22, shows he must have received a good education.

John Orr senior and his first wife Margaret Drummond had four children of whom only two survived: James who was born in 1786 and John in 1790. His first wife died, as when John Orr senior had a daughter, Margaret Maule in 1795, the mother is listed as Margaret Macgregor. She then became John's stepmother. Both his father and stepmother died when John was young. I have been unable to confirm this as there were few death records at this time; however, in an archive letter written in August 1841 John wrote: 'Mrs Orr [Jane Pollock, John's wife] and myself were early left orphans.'[2]

On leaving school, John became a soldier. The first record in the archive is his commission as ensign, when aged 19, he joined the Stirling Militia in July 1809.[3] John wrote in a note that he entered the militia as a volunteer. The Scottish Militia had been founded in 1797. It had become necessary as many fencible regiments were coping with a revolt in Ireland and the ever-present danger of invasion by the French was a concern. (Fencible regiments were British army regiments raised in the United Kingdom and the colonies for defence against the threat of invasion.) Conscription started with those under 30 who had no children. If John had not volunteered, he would have been conscripted. Each person so recruited would have been sworn in to serve for a five-year term. John probably volunteered as he had no money to buy a commission in the regular army. It was, therefore, a sensible plan to join a militia. He only stayed with the Stirling Militia for a few months. In November 1809, he was appointed to the Edinburgh Regiment of Militia which was under the command of the Duke of Buccleuch and in July 1811 he was promoted to lieutenant.[4]

While John had been growing up, Napoleon had become a successful army general and in 1804 he was proclaimed emperor. France was determined to extend its sphere of influence with Napoleon leading campaigns against Austria, Italy, Egypt, Prussia and Russia. In 1808, French troops invaded Spain and Portugal and Napoleon declared his brother, Joseph Bonaparte, King of Spain. It resulted in an uprising by the Spanish and Portuguese people. Britain supported these countries and sent troops to the Peninsula.

In the summer of 1811, militia regiments were deployed wherever they were needed to ease the demands of the regular army. On 18 July, the Edinburgh Militia sailed in four ships to Harwich where it was quartered. Three weeks later the troops marched to Colchester where they remained for nine months. (Colchester had been an army garrison since Roman times and because of the Napoleonic Wars new barracks had been built there in 1794.) The officer in charge of the militia was Lieutenant Colonel William Macdonald. In old age John wrote a note which is in the family archive:

> Embarked at Leith for Harwich, thence to Colchester and when there used to play chess with Mrs Macdonald, whose husband was Lt Colonel of the Regiment and she wished to purchase my lieutenancy but I refused and then volunteered into 1st battalion of the 42nd Royal Highlanders (Old Black Watch) and joined the regiment at Lewes.

From time to time, Colonel Macdonald and his wife will appear in John's life. They liked and supported this young orphan from Greenock.

The regiments were commissioning young officers without purchase in readiness for the fight against Napoleon. In October 1811, John joined the 42nd Regiment of Foot. He wrote in a note in the archive:

> I soon embarked from Portsmouth for Lisbon in 1812. Three frigates were required to convey the Regiment and we were sent to join the Army in Spain under command of the Duke of Wellington. On Lisbon, there marched to a convent and quartered there, supplied with horses and mules to carry our baggage. Lieutenant Young and I had one mule between us – this was the allowance for 2 Subs.[5] [Subaltern was another name for an ensign, the lowest officer rank.]

I have John's campaign diary for the eighteen months he was in the Peninsula. **(Illustration 02 monochrome)**.

It is written in ink in a little unlined notebook (4x6ins) which no longer has a cover. The writing is reasonably legible considering that on most occasions it would have been written after a day's march in poor light. It is a simple affair, often only a line or two about the place where they have camped or the countryside around. From December 1812 to April 1813 there are few entries. During the winter the fighting stopped and John wrote 'I have endeavoured to keep a kind of journal of my actions during the campaign. As to what happened since we got into winter quarters is no consequence.' From the start, therefore, he only intended it to be a campaign dairy. Yet he shows great interest and curiosity about his surroundings. There are, sadly, only a few personal remarks.

He started his diary on arrival in Lisbon on 19 April 1812. His description of the city is more positive than that of young Ensign George Bell who considered Lisbon the dirtiest town he had ever seen – full of beggars, wild dogs and chamber pots being emptied out of windows.[6] John writes:

> Lisbon is a very fine town but rather irregular and the streets dirty as they take no trouble in cleaning them although it would be very easily done. The town, with the exception of a small part, stands on the face of a hill on the side of the Tagus. The country all around is most beautiful and in a high state of cultivation. I went to see the church of Sao Roque and was shown some elegant silverwork and some beautiful mosaic paintings in the church. I also went to the opera and saw some fine dancing.

There is nothing in the archive about the clothing John took to Portugal. He probably had a similar kit to that of Ensign George Murray (later Wellington's Quartermaster) who travelled to the West Indies around a decade earlier. He took the following:

> 2 shirts, 2 pairs of stockings, 2 pairs of white trousers, 2 towels, 1 pair of boots, 2 shoe brushes, 1 clothes brush, 1 plate brush, 1 button brush,1 button stick, 1 pair razors, 1 pair scissors, 1 comb, 1 sponge, 1 simple fork and spoon, 1 blacking box, 1 soap box and shaving brush, 1 portable case for small articles and 1 great coat.[7]

I have at home a small wooden box (11x11x23ins) with iron corners and hinges which has a little brass plate on top engraved 'J Orr, 42nd Reg'. **(Illustration 02 colour)**.

It is possible he took it to Portugal or to Ireland in a later posting. The kit listed above, apart from the great coat, would fit into the box.

They were often hung one on either side of the donkey's back, in the same way as the kitchen equipment was transported – as described by James Thornton, the Duke of Wellington's cook, in an interview with Lord Frederick Fitzclarence.[8]

It is doubtful if John had any independent income as his parents do not appear to have been wealthy. Towards the end of the diary, he wrote: 'I might have gone home but being in debt could not go.'[9] An ensign, in about 1800, received £106 (£9,105) a year.[10] Out of this sum, he had to pay for his rations, living, dining and incidental expenses; a new officer might have in his hand only about 5d (£1.60) per day. Sir John Moore, a British army general who would be killed at Corunna, reckoned that a junior officer could not be expected to live on his pay and would need an additional income of about £100 (£7,720) per year.[11]

During 1810 and 1811, the combined British and Portuguese armies had been fighting the French, trying to remove them from Portugal. In April 1812, Wellington besieged and captured the Spanish town of Ciudad Rodrigo; the aim was to push the French further north through Spain. John and the 42nd would be marching through Portugal into Spain to join Wellington's other regiments.

On 8 May 1812, the 42nd 'got the route' and set off north along the Tagus. It took them two weeks, marching most days, to reach the Spanish border about 120 miles away. On the way, they stopped at the small town of Nisa where the regiments were to be reformed. The 42nd Regiment had two battalions. The 1st Battalion was to be re-recruited and the 2nd Battalion was to return to Scotland, together with junior officers from the 1st Battalion. John did not want to go back to Scotland. He had recently joined and was looking forward to the adventure ahead. He therefore asked Colonel Stirling if he could remain with his current battalion:

> as I did not wish to return I applied to Colonel Stirling to use his influence to keep me out and told him I wished to see some fun and if I go home I'll soon be ordered out

> again. On my asking him he said, 'Well Sir you put that in monochrome' and I did so. An order came at once for me to remain out. My request was granted and the following day, the Old Col said to me on the line of march, 'Well Orr I'm glad to see you have some spunk in you.'[12]

John's diary lists the names of the places where he stops most nights. Officers were often billeted among the population, but most of the soldiers bivouacked as no tents had been allocated at that time.[13]

After marching north through Portugal and into Spain at Ciudad Rodrigo, they arrived near Salamanca on 17 June 1812. The 6th Division was laying siege to the fortified convents where the French had left a garrison of 800 men. John said that his division, the 1st, was camped about a mile away. He managed to meet up with his cousin Captain Bogle and they dined together. (James Bogle would later marry John Orr's half-sister Margaret Maule Orr. He was an officer in the 94th Regiment of Foot.)

Two days later John wrote:

> On 19 June the army was drawn up in battle order on the heights on the north side of the Tormes [river near Salamanca] as the enemy was endeavouring to relieve the garrison. It was there that I first heard the roar of war and shot flying over me.

Wellington and Marshal Marmont, in charge of the French forces, spent about a month eyeing one another up and repositioning their armies. During this time, John had to go back to Ciudad Rodrigo to collect a detachment of sixty-one men to join the army. The 17 leagues (about 51 miles) back to Salamanca were difficult as they lost the mule that was carrying all their provisions and John had no money to buy more. He enjoyed seeing Salamanca and wrote that, 'the Cathedral is very fine indeed.' He was there when the magazine in the fortified convent blew up, destroying it. John wrote: 'which caused great confusion in the town. The shock was awfully grand.'

On the evening of 21 July, they crossed the river and 'marched to the heights on the side south of the Tormes and halted about 12 at night in a ploughed field. It there began to rain accompanied with thunder and lightning which seem to threaten both armies.' Another officer in the 42nd, Lieutenant Donald Mackenzie, confirmed that the storm was intense with not only rain but hail and sleet. Mackenzie had to spend the night sitting on the ground with no cover, no food and his hungry horse attached to his leg.[14]

On 22 July 1812, John wrote that about 4 p.m.:

> both armies came to close engagement and about 6, victory favoured the British, at 7 the French were in full retreat. They lost about 20,000 in killed, wounded and prisoners. Marmont was wounded. In short the French seldom or ever got such a drubbing. Then our division 1st, along with others, pursued the enemy up to Valladolid, but did not cross the Douro. The army moved on to Madrid, but our regiment being sickly were sent to Cuellar. [Spanish town 50km south of Valladolid.]

John's figure of 20,000 is a little high. It is now estimated that the French casualties amounted to 13,500 – about one-quarter of its forces. The allies had only 5,220 casualties.[15] Wellington in the end had out-manoeuvred Marmont's army and had won a decisive and important battle. The French had many armies under different generals and Wellington realised there would be more battles ahead before the campaign was over.

Salamanca must have made a great impression on John. It was his first battle. When he became superintendent of the Scottish Naval & Military Academy, he kept a press cuttings book which is in the family archive. Forty-one years later, next to the press report about the prize-giving which was held on 22 July 1853, John wrote 'Salamanca Day!!!'

Despite the difficult conditions, which many other Peninsular War diarists wrote about, John rarely complains in his diary. William Hay, an ensign in the 52nd Light Infantry, described the dreadful conditions which he had to endure and for several months never changed his clothes.[16] John will have faced similar circumstances but he accepted the life of a young officer fighting abroad. Occasionally, he writes 'a very fatiguing march.' His comment, however, is more often 'Was on the march about 10 hours; pass some delightful country.'

In many places where the regiment stopped for more than one night, John went out to explore the town. At Castelo Branco he went 'to see the Bishop's Gardens which are beautifully laid out'. In June the following year, during a forced march north, they camped briefly near Zamora. 'The town is finely situated on the side of the Douro and has an old castle which has complete command of the river and bridge. I also went to see the cathedral which is very neat indeed.' He frequently comments on his surroundings: 'The country all the way from Valladolid to Burgos is beautifully situated with fine vineyards and a delightful river passing down through the plain.'

After the Battle of Salamanca, the 42nd were given orders to march to Cuellar and then on to Madrid. They, however, had to remain two weeks in Cuellar as many of the men were ill. Lieutenant Donald Mackenzie wrote that he himself was ill with a fever and dysentery and many others in the regiment were poorly with different conditions, some due to their poor diet and lack of protection from the extreme weather conditions.[17] They eventually reached Villacasten, a town north of Madrid, where they were ordered to wait for the 1st Division, who would march to join them. On the 6 August, John showed a rare moment of emotion:

> But when at Villacasten we got orders to halt till the 1st Division would come to us as they were on the march to Valladolid. We feel much disappointed at being obliged to turn back when within 10 leagues [30 miles] of the place we were all so anxious to see.

The army was now going north to follow the French. John said, 'we entered the town of Valladolid out of which we drove the French where they thought themselves pretty snug.' The French continued north and established themselves in the fort and castle of Burgos. The medieval castle was on a large high plateau of land. Beside it, but separated by a narrow valley, was a hill called Cerro de San Miguel which had a little fort on top of it. The British army arrived there on 18 September 1812. Wellington knew that it would be necessary to capture both San Miguel and the castle if they were to take the city.

Since Wellington had not envisaged a major siege, he had left his siege train in Madrid. Despite having insufficient fire power to take Burgos Castle, he ordered a siege when they arrived in the city.

The castle was not as well fortified as it appeared, although the 2,000 soldiers in it had much better artillery. The small fort on the San Miguel hill was defended by a hornwork (a type of fortification with angular points defending the inner fort). It was decided to organise an assault on the fort and at the same time to have a diversionary attack on the main castle. John writes on 19 September:

> Our Regiment was ordered to support General Pack's Brigade in storming the out fort of the castle at Burgos, but getting to the top of the hill they thought it better that we should both storm and support. Then some of the companies supported and others stormed. The attack began after dark and lasted about 20 minutes. Our regiment entered in a style becoming the Royal Highlanders. We had two Lieutenants killed and a Captain and Lieutenant wounded. The company I was attached to lost some men next morning.

According to Victoria Schofield in the official regimental history of the Black Watch, Wellington praised the 42nd for having distinguished themselves in this assault.[18] The official regimental returns list many more killed and injured in the attack than the figures John mentions.

It was impossible to attack the main castle with the type of guns that Wellington had with him, as the sides of the hill were so steep. Siege trenches were dug, but the soldiers were inexperienced in this work and did not have the correct tools.[19] The castle was protected by several perimeter walls. The siege trenches made little progress, as they were filled with mud and the castle remained impregnable. There were many deaths and injuries.

There are several entries in John's journal describing being in the trenches. On the 4 October 1812, John wrote:

> Was in the trenches all night as a covering party and was pretty hot work of it. But thank God I got safe off, though the only remaining officer of the Brigade, for both the Captain and the Lieutenant were wounded. I lost about 10 or 12 men and some 20 to 30 wounded. I was out for forage this morning a very unpleasant duty. [underlined in his diary]

A break of over a week occurs in John's diary entries from 20 to 28 September. I later found out he was wounded in one arm during or after the assault on San Miguel. He may not have mentioned it in his diary, as he felt he had come off lightly compared with others. The next entry, 28 September, John writes: 'I have been in the hospital today at Villa Torro and the sight is melancholy indeed, to see fine stout young men laying some wanting legs others arms.'

I discovered about the wound in a letter in the archive dated 25 April 1825 where John requests some money because of this injury. Cox & Co, Army Agents, London, told him he had to obtain a certificate from the doctor that attended him and another from the adjutant in charge of his company. Dr Hamilton, the surgeon who attended him, wrote that the injury was:

> a severe contusion in his left arm from the splinter of a shell on 20 September 1812 … while he was occupying Fort San Miguel at Burgos, during the siege of the Fort. Although I felt an opinion being the acting surgeon with the regiment at the above period that I should report his having received an injury which was likely to render him unfit for duty for a considerable time, his zeal for the service and anxiety to do his duty prevented him from doing this and consequently from receiving any remuneration.[20]

This statement was not enough for Cox & Co who required precise medical details of the wound which the doctor could not supply as thirteen years had passed since he had seen it. The adjutant, Captain Alex Mackenzie, had died and therefore could not confirm what had happened.

In the archive is a letter written by John, in which he talks about his wound:

> I am certainly much to blame in not allowing my name to be returned as it would clearly have shown the fact, but at the time I was not aware of what might happen and did not wish to alarm my friends at home. Also had always a strong aversion to get to the rear [underlined in letter] when I was in any way able to do my duty with the Corps.[21]

John did not want to shirk his responsibilities. He wanted to remain with his regiment at the front where the action was. This determination to do the correct thing and exercising moral courage were attributes that would make him a good superintendent later in his career. The claim was not proceeded with as John was unable to obtain the two certificates.

On 3 October John wrote:

> This day twelve months I had the honour of being appointed to the 42nd Regiment. I was at work in the trenches the other day and thank God I came home without one of the party being hurt. At Captain Williamson's funeral. He was wounded at the same time poor Cullen got his mortal wound in the trenches when at work.

The deaths and injuries continued for nearly another three weeks. The siege lasted about a month from 19 September until 21 October 1812. It was Wellington's worst mistake in the Peninsular War. All attempts at taking the Castle had failed. When Wellington heard that the French army under Marshal Soult was only a few days' march away from Burgos, he had no option but to give the order to retreat. It must have been a bleak decision for Wellington. He later remarked that it was 'the worst scrape that I was ever in'.[22] The wagon wheels were bound with straw to muffle their sound and the retreat began. On 22 October, John wrote: 'through Burgos and passed under the fire of the castle but the enemy did not see us'.

On 24 October, John reported on the bad behaviour of some men, which he did not support. They had found where a town's wine vaults were situated:

> Our regiment (along with others) having broke into some wine houses during the night, were I am sorry to say, in a most unsoldierlike manner on the march. A number of our officers got all they had stolen from them as they pitched no tents, it being late before we halted.

They marched for days. Wellington hoped that they could hold Salamanca, but the French were near behind them and this was not possible. They therefore had to continue the retreat south to Ciudad Rodrigo. Many of the troops were captured. Others died during the forced march with few provisions and in appalling weather. William Hay, now serving with the 12th Light Dragoons confirms in his diary that it rained without cessation for six days and he survived on scraps of meat and acorns.[23]

On 17 November 1812, John comments:

> I was on the baggage guard the same night Sir E. Paget was taken prisoner and I near sharing the same fate. I marched all night and next day got into Roderigo, many a dead animal and body on the road. After passing Roderigo we got into houses at night which we stood much in need of, as the weather was very wet.

No fighting took place in the winter months. John and his regiment retired to the hills across the border in Portugal. He and his regiment were in the town of 'Cea'. (This is probably the town of Seia in the foothills of the Serra da Estrada, between Guarda and Coimbra.) He was pleased as he had been 'very fortunate in getting one of the best quarters in town and my landlord is very civil to me in sending me presents of wine and invitations to dine, but as I do not speak Portuguese I seldom or ever wait on him'. John was lucky as many were billeted in poor accommodation.

Lieutenant Donald Mackenzie wrote how depleted the regiment was after the dreadful toll at Burgos and the subsequent retreat:

> In six months the 42nd had been reduced from 1,200 to 300 fighting men, and had difficulty ever afterwards in mustering above 500: fatigue and bad feeding caused fever and dysentery, carrying off the men by scores, these diseases being far more deadly than the most bloody encounters with the enemy.[24]

Occasionally in the diary John showed a moment when he was low and this most often relates to not getting mail from home. Home means his half-sister in Scotland and his brother James who was in the Royal Navy.

In February he wrote: 'I have written to my sister four times without hearing from her.' A little later he wrote: 'I do not know what to think of my sister's silence.'

John became ill with a fever and on 1 April 1813 he noted, 'I had a letter from both brother and sister. I am still holding better thank God.' He had clearly been ill as two weeks later he wrote: 'I am still holding better and able to walk about.'

Towards the end of April 1813, the campaign resumed. On the 29th they set off and he wrote: 'I found my legs weak.' The 1st Division was now marching north again. In old age John wrote:

> On marching up to Vittoria from Salamanca our baggage was detained for 3 or 4 days. We officers had no change of linen. I took off my shirt and washed it in the Tagus and let it dry on the rocks when I was bathing. The lice are abundant in Spain and I had to take a stone and beat my shirt to kill the vermin. I have seen them crawling on the floors just thick like dust, some of them such big fellows. I've gone into a stable and come out, you could not tell what colour my trousers were, just covered with them. A sort of brown up to my knees.

It is strange that John mentions he was wearing trousers as the 42nd wore the kilt during this campaign. Anthony Clayton mentions in *The British Officer* that during the Peninsular War 'Fleas, lice and mosquitos were additional and severe summer and autumn problem.'[25]

Throughout June 1813 they were marching north each day. On 6 June, he is delighted to have word of his promotion and writes: 'I heard this morning of my being in the gazette as Lieutenant!' They passed Burgos on 14 June and started to climb into the Cantabrian mountains. On 16th he wrote:

> Was on the march about 10 hours; pass some delightful valleys. In short the scene is far beyond conception. The rocks are awfully grand and the valleys fine and richly furnished with fine villages. We halted on the Ebro along which I had been moving all day.

The advance north continued. Some days they were marching from early until late. On 29 June they started at 5 a.m. and did not reach their 'ground until eleven at night.' They passed through the town of Laguardia where 'the inhabitants hailed us with great joy, *viva'd* us as we passed.'

According to the historian Charles Esdaile, 'The march of the Allied army from the Portuguese frontier to the Cantabrian mountains is an example of strategic brilliance that is without equal in the annals of the Peninsular War.'[26] They had covered this distance of about 350 miles in less than a month. Wellington had learned lessons from the disastrous retreat from Burgos. He had organised better medical services for the sick. Amongst other improvements, there were more kettles and they were lighter, more tents and men no longer needed to carry their heavy greatcoats. They, however, missed these in the mountains when the weather became colder.

The next months involved sieges, skirmishes and battles with the French. John and his regiment arrived a mile from Pamplona on 5 July and spent a week 'throwing up redoubts'. A redoubt was a type of fortification made of earth, stone or brick. (The starving garrison in Pamplona held out until 31 October.) John's regiment was ordered north and on 31 July reached the top of the Pass of Roncesvalles in the Pyrenees, which is the border between Spain and France. On the way, John was shocked as the French army fleeing northward had plundered houses.

On 1 August he wrote:

> Some fine villages. Houses neatly covered with wood, but the French did not leave a house without plundering everything within. The people fled to the mountains.

On 1 September they heard that San Sebastian had fallen. The 42nd spent September and October in the western part of the Pyrenees in and round the Pass of Maya where they had skirmishes with parts of the French army. On 3 November, while still in the Pyrenees, John heard that his uncle had died. He asked for leave to return to Scotland; this was granted. As his parents were dead, his uncle was the senior family member. John wrote: 'On 21 November sail from San Sebastian and after a <u>very pleasant passage</u> got to Falmouth on 28 November where we were obliged to put in owing to the wind being ahead.' [John's underlining.] He had been in Spain and Portugal for nearly eighteen months.

Chapter 2

Quatre Bras, Waterloo and After

> 'The French cavalry were only a few yards off and I gave a yell and shouted 'Charge' and we did so and drove them off.'[1]
>
> John Orr. Family archive.

John's military career continued with a peacetime posting with the 42nd Regiment to Kilkenny, Ireland. In 1798 there had been a major uprising against British rule. The rebellion united radical Protestants and Roman Catholics and was fuelled by the French and American revolutions. From January 1801 the Irish legislature was abolished and the United Kingdom of Great Britain and Ireland was formed. British troops were, thereafter, regularly stationed in Ireland. The family archive has no comments written by John during his time in Ireland. I have turned for some background to the diary of Sergeant Anton, who like John, was in the 42nd.

Anton remarks: 'A considerable number of detachments are furnished from the garrison of Kilkenny to the different villages and hamlets throughout the surrounding district.'[2] John and Sergeant Anton were both in Kilkenny at the same time; however, it is not clear whether Anton was in John's detachment. Anton found the local people helpful. 'Were we scarce of fuel they would freely lend us until a supply could be found; if provisions were short, they would find some person to supply us.'[3]

In Europe the fighting continued. The allies offered terms for Napoleon to surrender but he declined. Eventually in April 1814, at Fontainebleau, he abdicated and was exiled to the island of Elba. On 26 February 1815, Napoleon escaped from Elba with the retinue that he had been allowed to keep. He landed in Antibes and arrived in Paris on 20 March having gathered thousands of supporters as he went north.

In the archive, there is a small print of Napoleon which may have been bought by John when he took his daughters to see the site of the Battle of Waterloo in 1853. **(Illustration 03 colour)**.

In Britain, regiments were sent to the Low Countries. The 42nd, under the command of Lieutenant Colonel Robert Macara, was called back from Ireland and sent to Brussels to be part of the 5th Division, one of the divisions in the Reserve under Wellington's personal command. The battalion marched from Kilkenny to Cork and sailed from Cobh on 4 May 1815. The weather was stormy and many ships took shelter in Milford Haven, but eventually the soldiers all landed at Ostend. They marched to Ghent and on to Brussels. Sergeant Anton remarked how flat the land was between Ostend and Ghent. It was a big contrast compared with the hills of Ireland where they had spent the previous months.[4]

The 5th Division was commanded by Sir Thomas Picton, an eccentric man, who rarely used military uniform. 'He generally wore a blue frock coat, very tightly buttoned up to the throat; a very large black silk neckcloth … and a round hat.'[5] According to Wellington, he was 'a rough foul-mouthed devil as ever lived'.[6] Yet he was a capable soldier. The 42nd was in the 9th Brigade commanded by Sir Denis Pack, one of Wellington's most able commanders who had received several decorations for his service in many countries.

The Duke of Wellington had been in Brussels since early April, coordinating the allied forces for their confrontation with Napoleon. He was in command not only of the British army but also of Dutch, Belgian and various German-speaking units. By June, the city was overflowing with British regiments, and senior officers, sometimes with their families, who joined the large British community already in Brussels. A general feeling was that the fight would be taken to Napoleon and the battle would be on French soil and so the rounds of parties and balls continued. The atmosphere is well described in Nick Foulkes' book *Dancing into Battle*:

> Wellington's flippancy and blithe confidence were a front that he presented to British expatriate society in Brussels. The slightly desperate tone of his letters to Horse Guards and the misgivings, concerns and even fears that he shared

> with a very small circle indicate a completely different man to the public image projected as he danced at balls, flirted in salons and strolled in the park.[7] [Horse Guards was a building in Whitehall which was the main office of the British army and where the office of the Commander-in-Chief was situated. It became used as a metonym for the British army headquarters.]

Since the border between France and Belgium was porous, there were French spies in Brussels, and Wellington hoped that this confident atmosphere would deter Napoleon from attacking. He could then choose his time and place to fight in France. Napoleon, however, was not deterred and came north quicker than many, including Wellington, expected.

Napoleon's plan was to split his opposition. On Thursday, 15 June he crossed into the Netherlands. On 16th he fought the Prussian army, under General Gebhard von Blucher, at Ligny, about 37 miles south of Brussels and due east of Quatre Bras. The French defeated the Prussians, yet they did not pursue the retreating army. Hence the remnants of the Prussian army, including the wounded Blucher, were able to reach Wavre in the north and regroup. Blucher had met Wellington in May and again before the battle of Ligny. They had both agreed to support one another in resisting an attack from Napoleon. Blucher, therefore, knew that the Prussian army would be needed in the main battle which was to follow. Napoleon sent the other portion of his army, under Marshal Ney, to the west to capture the strategic crossroads at Quatre Bras, south of Brussels.

The news of Napoleon's fast advance came on the evening of Thursday, 15 June during the famous ball in Brussels, hosted by the Duchess of Richmond, attended by Wellington and almost all British senior officers. Between midnight and 1 a.m., Wellington was shocked to be told that Napoleon had given orders to Marshal Ney to try to take the crossroads at Quatre Bras. It was, therefore, in the early hours of Friday, 16 June, two days before the battle of Waterloo, that Wellington ordered the 42nd, the 92nd and the 1st Royals to muster. Many officers in these regiments, who had been at the ball, had no time to change and had to leave to fight in evening dress.

At 4 a.m. they were due to depart, although the 42nd were late in joining. Sergeant Anton wrote how they 'were roused from our peaceful slumbers by the sounding of bugles, the rolling of drums and the loud notes of our Highland pipes'.[8] They were issued with four days allowance of bread and three days of beef and spirits and marched off to bands playing and the cheers of the watching crowds.

They followed the Forêt de Soignes south from Brussels until they reached Quatre Bras 22 miles away. When they arrived at the intersection, the 42nd settled down to prepare a meal, but suddenly 'the distant report of guns became more loud'.[9] The order came to fix bayonets and move forward through a field of rye which had stalks as high as their bonnets. They were then charged by a group of French lancers. John's recollection in old age describes the action:

> At Quatre Bras I commanded a company and did duty as Adjutant … The enemy had a gun on our flank we were formed into a square. A man was tardy and slow in turning and I took hold of him by the arm and said, 'Come up Sir.' I felt the wind of a ball whiz through the air and it struck the man, knocked his head off, the brains spattered about, some on my coat. The French cavalry were only a few yards off and I gave a yell and shouted 'Charge' and we did so and drove them off.[10]

The 42nd's experiences are confirmed in Lieutenant Percy Grove's *The History of the Black Watch*:

> By 4 a.m. on 16th Picton's Division was on its way to meet the enemy. After a march of 22 miles, the 42nd arrived at the post of Les Quatre Bras just as the 2nd French Corps, under Marshal Ney, was developing a serious attack on that position. The British regiments formed for action as they came on the scene of conflict, and being assailed by enemies advancing from different points, each regiment had to fight independently, and, in many instances, to stand or fall by itself. As the 42nd was advancing though a rye-field, it was charged by a body of French lancers before it had time to form a square. Though taken at a disadvantage, the

> Royal Highlanders were not dismayed and fighting back-to-back, they repulsed their antagonists.[11]

The fighting continued until dusk. That night an order was given that no fires should be lit. 'Round us lay the dying and the dead,' Sergeant Anton later recorded, 'the latter not yet interred and many of the former, wishing to breathe their last where they fell.'[12]

Quatre Bras was a messy battle and technically a stalemate. The French, however, neither won nor gained ground and this proved to be of immense importance to Wellington for the main battle that followed two days later. The Allied casualties were about 4,800 and the French in the region of 4,000. The 42nd started off the day with over 500 men and 39 officers. One after another, three of their commanding officers were either killed or severely injured. During the battle, four officers and forty men were killed. Fifteen officers and 213 men were wounded.[13] Wellington listed in his despatch to Earl Bathurst those officers and regiments that had distinguished themselves in the battle and he ends by writing: 'I must particularly mention the 28th, 42nd, 79th and 92nd regiments and the Hanoverians.'[14] Wellington ordered those who had fought at Quatre Bras to retreat north, to near the village of Waterloo which was about 10 miles south of Brussels.

According to Sergeant Anton, before leaving, they did what they could for the wounded and buried the dead. They managed to eat well, as apart from the meat ration they had with them, they killed geese, duck and chickens and used vegetables from a nearby farm.[15] They found that the breastplates of dead French cuirassiers killed during the battle made ideal frying pans.[16]

Rain fell heavily during the night of 17 June. The miserable conditions are described by Captain George Ulrich Barlow of 69th Foot Regiment when he wrote to his father in India. (His regiment was not so lucky with finding supplies of food.)

> Night came on and with it the flood gates, it however seemed to be opened as it poured in torrents without intermission. We had no canopy but the sky, nothing to eat, thus hungry; drenched and sleepless around a fire which barely emitted heat would scarcely burn, did we await in a cornfield the dawning of the 18 June.[17]

John has left us no first-hand account of the battle of Waterloo but sufficient records remain by others to explain what he and the 42nd experienced. On the morning of 18 June 1815, Picton's 5th Division, which included the 42nd, were placed to the left side of the Charleroi Road which had a hedge running along its side. Immediately behind the hedge and in front of them was the 95th Rifle Brigade made up of Dutch and Belgian soldiers. Sergeant Anton wrote in his memoir that it was a 'stunted quickset hedge' which formed 'feeble cover from the enemy's view, but no defence against his shot, shell or musketry'.[18] The French were unaware of their presence.

The fighting did not start until about 11 a.m. The 42nd and the other regiments in their area did not enter the battle until about 2 p.m. There are differing reports as to what happened next. It seems that sometime after 2 p.m., Napoleon ordered an assault which was countered with a bayonet charge by Pack's brigade.[19] Picton was immediately struck on the right temple by a musket ball and died instantly. After the battle, Wellington noted in a despatch: 'Sir Thomas Picton … fell gloriously leading his division to a charge with bayonets, by which one of the most serious attacks made by the enemy on our position was repulsed.'[20]

Sergeant Major Cotton describes how the remains of 92nd Highlanders 'aided by the Royal Scots and 42nd Highlanders immediately advanced in order to come to close quarters with the enemy, whose fire they received without returning until within 30 yards, they then threw in a concentrated volley which completely staggered the French'.[21] Sergeant Anton writes that it was 'a scene of vehement destruction, yells and shrieks, wounds and death; the bodies of the dead served as pillows for the dying'.[22] Ensign Edward Macready later said, 'The battle was now not a trial of skill or soldiership … but who could "stand the killing longest".'[23]

At some stage during this melee, John was injured, receiving a musket ball wound to his left knee which badly damaged it.[24] One of John's obituaries says he 'was carried from the field'.[25] Many of the wounded were taken to the farm of Mont St Jean which acted as a field dressing station, John was probably taken there as it was not far from where the 42nd were positioned on the battlefield. In their book about how the injured were cared for during and after the battle, Michael Crumplin and Gareth Glover observed:

> What made Mont St Jean a good field hospital was not only its proximity to the combat zone, but also its structure. Although the roof was damaged by stray ordnance, there are no records of any casualties being further injured whilst resting in the farm … The dead were collected in outhouses and the human detritus from numerous amputations was simply thrown on the farm's midden … A vitally important issue was an adequate water supply and this was provided by a centrally placed well.[26]

The water was needed for washing the wounded and because most of the injured were badly dehydrated. Each only had a wooden canteen which held a little over a litre (1.75 pints) and most had set out with alcohol in it. John would then probably have had an uncomfortable journey in an unsprung requisitioned farm cart, to one of the hospitals in Brussels. He was lucky that no one tried to amputate his leg. The death rate amongst amputees was high.

The battle and the killing went on all afternoon. Wellington was anxiously awaiting the support of the Prussian army. Their arrival from Wavre was slowed by the muddy conditions due to the torrential rain that had fallen. They appeared, eventually, to the far east of the battle area. Instead of advancing to where the main fighting was taking place, they engaged part of the French army near the village of Plancenoit, which caused Napoleon to send most of his reserves there.

At this time, Napoleon's main forces made an important advance and took the farm of La Haye Sainte. Marshal Ney immediately asked Napoleon for more troops for a central attack on the allied forces. The only troops which Napoleon had in reserve were his top regiment, the Imperial Guard. They were kept for deployment in an emergency and so he declined Marshal Ney's request.

About 7.30 p.m. Napoleon had to decide whether to withdraw and plan to fight a future battle, or stay in the field and send forward the Imperial Guard. He decided on the latter. The Imperial Guard was caught in crossfire by the allied artillery and was mown down. Victoria Schofield says, 'when, after trying to break through, the Imperial Guard began to withdraw, panic set in among the French army. Seeing the disorder, Wellington decided on a general advance against the retreating

French.'[27] The battle was over. Total losses of the Grand Allied army at Waterloo were recorded at 15,000, those of the Prussians 7,000 and the French losses were estimated at 25,000 dead and wounded and 8,000 prisoners taken.[28]

After the battle, the 42nd with all other regiments marched to Paris and were encamped in the Bois de Boulogne.[29] John was sent to the recently opened British military hospital at Saint-Denis, which was a northern suburb of Paris. A letter from the hospital, dated 25 August 1815, is in the family archive. It states that:

> John Orr received on 18 June in action with the enemy a severe contusion of the left knee by a musket ball, which confined him to his bed for three weeks, his knee and leg were much inflamed, at present is considerably weaker than natural. Cannot march any distance without feeling great pain in his leg and incipient inflammation.[30]

The British army remained on the outskirts of Paris until November 1815. (I presume John was fit to march home with the rest of the regiment, as there is a document in the family archive that he received while marching north with his regiment the following year.) On 17 December, the 42nd sailed from Calais. The weather was bad and so, instead of arriving at Dover, they landed at Ramsgate. The slow journey marching north took many months. They spent two weeks in Chelmsford Barracks and left there on 17 January 1816. They went north via Cambridge where Sergeant Anton writes that the bells 'welcomed us with joy'. The city supplied food and drink and gave 'a donation equal to two days' pay to each man'.[31] The regiment continued their march north, roughly following the road which is now the modern-day A1. According to Sergeant Anton, they were greeted along the way with bells ringing and 'joyful shouts'.

They left Sunderland for Ednburgh on 8 March. A big welcome awaited them: a reception in the castle, free tickets for the theatre and a large dinner in the Assembly Rooms in George Street. Anton says they 'staggered out, bonnets falling off in all directions'. The regiment left Edinburgh for Glasgow on 8 September 1816. They remained in Glasgow until deployed to Dublin in the following April.[32]

While marching north, John was sent a letter from the Waterloo Subscription, dated 16 April, telling him that he had been awarded £45 (£3,665) as compensation for having been wounded at Waterloo. The award is 'in testimony of the gratitude of your countrymen, and of their admiration of British valour, so eminently displayed in the late ever-memorable campaigns'.[33] The Waterloo Subscription was funded by the public and was administered by Hoare's Bank where an account had been opened on 29 July 1815.[34] The major initial donors were merchants, bankers and brokers, but contributions continued from every part of society.

I have John's Waterloo Medal, which was issued between 1816 and 1817. **(Illustration 04 colour)**. The medal is made of solid silver and has the Prince Regent's head facing left on one side. The reverse has the figure of Victory seated on a plinth. The words engraved on this side are: **WATERLOO, JUNE 18 1815** and **WELLINGTON**. It has a crimson ribbon with blue edging. John's name and rank are engraved around the edge:

> Lieut. John Orr 42nd or R. H. Reg. Infantry.

The Waterloo Medal was the first genuine campaign medal to be issued to all soldiers who took part in the fighting that weekend regardless of their rank. It was also the first medal to have the soldier's name, rank and regiment engraved round the edge. It was supposed to be awarded to families and next of kin of those who had died but the Mint was halted from printing the Waterloo Medal for relations of dead officers and soldiers. It was left to these families to apply for the medal.[35] The 'Waterloo Men' were also to have two years' additional service in the reckoning of pay or pension. This meant that soldiers could take up their pensions two years earlier. There were additional benefits for those who had been injured.[36]

On 2 December 1816, a few months after John got back to Glasgow, aged 26, he married Jean Pollock (later called Jane.) She was 24 and the youngest of three sisters. Her father, Alexander Pollock, was a wealthy manufacturer. The Pollock family lived in a large house in the Anderston area of Glasgow. I have come across a miniature which I think is of John Orr and was probably painted about this time. **(Illustration 05 colour)**.

It was advertised for sale online with a pair of pistols belonging to his son John William Orr.[37] The owner wants to remain anonymous.

On 26 December 1816, John was retired on half pay from the 42nd Regiment due to a re-division.[38] (Between 1816 and 1821, thirty-five infantry and eight cavalry regiments were disbanded and others were the subject of re-division to make them smaller.)[39] The following four years were to prove disjointed and unsettling for the couple. John was unlucky as three of the regiments he was enrolled with, were either divided or disbanded. He had to face months of being on half pay between military appointments. After Waterloo, the British army was reduced from 149,000 in 1816 to 100,000 by 1821.[40]

John was determined to try to remain in active service. In March 1817 he wrote to the Marquis of Lothian, a colonel in the Edinburgh Militia, asking him if he would approach Lord Huntly on his behalf with regard to his rejoining. Lord Huntly was colonel in chief of John's old regiment, the 42nd. The marquis declined to help as 'my acquaintance with his Lordship is not such to entitle me to take the liberty.' He goes on to urge John to approach Lord Huntly directly:

> The character you bore in my Regiment justly entitles you to every recommendation I can faithfully give you; and your Services in the 42nd Regt for which I saw by the Gazette you were wounded will I hope entreat his Lordship in your favour.[41]

The archive has no copy of a letter to Huntly, but there is one from John to the Duke of York asking for a placement.[42] The Duke of York was in the process of overseeing the reorganisation of the British army. Either as a result of this letter or other letters, which are not in the archive, John joined the 94th Regiment of Foot (the Scotch Brigade) on 2 August 1817.

The Scotch Brigade was stationed in Dublin. John and Jane were there for eighteen months. He had served in Ireland before, but now the country was wracked with famine and disease. That summer had been much colder and wetter than usual and had destroyed the grain and potato crops. Many became hungry and were more susceptible to typhus which was taking hold. Jane was pregnant with their first child when they arrived. John Drummond Orr, was born at Richmond Barracks, Dublin, on 19 February 1818. Ten months later, on 25 December 1818, the Scotch Brigade was disbanded. Items from the mess were distributed to officers and John was able to keep, as a memento of his service with the Brigade, a large engraved glass goblet. **(Illustration 03 monochrome)**.

The Orr family moved to Edinburgh, where Jane's recently married sister, Agnes, was living. John and Jane's second child, Jane, was born in Edinburgh on 1 November 1819. Both little John Drummond and daughter Jane died young. John was now on half pay for a year and a half.

Eventually, on 6 July 1820 he joined the 8th Royal Veteran Battalion and the family returned to Ireland, on this occasion to Belfast. This posting only lasted eight months as the regiment was disbanded in late March 1821. In a metal box of army uniforms belonging to the family were two parts of his kit from this period of his service with the Veteran Battalion. One is his shako badge and the other is his gilt shoulder belt plate. The badge was attached to the tall cylindrical cap made of felt and leather which was called a shako. The shoulder plate joined two pieces of the belt from which hung a sword or cartridges. **(Illustration 06 colour)**.

John, aged 31, was placed on the retired list, but luckily was kept on full pay. Between July 1822 and April 1823, he received four payments of about £34 10s each, making an annual sum of £137 17s 6d (£13,370).[43] His military pension remained the same for the rest of his life, paid in quarterly instalments. He was a 'retired' officer for ten years as he was offered no other appointment and without funds he was unable to buy himself a higher commission. John would know many of his army friends in the same position. As we will see he was about to enter a difficult decade with the family moving three times and another child dying.

The first of these moves was back to Edinburgh where they stayed in a house on the estate belonging to his old friend, Colonel Macdonald. This is the same family that supported young John when he was 19 and had enrolled with the Edinburgh Militia. The Macdonald estate, called Powderhall, was on the northern outskirts of Edinburgh's New Town. The Orr family stayed in East Powderhall House from 1821 to 1824. (Both houses were demolished in the late nineteenth century to make way for a refuse dump.)

Two more children were born while they were in Edinburgh. Alexander George in May 1821 and James in June 1822. James was the first of their children to survive childhood. While they were living in Edinburgh, John and Jane could both see their relations. John's brother James had left the Royal Navy and was now a druggist in Edinburgh. Jane was able to visit her sister Agnes and her young family.

In 1824, John took his family back to Glasgow and stayed there for two years. During this time a post-nuptial marriage contract was registered which is in the family archive.[44] (Marriage contracts were a means of ensuring that wives could pass on an inheritance to their children.) The trustees bought property in Monteith Row for the young couple so that they could get income from the rent. Monteith Row was a single terrace overlooking Glasgow Green. For a time, it was the most fashionable residential street in Glasgow. Jane's marriage contract was probably funded by money left to her by her father.

John and Jane had another child, Margaret Mather, who would be known as Maggie. In 1825, John applied for money in recognition of his wounds both at Waterloo and at Burgos.[45] He ultimately received a warrant for £73 (£6,375) from Greenwood & Sons, army agents 'to complete a year's pay for a wound received by you at Waterloo.'[46]

Early in 1826, their 4-year-old son Alexander George died. Margaret Bogle wrote to her sister-in-law Jane, John's wife:

> The hand of affliction has indeed been upon you. God sanctify your sorrows and mend our hearts to bear with humble resignation His merciful and wise dispensations. Your poor boy has been a sufferer from his birth, his constitution never would have been strong – he has been taken from the evil day! How deeply I feel for you.[47]

The Orr family left Glasgow shortly after Alexander George's death and moved into Dove Cot in Inveresk, a village near Musselburgh on the outskirts of Edinburgh. During this period two other children were born, William Pollock and John William. William Pollock died when a baby. John William Orr (latterly called Jack or sometimes Johnnie) survived and would become my great-grandfather. Of their first seven children, four died between the ages of 2 and 4.[48] I have a simple watercolour, painted about 1829, of John and Jane with the Maggie and James, who is holding a cricket bat. **(Illustration 07 colour).**

John enjoyed woodworking as a hobby. In 1830, Margaret Bogle wrote to her sister-in-law Jane to ask how John was doing, does he 'not appear to long for employment?' She went on: 'He must have turned and carpented a great deal since I left. I shall expect some very nice little *cosa* when I come back.'[49] (A *cosa* is a small item in Italian.)

A paragraph about John Orr in the Waterloo Roll Call sums up his military career:

> Accompanied the 1st Battalion, 42nd Highlanders to the Peninsular; was present at Salamanca, the siege of Burgos, storming of St Michael; the retreat to Portugal, and all the actions in the Pyrenees. Was wounded at Burgos, and again severely at Waterloo. On the reduction of the army after Waterloo, he joined the 94th (the old Scots Brigade), and on a further reduction, was appointed to the Royal Veteran Battalion.[50]

On 2 June 1831, John, aged 41, rejoined the Edinburgh Militia as a captain.[51] Lieutenant Colonel Macdonald was still in charge and wrote to Horse Guards to find out if John's pension would be affected. Horse Guards wrote back saying they had consulted the Secretary of State for War and had been told that if a lieutenant or a captain joined a militia, he would continue to receive his full pension.[52]

It may be that Colonel Macdonald encouraged John to rejoin the militia. He was an early subscriber to the SNMA and had been an ordinary director since 1829. He knew that the Academy was urgently looking for a new superintendent. If John were to become a captain, it would give him a more appropriate rank to be superintendent.

In the metal uniform box, I found John's scarlet militia jacket or coatee with his name in the inner part of the collar. (A 'coatee' was a tight-fitting military uniform coat or jacket.) Still in their proper box were his militia silver bullion epaulettes with their tassels. They attach by laces fed through holes in material of the coatee. One of the epaulettes has 'Left' written on it, so each must be slightly different.

The jacket is small, but I can just get into it, although the sleeves are too long. I am size 14, John must have been a slight, but tall man. In the uniform box were also his sword with the cipher of King William IV on the guard and its lace sword knot, black leather scabbard and carrying case. **(Illustrations 08, 09 and 10 colour)**.

Soon after joining the Edinburgh Militia, John was formally approached to become the superintendent of the SNMA. He accepted and was to remain in this role for over thirty years. He would see it grow in size and renown and then, sadly, witness its eventual decline.

Chapter 3

Becoming Superintendent of the Scottish Naval & Military Academy

> In Captain Orr, the Directors believe they have found a gentlemen possessed of the necessary qualifications; to great firmness they observe that he unites the conduct and proper feelings of a gentleman.[1]
>
> Sir Henry Jardine, Vice Chairman.

In order to explain how and why John became superintendent of the SNMA it is necessary to look back at the start of military education in Scotland. The first college to be established was the Scottish Military Academy which was founded in 1823 by Captain George Scott. It is not clear why Scott wanted to start a military academy. He had been placed on the retired list in 1816 and may have wanted to augment his pension or perhaps, like John, he was bored in retirement. He may well have realised he was not likely to get another military appointment due to reductions in the army's size.

Scott had served eleven years as adjutant to the 1st Battalion of the 91st (Argyllshire Highlanders) Regiment. He was commissioned as lieutenant in 1810 and served as adjutant at the Battle of Waterloo. Scott was a good linguist; his French was so fluent that while he was serving in France he was regularly used as an interpreter at courts martial.

Scott's military academy, a day school, was established partly to better equip young men who wanted to enrol in the British army by buying their commissions and also to make it easier for others to join the East India Company (EIC) as foot soldiers. They would still need to go to Addiscombe Military Seminary in England, the training college for the EIC, if they were planning to go into the artillery or become engineers. There appears to be no extant register of pupils who were at Scott's Academy so it is not known who they were or what career path they followed.

The Academy started in a small way and soon expanded by moving to larger premises at 24 Waterloo Place, near Calton Hill. It taught broadsword, small sword, firelock tactics, fortification and gymnastics. The academic subjects were practical mathematics, drawing, geography, history, French, Italian and German. It was a successful and popular institution. The first public examinations were held over four days in July 1824. At the prize-giving, Captain Scott announced that 165 young men had received instruction since the examinations had been held the previous summer.[2] All reports mention that Scott did most of the teaching himself.

In August 1824, an article appeared in *The Scots Magazine* emphasising how excellent it was that at long last Scotland had its own military academy. Young men could be taught all the other professions in Scotland such as law, the church, and medicine but had to go to England for a military education. 'What we desire is that the youth of Scotland may have the same advantage' and be able to study in their own country. Up until then most 'young men were transformed into officers by the co-operation of the army clothier and the drill-serjeant'. It then said that:

> The general proficiency of the pupils in Mathematics, Fortification, Languages and the Sword and Firelock Exercises in all their branches, reflect the highest credit on the zeal and ability of Mr Scott, and give promise that this infant Institution will at no great distance of time rival the old and lavishly patronised Military Academies in the south.[3]

The article is referring to the Royal Military Academy, Woolwich (RMA), the Royal Military College, Sandhurst (RMC) and Addiscombe Military Seminary. It went on to welcome the teaching of gymnastics and fencing.

Towards the end of October 1824, the Academy announced that its new term was underway. Scott repeated that his object was 'to unite Physical and Mental education'. He was happy that students enrolled for only one subject or they could choose more, if that was their preference. 'Pecuniary motives not being principal inducements to this Institution, the terms are moderate.'[4] Each class would have been paid for individually. Lord Kerr in 1830, by then the SNMA chairman, commented that Scott's Academy succeeded 'beyond expectations' due to Scott's 'unwearied' and 'unaided exertions'.[5]

George Scott died after a short illness in the middle of a term on 9 July 1825. He had run the Academy for only two years. He was buried in the graveyard at St Michael's Church, Inveresk, where one of his sons had been interred nearly fourteen years earlier. He left an elderly mother, an orphaned son and pupils with no teacher. The military, nobility and influential men of Edinburgh were concerned about the potential closure of The Scottish Military Academy. They considered it essential that Scotland should continue to have its own military college.

On 22 July, only thirteen days after Captain Scott had died, a public meeting was held in the Waterloo Hotel to discuss the establishment of a new military academy. The chairman was the Right Honourable Lord Robert Kerr. A group of about twenty-four 'Nobles and Gentlemen' gathered to hear what he had to say. Lord Kerr had had a long career in the army and was now adjutant general. He said that the 'metropolis of Scotland' should have a military seminary. Sir Patrick Walker, an advocate and landowner, who was the honorary secretary spoke next:

> Captain Scott had the merit of making the first experiment, and his success, under all disadvantages, proved that such an establishment, if properly conducted, would succeed on a much larger scale. Indeed it was hard that gentlemen, who wished to prepare their sons for a military profession should be compelled, at great expense, to send them to England for the want of a seminary in Scotland.[6]

All present agreed that a new seminary should be established, similar to Scott's Academy, and provision should be made for his aged mother and his orphaned son. A committee would be appointed to run the organisation with Lord Kerr as the chairman. Other members would include the Lord Provost, Sir Henry Jardine (a solicitor and antiquarian), Sir Patrick Walker (lawyer and landowner) and various well-known

Edinburgh and military figures, some of whom had been involved in Scott's Academy. Various proposals were agreed, which included that premises had to be found a superintendent appointed.

The following month another meeting was held, which resulted in a prospectus being published in the *Caledonian Mercury* of 24 August. It stated that the new academy was to be funded by asking people to participate in a share subscription scheme. One hundred and twenty-seven people had already subscribed for 191 shares which gave a total sum of £1,910 (£166,800).[7] The transactions are not dated and the value of one share was £10 (£877).

The list of subscribers is impressive because they came from both the nobility (the largest proportion) and the professions. Many of the nobility had served in the army. As well as the Duke of Argyll and the Marquises of Lothian and Huntly, there were other titled men such as Earl of Glasgow who was a Tory peer; Major General Sir George Leith who had fought in India and had become the Governor of Penang; and Sir Robert Keith Dick had served in India and was a well-known Edinburgh landowner who lived in Prestonfield House.

Ten lawyers, including a sheriff, an advocate and several Writers to the Signet subscribed. (Writers to the Signet are members of a private society of Scottish solicitors dating back to 1594.) There were six medical men including Dr David Maclagan, the president of both of the Royal College of Surgeons and the Royal College of Physicians, and Sir George Ballingall, the Regius Professor of Military Surgery at Edinburgh University. On the list was also the Very Reverend Baird, who was the Principal of Edinburgh University and William Burn the architect of the Edinburgh Academy school and John Watson's Institution (which is now Scottish National Gallery of Modern Art). Several army and naval officers were subscribers. Its name would be Scottish Military & Naval Academy. (When John became superintendent in 1831, the name was changed to the Scottish Naval & Military Academy – to reflect that the navy is the senior service. It is called SNMA throughout this book.)

The directors planned to have a fund which would enable 'a fair interest to be paid on the capital advanced'. In addition to shares being bought, it was hoped that some people would give donations. Gymnastics would be included, a novel idea in the UK, but well known in Sweden and Germany:

> Gymnastic Exercises have not only been found extremely advantageous by Gentlemen following Military and Naval professions; but are well known to tend much to the improvement and preservation of health. Gentlemen in every class of society, therefore, are interested in the present institution, especially those of a weakly constitution, or of sedentary habits, to whom Gymnastic Exercises are particularly beneficial.[8]

On 13 October 1825, the acting secretary wrote a public letter on behalf of the directors.[9] He announced the establishment of a new military seminary. It, like Scott's Academy, would be a day school and would use the Scottish educational system 'which has been so much approved of and has procured for Edinburgh such high celebrity'. The subjects to be taught were: military and naval tactics; practical mathematics; French; Spanish; Italian; German; Persian; and Hindustani. In addition, were listed military, landscape and architectural drawing, elocution, composition, history, writing and geography.

The fees were to be 'as moderate as the interests of the Establishment will admit of'. There would be no fixed curriculum, students could enrol for the classes which they wanted to attend. If, however, they were planning to have a military career, they would be required to take all the necessary classes for that purpose. The Acting Secretary Mitchell Patison suggested that the SNMA should use premises that he owned. They proved to be inadequate and the Academy soon moved into what had been a terraced house in George Street in the centre of Edinburgh's New Town.

The Academy needed a superintendent. At this time John was living in Glasgow and may well not have been known to any of the directors, he was also still a lieutenant, too low a rank to be considered for the position of superintendent. Major General Stewart of Garth, an ordinary director of the SNMA was going to visit to London and was asked to check with his military colleagues regarding possible applicants for the post. (Major General David Stewart was a well-respected officer who in 1822 had written *The Sketches of the Character, Manners and Present State of the Highlands of Scotland* which included a history of the 42nd Regiment.) He first suggested Colonel Ryves, who proved to be too expensive. Major General Stewart next proposed they should interview Major Charles Downes who had served under him in the Peninsular War. Downes travelled to Edinburgh, was interviewed, and appointed superintendent. In addition, he would teach military fortification, drawing, surveying and landscape drawing. The directors agreed to pay Downes a salary of £150 (£13,400). In addition, he would earn money from his teaching fees.

Downes had been assistant military draftsman at the RMC, and while there in August 1819 had been promoted to brevet major. He served in the Peninsular War with the 40th Foot, but he is recorded as being retired on full pay from 1st Royal Battalion. He was good at teaching military drawing, but as will be seen later in this chapter, Downes was the wrong choice for the role of superintendent. His idea of how a military college should be run was at odds with views of the directors.

Two years later, in 1827, disciplinary problems started to occur when the Academy was based in George Street. According to Downes, in a retrospective report in the press, it began with an incident regarding uniform.[10] Downes had criticised a pupil about the cap he was wearing and the boy left the Academy. The directors were unhappy with the way he had dealt with the situation and criticised his action. Downes considered he had been over-ruled and stopped disciplining the students. He confirmed that the pupils had started to behave badly, but he felt it was no longer his role to control them 'others sat with their hats on at the upper windows, throwing cinders into the street at the passengers'.

The directors became increasingly dissatisfied with Major Downes' lack of discipline. In 1828, he was demoted to only teaching military fortification, drawing, surveying and landscape drawing. He was no longer to be the superintendent and he would not receive his salary for that role. Yet the directors allowed Downes to continue to call himself superintendent and did not appoint a new one. This was a weak decision which was to cause trouble in the months and years ahead. With Downes no longer acting as superintendent and no one in charge of exercising daily discipline, the bad behaviour of the pupils was obvious to Edinburgh citizens living nearby and regularly passing their building in fashionable George Street. Had there been a functioning superintendent in place, these issues would not have occurred.

A worry for the directors was that enrolment was steadily going down. I have found no note of the number of pupils who joined during the first six years of the SNMA. (The Roll Book in the family archive only starts when John became superintendent in 1831.) There is, however, a record of the total amount of entrance money the Academy received each year for the first four years. Every pupil had to pay an entrance fee of £1 1s (£101). It is therefore possible to get an approximate figure for the numbers enrolling each year.[11] These figures indicate that the enrolment nearly halved between 1825 and 1828, reducing from 173 to only about 95.[12] The numbers apparently continued to fall during the following two years.

The diminishing numbers enrolling during the first years of the SNMA may well have been due to the poor leadership while Downes was not an active superintendent. There were, however, wider causes such as the deliberate policy of reducing the size of the army after the defeat of Napoleon, which meant fewer officers were needed. After Waterloo, as John found out, many regiments were disbanded and others contracted.

Another problem was that Major Downes was against the teaching of non-military subjects. He was not supportive of the broad curriculum that the directors thought important. He was strongly opposed to the widening of the enrolment to include younger pupils. In a public letter written later, he said, 'The introduction of minor branches of education would be the means of introducing little boys into the Academy, who would come with satchels on their backs, and thus destroy the respectability of a regular military establishment.'[13]

The situation worsened and the directors realised that they had to find a replacement superintendent. Press reports and letters in May and June 1832 revealed retrospectively how bad the situation had become. Downes admitted in a letter to the *Caledonian Mercury* that during this period, 'The hours which should have been devoted to study were spent in idleness and riot, disorders of all kind increased' and the students were 'walking about the Academy, smoking cigars and setting off Waterloo crackers'. (Waterloo crackers were explosive crackers that required pulling at both ends, similar to a Christmas cracker.) This could not continue, a new superintendent had to be appointed as soon as possible.

In June 1831, at a general meeting of directors, Lord Robert Kerr spoke of the necessity of appointing a new superintendent of the Academy. It was debated and Major Downes' incompetence was unanimously acknowledged. Captain Orr's qualifications were discussed and Colonel Macdonald would have been able to speak about John's distinguished military service. It was agreed to offer him the role of superintendent and John accepted. He was appointed in the summer of 1831 and was in post for the opening of the new term on 1 October.

The term started off badly as directors did not tell Major Downes that a new superintendent was in place. Downes wrote subsequently in a letter to *The Scotsman* that the first he knew of it was when 'a person, whom I had never seen before, entered my classroom, and told me he was the appointed superintendent.'[14]

The directors quickly put a notice in *The Scotsman* of 8 October to announce that John Orr was the new superintendent of the SNMA. They added some mollifying words, thanking Major Downes for his years of service as a teacher. The announcement stated:

> Major Downes having retired from the situation of Military Superintendent of the Academy in consequence of his arduous duties as a Teacher, in three of the principal branches of study, rendering it impossible for him to attend to the detail and interior economy of the Establishment, the Directors take this opportunity of publicly expressing their entire satisfaction with the manner in which Major Downes has discharged his various duties ever since the commencement of the Academy.[15]

Major Downes did not accept this attempt by the directors to explain the situation. He was annoyed about what had happened and resented a captain replacing him, given that he was a major, albeit a brevet major.

During the first six months of the new session, the pupils at the Academy had become more disciplined under John's superintendency. In March 1832, the masters were so pleased with the way the first few months had gone that they gave John a dinner in the British Hotel to thank him 'for the eminent services rendered by him' to the Academy.

Mr Lees, the mathematics master, who was in the chair, proposed the health of Captain Orr. He 'passed a very high and well-merited eulogium, on him for the many excellent and judicious arrangements which he had introduced since he filled the office of superintendent'. [16]

The directors had a problem. The angry presence of Downes could no longer be tolerated and they gave him duties which he resented as being too demeaning; this forced his resignation on 1 May 1832. He did not go quietly.

Major Downes was seething with anger and wanted to make public his displeasure about the way he felt that he had been treated. He announced in the *Caledonian Mercury* that he would be publishing a letter stating his reasons for leaving the Academy. Before printing excerpts from Downes' letter on 12 May 1832, the paper issued a hostile leader against the SNMA. The newspaper had believed everything that Major Downes had said and had not verified the letter's contents. I have quoted at length from the leader to show how critical it was:

> This Academy, we fear, is going to the wall, if it be not gone already. We have before us a printed 'Letter to the Subscribers of the Scottish Naval and Military Academy on the Management of that Institution, by Major Downes', the late superintendent, which makes disclosures at once painful and humiliating. By mismanagement on the part of the Directors, insubordination on the part of the students, caballing among the masters, and, worse than all, the adoption of a system of education at once vicious in principle and imperfect in its details, the Academy, considered as a military school, has been utterly ruined; the only man connected with it who, by his scientific acquirements and his military experience was fitted to raise it to the rank which we fondly hoped it would one day attain as a national establishment for the education of such of our youth as were destined for the profession of arms, has been driven from it by a series of ill usage and petty annoyances, which reflect but small credit on those who either sanctioned, or tolerated them. But we must let Major Downes speak for himself.[17]

In the same edition of the newspaper, Downes put forward his case. He started by saying he was specially sought for the position of superintendent because of his experience. He was deeply critical of the uniform that the directors had chosen as it was too ornate. He then listed many other criticisms, for instance gymnastics should not be taught and he was against elocution being included in the syllabus. 'We are yet to learn that there is anything either in the theory or practice of war which requires the aid of spouting.'

He explained that he had never been told that a new superintendent had been chosen. He claimed that John's appointment had been made without the directors' knowledge and behind his back and he had never resigned the position. He was disparaging about the new duties of the superintendent. He thought they were demeaning to the role.

In May, the SNMA made two announcements in the *Caledonian Mercury* firstly that 'Major Downes' connection with the Academy was about to cease', and later that they were pleased to confirm the appointment of Captain Shaw of the Royal Artillery to teach fortification and military drawing.

A supportive letter for the Academy was published in the *Caledonian Mercury* on 21 May, signed by a 'Well-Wisher of the SNMA'. It stated that much of what Major Downes had written in the letter was 'unfounded and defamatory'. The Academy had found that 'teaching occupied him the whole time' and he was, therefore, not able to be superintendent as well. It was because of this the directors had wanted to remove him from being the superintendent and that portion of his salary cut. Yet Downes was allowed to keep the title of superintendent, 'as the loss of that seemed to touch his feelings'. The letter confirmed that he held such things as gymnastics in great contempt.

On 28 May 1832, Downes published a second angry missive in which he was replying to the well-wisher's letter. He said that the directors, despite their titles, could easily not be telling the truth. 'And does the writer really conceive that no man can speak the truth but a person with a title?' He agreed he did not teach gymnastics. 'I really do not think it exactly the sort of thing for an officer to do.' He denied everything in the 'well-wisher letter' and aggressively defended what he had written in his earlier letter of 12 May and threatened legal action.

A second letter from a 'Well-Wisher' was published on Saturday, 9 June. The writer stated that, 'In the beginning of June 1831, that is, one year ago, Major Downes was voted incompetent at a general meeting of Directors, Lord Robert Kerr in the chair.' The well-wisher went on to write how important were subjects such as the First Books of Euclid, writing, arithmetic and bookkeeping, elementary French, elocution, history, geography, Latin and Caesar's Commentaries. (First Book of Euclid was a book on geometry and was the first of thirteen books attributed to the mathematician Euclid *c*.300 BC.) All these subjects were ridiculed by Major Downes. The well-wisher ended by saying 'that the Major's letter is, in toto founded on mis-statement and distortion of facts'.

There followed a note from the editor defending publication of Downes' letters. 'We found it duly authenticated by his name, we never for a moment doubted that the facts were accurately stated, and, upon this assumption, proceeded to argue the case, which, ex facie of the Major's statement, appeared a very hard one indeed.' It was signed, 'Editor, *Caledonian Mercury*'.

On 21 June, the *Caledonian Mercury* had a volte face and printed an apology for believing all that Major Downes had said. The newspaper retracted its previous statements:

> But, as the whole case is now before us, and as the complexion of the question at issue between the late Superintendent Major Downes, and the Directors of this establishment, has proved very different the whole indeed from what we were at first let to anticipate, we deem it incumbent upon us to state generally, for the information of the public what respects, and to what extent, the original statement of Major Downes has been shown to be erroneous and unfounded.
>
> We could not imagine that the Major had reconnoitred his ground so badly as to take up a position upon the quicksand and it certainly never entered our imagination that, although his inferences might be denied, his facts could be refuted. The event has shown however, that we were mistaken in both respects.
>
> The case he made out has been annihilated, partly on evidence supplied by himself he cannot wonder that his

> authority should cease to command respect, and that his complaints should be disregarded as at once groundless and frivolous.

It had been a difficult time for the Academy and for John. Major Downes did not leave until 1 May 1832. From 1 October 1831 until then Downes was an angry and disgruntled presence at the Academy. During May and June 1832 many who read the *Caledonian Mercury* would have thought that the SNMA was a troubled institution.

It should be mentioned that some of the cadets liked Major Downes and gave him a presentation of 'a large and valuable silver snuff box' on his departure. Downes was good at teaching the military courses and some of the students regretted his departure.

Before John became superintendent, the Academy was not being competently run. The Downes saga was an example of this. The directors, in addition, made another poor appointment in choosing Mitchell Patison as their acting secretary. Patison while employed by the SNMA became bankrupt.[18] Accounts published in 1830 say 'SUM lost by Mr Patison as far as yet ascertained £145 9s (£13,850)'.[19] (These are the only SNMA accounts that I have found.)

Furthermore, in November 1829 an annual shareholders' meeting took place which was reported in *The Edinburgh Evening Courant*.[20] A man called Peter Campbell questioned how the Academy was being organised. He was not a director but had subscribed as a shareholder when the SNMA was founded. He asked why shareholders were not circulated with annual reports. He had not seen the Rules and Regulations and he had no idea of the financial position of the Academy. He did not consider it enough that notification of the date of the annual meeting was only reported in the press. He tried to form a new committee. In the end he agreed with a proposal by Dr Maclagan, one of the directors, that an annual report should be circulated to shareholders annexing the Rules and Regulations of the Academy and giving an abstract of the financial position. This resulted in the *Report of the Ordinary Directors of the Scottish Military & Naval Academy* being approved which was printed in 1830.

The first public approval of John as superintendent came at the prize-giving in July 1832, ten months after he had been appointed. The prizes were presented by Lord Kerr and afterwards the Vice Chairman Sir Henry Jardine spoke. He concluded his remarks by saying:

> In Captain Orr, the Directors believe they have found a gentlemen possessed of the necessary qualifications; to great firmness they observe that he unites the conduct and proper feelings of a gentleman; and they take this public opportunity of expressing the satisfaction with which they have observed the zeal and unremitting attention which he has displayed in discharging the duties of an office which under the particular circumstances of his appointment, were, at their commencement, attended with peculiar difficulties.[21]

The next chapter goes into more detail about how the Academy was established and how it was run after John became superintendent.

Chapter 4

How the SNMA was run after John became Superintendent

> Shepherd: 'Pray, what is this new Military Academy? Is it a gude institution Mr North?'
>
> North: 'I think it is. It will not only give young soldiers some useful knowledge, but put spunk into them before they enter upon service.'[1]
>
> Ettrick Shepherd to Christopher North in *Blackwood's Magazine*.

John's appointment as superintendent proved crucial to the improved running of the Academy. His way of working is mentioned at a dinner after the prize-giving in July 1841, which was held in the Waterloo Hotel and was reported in the *Caledonian Mercury* of 26 July. After the meal there were toasts and speeches. George Lees, the mathematics master, proposed the health of the superintendent. Mr Lees started by describing how, from his first day in office, Captain Orr had shown 'the very qualities which were essential to the right discharge of the very important trust committed to him, qualities by which he brought out the retiring, and difficult student while he reined up the more forward and self-confident.'

He went on to illustrate this with an example:

> The Directors might have got a superintendent more acquainted with Hindustani, or one who could have conjugated a Greek verb with fewer blunders, but also they could not have got one possessing more kindly manners with a sounder judgement than did Captain Orr.

> (Much applause.) Down comes the captain to the Academy in the morning – his bland countenance beaming with goodwill to all – the students soon catch the spirit of his expression – the master strives in vain to maintain a stern countenance – he too gives way and the whole class-room becomes a scene of unclouded joy. [Cheers.] The captain, however, could also rebuke with great effect. Let there be a delinquent among the assembled pupils and woe betide the unhappy offender. (Laughter and cheers.)

John replied to this warm toast and thanked George Lees and went on to say how much pleasure he took in conducting his department of the Institution and discharging his duties. He said he was helped by so much kindness from all concerned and ended by saying 'he would not relax his endeavours to promote the interests of the Academy'. He thought if the government would let one or two of their best students to receive commissions then 'the Scottish Naval & Military Academy would become an institution worthy of the military character of the Scottish people.' This resulted in cheers from all those at the dinner.

I wanted to find out more about John's responsibilities. Luckily, I discovered at the National Library of Scotland a copy of the *Rules and Regulations of the Scottish Naval & Military Academy*, dated 1834; this helped explain John's duties and the way the Academy was organised.[2] (The nineteen sections listing the duties of the superintendent are in Appendix 4.)

The directors delegated the running of the Academy to John. He attended the weekly directors' meetings and brought them up to date with what had happened since the previous one. He had to ensure that discipline was maintained, keep an audit of the Academy's expenditure, see parents and guardians and insert advertisements in the press. He was in charge of the library and all property belonging to the Academy. A major duty was producing quarterly reports on the students and in addition he had to prepare the final certificates for those pupils who had passed the necessary examinations. The directors trusted John's judgement and he was given a mandate to act on his own initiative should a particular emergency arise that needed to be dealt with immediately.

On 15 December 1832, fifteen months after John became superintendent, a report was printed in the *Caledonian Mercury* which indicates how much John had achieved during this period. It congratulates the SNMA for the changes which had been recently made in eradicating the problems that had occurred under Downes:

> There is not now a better regulated establishment of the kind in any part of the kingdom, or one which is carried on with greater harmony and efficiency in all its departments. Various changes for the better have been recently effected in the details of the institution, the general system has been extended and improved in several very important points; the discipline also has at length been placed on a footing which insures perfect subordination, without the employment of undue severity; and, by the adoption and enforcement of a judicious system of rules, the whole of the machine, which not long ago seemed about to run riot if not break into pieces, has been reduced into excellent working order.

One of John's main concerns immediately after his appointment would have been the poor discipline of the pupils, which had started under his predecessor and had discredited the Academy. Unless this was improved it was possible that not enough students would enrol and the Academy might fail.

John used the Academy Prospectus to attract new pupils and issued it to parents who enquired about the SNMA. The family archive has three copies, each from a different year. They provide information about the office bearers, subjects studied and fees charged. The details from the Prospectus of 1833 can be found in Appendix 1, Table 2 and a photograph of the Prospectus for 1843 in the monochrome section. **(Illustration 04 monochrome)**.

John must have been delighted in 1832 when King William IV became the patron of the SNMA and in the same year the Duke of Wellington agreed to be one of the two presidents. Wellington was to remain a president until he died twenty years later. The SNMA had many tiers of office bearers, which was not uncommon at the time, particularly with institutions that had been funded by private benefaction. The tiers were:

Patron, President, Vice Presidents, Extraordinary Directors, Ordinary Directors and Superintendent.

The vice presidents were mainly those who had contributed to the initial funding of the SNMA and were members of the nobility, such as the Duke of Argyll and the Marquises of Lothian and Huntly, and others were wealthy landowners. Extraordinary directors included the Lord Provost of Edinburgh and rectors of two of Edinburgh's famous schools – The High School and Edinburgh Academy. None of these men were involved in the administration of the SNMA as it was the ordinary directors and the superintendent who were the people who ran the Academy. There is a list of office bearers for 1831/32, the year that John joined, in Appendix 3.

It was important for the credibility of the institution that the Academy should have several senior and respected army and naval officers as ordinary directors. These included Major General David Stewart who had joined the 42nd Regiment in 1778 and was the man who suggested choosing Downes. Vice Admiral Sir David Milne became a midshipman in 1779 and served in the Royal Navy for over sixty years. The Academy also had, as ordinary directors, retired officers from the East India Company. In 1831, there were two prominent politicians who both had military connections. One was General Duncan Campbell of Lochnell who was a Whig Member of Parliament for Ayr Burghs. The other was Sir John Hope of Pinkie who was the Conservative Member of Parliament for Midlothian.

To support John, a quorum of five ordinary directors would meet once a month and a committee of three would convene weekly, according to a roster. John attended all these meetings. The SNMA were fortunate to have two prominent men as chairman and vice chairman.

The chairman was Lieutenant Colonel Lord Robert Kerr (1790–1843) and it was due to his strong character that the SNMA was founded after the death of Captain Scott. Lord Kerr became an officer in the British army in 1798 and had served all over Europe and in Egypt. He was currently the assistant adjutant general on the North British Staff, a position he held until his death. Lord Kerr proved to be an excellent chairman, due to his many years' experience of army administration and his long military service. He and John had a good relationship and worked closely together.

After my parents died, I was intrigued to find at the back of a cupboard a small unsigned oil painting, which was slightly damaged. Low down on the front is written 'a sketch for a larger picture'. **(Illustration 11 colour).**

A note on the back says:

> Sketch for the Whole Length Portrait of Lord Robert Kerr in the Naval & Military Academy Edinburgh.

A full-length painting of Lord Kerr was executed by Robert Innes in the early 1830s. This painting is presumably Innes's preparatory sketch which was given to John's family.

Lord Kerr died on 23 June 1843 at his home, 38 Moray Place.[3] His death was officially announced by Major General Neil Douglas, the Governor of Edinburgh Castle. Major General Douglas would succeed Lord Kerr as chairman of the SNMA.[4] Lord Kerr's widow sent a memorial of her husband to John via their son Robert Kerr. John's letter book contains a copy of the note John wrote back to Robert thanking him for the memorial:

> I invariably received from him [Lord Kerr] that countenance and support which were the dictates of a heart and mind rarely possessed by any individual whose memory must ever be held in the highest respect by all who had the honour and happiness like myself to know and appreciate his superior worth.[5]

Sir Henry Jardine (1766–1851) was a good choice as vice chairman. He was a genial, popular man who had a great deal of energy and knew most influential people in the city. He qualified as a lawyer and had become an office bearer of several of the literary, scientific and charitable institutions in Edinburgh, many of these as a working director. He held two prestigious offices: one as the Solicitor for Taxes in Scotland and the other was the King's Remembrancer during the reign of King George IV (The King's or Queen's Lord Treasurer's Remembrancer is an officer in Scotland who represents the Crown's interests in certain areas. It is a post normally held by a lawyer.) He was a long-time friend of Sir Walter Scott. Scott asked Jardine to join him when he was given instructions to look for the long-lost Scottish regalia. They searched in various places in Edinburgh Castle and eventually found the crown jewels locked in an old oak chest in a small strongroom.

Sir Henry trusted John and his way of running the SNMA; this was confirmed at a prize-giving in 1835 when he said that John's 'intelligence, firmness and good sense rendered the duties of the Directors comparatively easy, and without whose assistance he believed the utmost and united exertions of the Directors and Masters would be in vain'.[6] Sir Henry died in Edinburgh on 11 August 1851. His obituaries all mention 'his kindness of heart and amiable disposition'.[7]

John's work as superintendent will have been made easier, as the Academy was now based in a different property. In 1830, they had moved into part of the new Royal Academy Buildings in Lothian Road **(Illustration 05 monochrome)**.[8]

This was the headquarters of the Royal Riding School, formally known as the Royal Academy of Exercise. It had been founded in 1760 by the nobility and gentlemen of Edinburgh for the methodical training of horses and riders. A few years earlier, they had decided to move from their original premises and commissioned an attractive custom-built property in Lothian Road. It was too large and they were happy to share it with the SNMA. This three-storey building was better suited to the SNMA's needs than their previous home in George Street **(Illustration 06 monochrome)**.[9]

The ground floor was used mainly by the Riding School, but the covered exercise area could be used by the SNMA for gymnastics and drill. The middle floor, known as the principal floor, was used by both the Academy and the Riding School and the top floor was for the sole use of the SNMA. The Academy had, at last, the appearance of a significant and well-established institution.[10] The rent for the SNMA portion of the building was £150 (£14,290) annually for seven years, which was less than they had been paying in George Street. Colonel Leatham, who ran the Royal Riding School, agreed to waive the fee of £3 3s (£300) for use of the stables. This meant that the Academy could now offer riding as an activity for its pupils. Colonel Leatham became an extraordinary director of the SNMA.

The Royal Academy Buildings were not large enough to provide student accommodation, therefore the SNMA continued to be a day school. It was John's responsibility to help parents find lodgings for their sons if they did not have family or friends to stay with in Edinburgh. John and some masters took in pupils as boarders. John charged 120 guineas (£12,170) for a single room and 100 guineas (£9,709) for a shared bedroom for ten months, but lodgings could be obtained for as little as £60 (£5,796) elsewhere in Edinburgh. All accommodation recommended by the SNMA had been checked by John.

The Academy syllabus was varied and parents could choose which subjects they wanted their sons to study, but those pupils planning to have a military career had to take prescribed classes. This regime meant that there were no fixed annual fees at the Academy; each boy's fees would be different, depending on which classes he took. The charges for classes varied, many of the standard subjects cost a guinea, £1 1s (about £101) per quarter, but foreign languages were often more than double this sum. The fees for each boy would be calculated and the parent had to pay the sum in advance. Subjects and fees are looked at in more detail in Chapter 6.

The masters had some measure of independence; they had to use textbooks that had been approved by the directors, but otherwise they could teach 'according to their own method'. They had to keep a daily record of pupils' conduct, progress and attendance in a report-book. This had to be shown to the superintendent so he could compile quarterly reports on the pupils. It was their duty to note any pupil's disobedience.

By the time John became superintendent, the Academy already employed some experienced teachers. One of these was Dr John Lees (1797–1886). He would become the longest-serving master at the SNMA. He started teaching mathematics when it opened in 1825 and taught there until 1853 when he became the assistant professor at St Andrews University. He wrote a number of mathematical books and was described as being an 'eminent, experienced and zealous teacher'.[11]

George Roland (1809–1862) started teaching fencing at the Academy in 1828. He was one of the foremost fencing teachers in the UK and both his sons taught at the Academy. He published *An Introductory Course of Fencing* in 1832 and in addition wrote a book on modern gymnastic exercises.[12]

Roland introduced Fencing Assaults to Edinburgh; they had been started in London by his father, who was French. These were fencing displays and not competitions. Each school sent its top fencers, who fenced each other. John agreed that the SNMA should take part; the other schools were usually the Royal Academy and the Edinburgh Academy. The event was held in the prestigious Assembly Rooms and was a popular social occasion, similar to the Academy's prize-giving. It concluded with a fencing display between George Roland and his sons. Prizes were awarded to the school who had the most skilled fencers. In the Assault in 1834 Mr W. Campbell, who was awarding some of the prizes, said, 'That while Mr Roland was himself one of the best fencers in Europe, the skilful fencing of his pupils proved him to be the best teacher.'[13]

A major new appointment after John became superintendent was that of James Ballantyne (1813–1864). He was one of the well-known orientalists of his day and was a master at the SNMA from 1832 to 1845. He was born in Kelso, Roxburghshire and studied Oriental languages at Haileybury where his uncle was a teacher. (Haileybury was the East India Company's college for the education of pupils who had been chosen to train for the Indian Civil Service.) He then taught Hindustani and Persian at the SNMA and offered to teach other languages of the Indian sub-continent.

Ballantyne was interested in both science and religion and had a genuine respect for Indian philosophy and thinking. His knowledge of languages enabled him to translate Indian philosophy texts into English, enabling people in the West to read them for the first time. It worked the other way round and he was able to bring European thought and ideas to people in India.[14] He wrote a book, *Christianity Contrasted with Indian Philosophy*, and translated English scientific texts into Sanskrit. He was, however, a committed Christian and believed that all should be converted to Christianity.

Other works included books on Hindustani, Sanskrit and Mahratta languages and grammar; some of these were written while he was teaching at the SNMA. In 1845, he was awarded an LLD by Glasgow University and in the same year travelled to India to oversee the reorganisation of the Government College in Benares. In 1861, his health began to fail and he returned to Britain and became librarian of the India Office in London, a position he held until his death in 1864.

When James Ballantyne stopped teaching at the SNMA, the post was filled by another eminent lecturer. He was the Reverend David Liston (1799–1881), Professor of Oriental Studies at the University of Edinburgh.

The best known of the Academy's teachers was Sir Henry Yule (1820–1889) who became a famous polymath **(Illustration 07 monochromc)**. In retirement, he wrote a book on Marco Polo and then in 1886 with the help of Dr H. C. Burnell, he produced *Hobson-Jobson*, a dictionary of Anglo-Indian colloquial phrases, which is still in print.[15] Sir David Gilmour comments in *The British in India* that *Hobson-Jobson* is 'one of the most remarkable literary products of British India'.[16] As recently as 2021, Sathnam Sanghera in *Empireland*, calls it 'the glorious *Hobson-Jobson* Dictionary'.[17] A few years ago, I saw it in a Waterstone's bookshop. Beside it was this notice:

> Bungalow, pyjamas, tiffin, veranda, curry, cheroot, chintz, calico, gingham, mango, junk and catamaran are all words which have crept into the English language from the days of Britain's colonial rule of the Indian sub-continent and the Malaysian Peninsular.

It is an essential book for all who are interested in English etymology and the development of the language.

Yule was born at Inveresk, near Edinburgh, on 1 May 1820. His father was a major in the Indian army. After being a pupil at the SNMA for a year in 1836, he went on to study at Addiscombe and Chatham. He is listed in John's Roll Book as planning to join the EIC. This proved to be correct as he was commissioned into the Bengal Engineers in 1840 and returned briefly to the UK to marry in 1843. He served in both Sikh wars, 1845–6 and 1848–9.

In 1850, Yule took three years' extended furlough and returned to Edinburgh to teach at the SNMA. (A furlough of two years was allowed after serving eight years with the EIC.) During this period, he wrote a book on fortifications which was later translated into French.[18] It received an enthusiastic review in *The Edinburgh Evening Courant* of 9 September 1851 which noted: 'he writes with great ease, with excellent taste and with abundant spirit, he has produced a volume which we cannot hesitate to pronounce an exceedingly interesting one, even to those who are not soldiers.'[19]

He returned to India and was involved with various public works including irrigation schemes and a new railway system. Henry, aged 42, retired from the EIC in 1862 with the rank of colonel. He was created a CB in 1863. (The Most Honourable Order of the Bath, a reward for outstanding military or civilian service.) He then devoted his time to researching medieval and oriental history of Central Asia and became a leading authority on these subjects.[20] Due to his wife's ill health, they went to live in Palermo. He published many travel books; two of these were *Cathay and the Way Thither* (1866), the *Book of Ser Marco Polo* (1871–75). He received the gold medal of the Royal Geographical Society for the latter book.

Sir Henry Yule received many accolades during his life, including an honorary doctorate from Edinburgh University, and he was created Knight Commander of the Order of the Star of India in 1889. He died later that year in London. Henry's entry in the Oxford Dictionary of National Biography finishes with these words: 'Next to cruelty what roused his anger most was the neglect of an author to make an index to his work.'[21]

The quality of teaching at the SNMA was impressive. Joseph Panton, who was a pupil from October 1847 until July 1850, wrote in his memoir: 'Our professors were scholars and gentlemen. It was a pleasure to associate with them and altogether we felt it was our duty to work for the honour of the institution.'[22]

Panton talked with affection and admiration about his teachers. He said, 'That was one great thing amongst the students; there could not have been a more loyal lot of young gentlemen. It was a point of honour never to give offence to any of our masters.'[23] More will be revealed about Joseph Panton in Chapter 9.

Chapter 5

Orr Family Life

'He was a very strict disciplinarian, but at the same time a dear kind-hearted old fellow, and a real companion.'[1]

Joseph Panton.
Strength in Battle.

What was life like in the Orr family? How did they cope with having five or six boarders in the house for ten months of the year? The family archive is limited regarding daily family life as there are only a few personal letters and little written by John himself, except for a few valentine cards to his children. I know very little about his wife Jane as there are none of her letters in the archive. I have paintings of John and Jane, a few photographs of John, and his London passport issued to travel abroad with his daughters in 1853.

Much of the information about the Orrs has come from public records and it's a bit like trying to do a jigsaw without all the pieces. Luckily, the edited memoirs of a pupil who stayed with the Orr family for three years, *Strength in Battle, the Memoirs of Joseph Panton*, give us an entertaining first-hand account of life with the Orr family.

Before John became superintendent, the Orrs had been living in a cottage in Inveresk, a little village outside Edinburgh, but on his appointment they moved into the city, to 43 St Cuthbert Street, with their three surviving children: James, aged 9, Margaret (who was known as Maggie) 6, and Johnnie (latterly Jack) who was 3 and who would become my great-grandfather. This street was in the process of being formed and was part of the West New Town of Edinburgh. The development was built over ground called Morrison's Park which lay between Maitland Street, Castlebarns and the Lothian Road. The land was offered for sale as feuing lots in July 1824.[2] It would only take John a few minutes to walk along St Cuthbert's Lane to the Royal Academy Buildings in Lothian Road where the SNMA was now based.

The Orr children must have attended school in Edinburgh but I have found no record as to where they went. In April 1835, Jane gave birth to their last child, Helen Jane; she was born six years after Jack's birth, when Jane was 43 years old. John was fond of his children and in the archive are various valentine's wishes which he sent as loving jokes to Maggie and Johnnie (Jack). Although none of them is signed, the handwriting is recognisable. Two were posted anonymously in 1838, in each John has composed comical verses written beside the picture.

(Illustrations 12 and 13 colour). In the one sent to Johnnie, who would have been 9, the verse was written below the picture of a fashionable young lady:

My bonnie little Johnnie
I love you best of ony
Dinna leave me lang to pine
But choose me for your Valentine.

Maggie's valentine has the picture of a young sailor with an oar in his hand and his boat behind him. Maggie would have been 13. Here the verse is:

My dear Miss Orr
I've come ashore
For you alone I sigh,
Oh be not cruel
My dearest jewel
Nor bid your Jack goodbye.

When sails ascend
And main mast bent
And billows mounting high
I'll prize my Oar!!!
So much the more
And winds and waves defy.

(The exclamation marks are John's – playing on the pun of their name.)

John chose a large house when he became superintendent as he knew he would take in some of the pupils as boarders, most would stay for ten months until the following July. In October 1832, the Orrs had three boys staying, from then on it was normally five or six pupils each year. Two boys usually shared a room and they were all treated as part of the family.

John had duties at the end of each session that occupied him after the prize-giving, but in September he often took the family across to Fife for a few weeks' holiday. They normally stayed in one of the coastal villages such as North Queensferry, Inverkeithing, Dysart or Elie.[3] In a letter to Mrs Tomkinson, a mother of a pupil, he wrote: 'I am as usual in a great bustle clearing up accounts to be off to the country.'[4] In another letter written from Dysart, in 1840, he wrote: 'I intend to remain at this place till 21 September with my family for the benefit of sea bathing.'[5]

Sea bathing had become popular in Victorian times, as it was believed to be good for one's health. In some places, men and women had to be at least about 300ft apart on a beach, and women used a type of small, wheeled hut to get into the water, called a bathing machine. In the village of Portobello, on the outskirts of Edinburgh, sea bathing also took place. In 1832, the judge Lord Cockburn, who sent two of his sons to the SNMA, was not a fan of the pastime and wrote a letter to his daughter Elizabeth commenting on the 'the maritime indecency of Porto Bello is more than I can endure. It should be called Porto Nudo.'[6]

I have a pair of small water colour portraits of Jane and John painted in 1838, each 11x12ins **(Illustrations 14 and 15 colour)**. They were executed by Felice Piccioni, an Italian artist who was known for his portraits and normally worked in Ireland, but was living in Edinburgh that year. John is wearing his SNMA jacket, his red sash and his Waterloo Medal. He would have been 48. Jane, who was 46, is wearing a dark-blue dress with a gold brooch at her neck and on her head is a lace and ribbon cap which would be worn in the evening. She looks calm, composed and slightly matronly.

An engraving of John in his superintendent's uniform, painted much later in his life, hangs in my hall **(Illustration 01 monochrome)**. As a child I was interested in this picture and was told it was of my great great-grandfather, Captain John Orr. He looked a kind, but strong man gazing out at me. He is wearing a single-breasted frock coat with a high collar and he has a crimson sash over his left shoulder, The sash is in the archive box. He is holding his gloves in one hand and his cap and sword in the other and he is wearing the SNMA shoulder crescents **(Illustration 16 colour)**. Pinned on his frock coat are the Waterloo Medal and the General Service Medal. The portrait is an engraving by Thomas Dick of an oil painting by Robert Innes whom the directors had previously commissioned to paint Lord Kerr.

As a family we did not know when John Orr's portrait was painted. One day when I was examining the picture, I realised that one of the medals he was wearing was the Military General Service Medal which was issued to officers in 1848. The portrait, therefore, had to be painted after that. I approached the Royal Scottish Academy to see if anyone there had information about the painting. Agnes Wood, one of their collections volunteers found that the painting was exhibited by Robert Innes in the 1850 RSA Exhibition. It may have been commissioned by the directors to mark either John Orr's sixtieth birthday on 1 April 1850 or because in 1851 he would have been the superintendent for twenty years.

Robert Innes was a popular Scottish portrait painter and his paintings were in many collections. He was the president of the Edinburgh Society of Artists in 1843. Thomas Dick, the engraver, worked in Edinburgh from 1839 until 1879 and produced several engravings of paintings of prominent Edinburgh figures.

The oil portrait was in the possession of my family but sadly is now lost. In 1916, it was listed in the inventory taken after the death of Major General John William Orr (Johnnie or Jack), John's son. Jack's estate was handled by his son, Dr James Orr (my great uncle Jim), who did not have time to attend to the contents of his father's house and put everything into store. All the pictures were sent to Doig, Wilson & Wheatley, 90 George Street Edinburgh, who were fine art dealers, print sellers and frame makers. When great uncle Jim died in 1942 the oil portrait could not be found by Doig, Wilson & Wheatley and they ceased trading in 1957. The Scottish National Portrait Gallery has a copy of the engraving and I hope one day the original oil painting may turn up.

The 1841 census helps to explain how the Orr house was run. It was taken on 6 June and lists John, his wife Jane, and three of their four children Maggie 16, Jack, 11 and little Helen Jane aged 6. (James is not listed although he did not finish at the SNMA until July of that year.) The six pupils who were boarding are all named. There were five servants in the house. The first named was Jessie Eddington and then there were four names, two of whom were sisters, Mary and Ann Blackhall. In a reasonably well-off Victorian household, there would have been a housekeeper, a cook, a housemaid (who cleaned), a kitchen maid, and a laundry maid. (When I told my daughter this, she said the last three have now been replaced in most homes by the vacuum cleaner, the dishwasher and the washing machine.)

'Old Jess' Eddington, who was 32, started off as the children's nurse, was now called the housekeeper. She continued to work for them after John retired and died, aged 69, in April 1876. She was very much part of the family and was buried in the Orr lair in Warriston Cemetery, Edinburgh. (Burial plots in Scotland are called lairs.) On the gravestone is written:

> Jess Eddington
> Who died 19th April 1876
> For 53 years
> A faithful nurse and esteemed friend
> In Captain Orr's family.[7]

The 1851 census still lists the Blackwell sisters, and Mary Watson is named in both the 1851 and 1861 censuses; this suggests that the Orrs were good employers. To be in the census they must all have been living in the house. Their accommodation may have been basic, yet these women seemed to be happy to be living with and working for the family for many years.

The Orr's eldest son, James, enrolled at the Academy in 1836 when he was 13 and was there for five years. He set off to join the EIC in 1842 and John equipped him before he left. It was expensive to provide all the kit for a young man to go to India and in a letter in 1842 written before James departed, John apologises for having to remind a parent to send the payment for their son's boarding fees as he had recently equipped his eldest son, James.

> I would not have taken the liberty I did in my last which could not have reached you when you wrote to me had I not been unusually pursued for money arising from my having

> some time ago been obliged to advance for a considerable sum for the outfit of my son as a cadet to India.[8]

It was sensible of John to provide his sons with all that they would need before they left to join the EIC. Buying what was required when cadets arrived in India would put them in debt immediately. Many of those who enrolled with the EIC in their Native regiments could not get out of debt until they had reached a much higher rank. Another part of the family archive contains papers relating to a cousin John Campbell. He did not know the Orr family and did not attend the SNMA. He joined the EIC in the 1840s and before he left the UK he bought his kit, which cost £148 3s (£15,760). It was provided by Grindley & Company in London.

James served in India with the Madras Native Infantry all his working life, retiring as a major general. He came back to Scotland on a furlough in 1856, aged 30, and married Catherine Younghusband Moir. She was the 18-year-old daughter of the doctor in the village of Inveresk where they had lived before moving to Edinburgh.

In 1843, John and Jane bought a nearby property at 42 St Cuthbert Street, using funds from their Marriage Contract, presumably by selling the properties in Monteith Street, Glasgow. Its purchase was to cause problems when John died because not enough money was left in the Marriage Contract to fulfil all the bequests. There is a statement in Maggie's death papers which says that 'considerable sums were expended on improvements thereon and the erection of outhouses connected therewith'. The Sassine records describe it as a 'tenement with other buildings thereon and back ground thereto on the south side of St Cuthbert's Street'. (Sassine records are a Scottish land register.)

The tenement houses in St Cuthbert Street would have been erected individually as the feuing lots were sold. They were probably four-storey houses to be formed into a terraced street when all the sales had been completed. The west end of street is built like this and is still standing. The ground floors usually had the dining room and possibly the master bedroom or a morning room. On the first floor there would have been a large drawing room and one or two other rooms and the top floor would have had further bedrooms. In the basement were the kitchen, scullery, pantry, wine cellar and space where the servants slept.

The Ordnance Survey map of 1853 shows the south side of the street called St Cuthbert Street and the north side named Torphichen Street.[9] The entire street became known as Torphichen Street in 1868. The houses were renumbered and the Orrs' house at 42 St Cuthbert Street, became 24 Torphichen Street. Their house no longer exists and in its place a Premier Inn Hub has been erected. It would have been a house of a similar size to their previous one in the same street.

The Orrs continued having five or six boarders staying each year. As mentioned earlier, much of the information of life in the Orr household comes from the Panton diaries. He describes the Orrs' house as having a large withdrawing room with a piano at one end and whist tables at the other. Pupils, the Orr family and guests, all had dinner together at the dining table which was large enough to seat twelve.

I have an attractive gold locket which has tiny fronds of curled brown and grey hair on the front and inside is a miniature painting of John (**Illustration 17 colour**). He looks to be in his fifties and is only wearing his Waterloo Medal and not his Long Service medal, so it must have been painted before 1848. It is not a traditional mourning locket, as Jane predeceased John, and it was possibly commissioned by him as a present for Jane on her fiftieth birthday in 1842.

On 20 December 1844, John's wife Jane died. She was only 52 years old. The death registration says she died of a burst blood vessel, now known as an aneurysm. She was buried on Christmas Eve in Warriston Cemetery which was Edinburgh's first garden cemetery and had been opened the previous year.

As was usual in the Church of Scotland, at that time, there would have been no church service, simply an interment. The coffin would have been taken from the house directly to the cemetery. The Protestant Church in Scotland considered that burial was not a sacrament and a minister was not involved in the funeral rites.[10] It was not until 1865 that it became a legal necessity for even a death certificate to be issued.

The account from the Warriston Cemetery Company is in the family archive which shows the cost of Jane's funeral was £9 3s (£976) which included £2 2s (£226) for a hearse and £4 4s (£449) for coaches. John's lair was 16D on the Cemetery plan and eventually nine people were buried in this plot. It was '6 square yards' and cost John £10 13s 4d.

(£1,135). (The graves could be 12ft deep.) A year later his brother, James, bought the adjacent lair, 17D.

It must have been a difficult time for the household as most of the boys would have been staying over Christmas. John considered it an unwelcome break in their studies if the pupils went home. (In Scotland at that time Christmas was not an important religious festival.) He wrote, for example, to Sir Thomas Whitehead in Lancashire, in 1841, talking about his son John:

> He wishes to (and I own naturally) to go home at the Christmas holidays but our vacation is then only for a week and I would regret if he was taken off his studies for that time. I think it would be for his advantage to remain.[11]

After Jane's death, life had to continue at 42 St Cuthbert Street. Jane had been an important part of the pupils' world and in almost all the letters to parents and guardians, in John's letter book, Jane is included as sending good wishes. After her death, the running of the household passed to John's eldest daughter, Maggie, who was 19. She had the help of Jess Eddington, the old family retainer and the other servants.

In 1847, three years after Jane died, Joseph Panton enrolled at the SNMA. He was 16 and came from Aberdeenshire. Joseph was at the Academy for three years and for all these sessions he stayed with the Orr family. At the start of his memoirs Panton wrote about his early education, several pages are devoted to his time at the SNMA describing what it was like living with the Orr family. His early schooling had not been pleasant with strict discipline when he was frequently beaten. On joining the SNMA, he wrote: 'here I found myself in quite a different atmosphere, more congenial in every respect.'[12]

At his first dinner in the Orr's house, he was seated at Maggie's right hand, being the newest boarder. He anxiously looked around the table to see who else was there. He noticed the 'Old Captain' at the other end who had a twinkle in his eye. He was then both shocked and surprised as John suddenly opened his mouth, popped out his false teeth, then smartly clicked them back in again and went on as if nothing had happened. Joseph did not know what to think, he looked at John again and saw another twinkle in John's eye. Joseph said he then realised that the 'Captain' had a great sense of humour and he knew he was going to enjoy living in his house.

Joseph described that the boys normally drank beer at dinner time, yet if there were guests or it was a special occasion, wine would be offered. He wrote:

> After dinner in summer-time we would have a bowl of cold sangaree punch, and big green glasses to drink it from. The great china bowl would be brought in with a little water, a block of ice floating on the surface, and a wooden bridge with a cup in the centre for straining the lemon through. The old captain would tap the bowl with his ladle, and our green glasses were pushed down the table and formed round the bowl to be filled and passed back.[13] [Sangaree punch is thought to have been brought to Europe from the Antilles Islands by Spanish merchants about 1700. It was a mixture of red wine, citrus fruits, sugar, nutmeg, and water.]

Sometimes, in the winter, hot whisky toddy was served in a similar way but from a brown jug. Panton remarked that a person today (he was writing in 1916) might think that too much alcohol was being served to such young men. He goes on to say that in those days more alcohol was drunk by everyone. (These drinks were probably safer to consume than drinking water.) It was helpful for young men to learn to drink sensibly as in some regiments an initiation prank took place, when older officers tried to make a new recruit drunk.

After dinner, the pupils had to go up to their rooms for at least an hour to do homework. They were then encouraged to come down to the sitting room where Maggie and Helen played the piano and sang, while whist was played at the card tables. Panton says, 'We susceptible youngsters were all in love with Maggie, the elder daughter, who, by the way was considerably our senior.' (Maggie would have been about 24 years old in 1847). Joseph was much keener at being at the piano end, near Maggie, and so played whist deliberately badly.

Panton wrote of frequent visitors who joined the family and the pupils at dinner time. He mentions that, 'Veteran guests were always entertaining when they referred to their campaigns.' He remembers one guest who shocked him when he talked about the British soldiers looting after the battle of Badajoz in the Peninsular War.

Two guests that Panton mentions are James Grant (1822–1887), a son of an officer who served in the Peninsular War, who wrote the well-known book: *Old and New Edinburgh* and over fifty novels, many of them involving military stories,[14] and Dr David Macbeth Moir (1798–1852), who was a physician in Musselburgh on the outskirts of Edinburgh, and wrote prose and poetry for *Blackwood's Magazine* under the name of Delta. (His daughter married to John's son, James.) Both these guests played whist after dinner.

Panton's accounts of life at 42 St Cuthbert Street indicate how well John got on with the pupils and how they were a big part of his life. They also show he was sociable and liked to have a lively number of friends around him. In July 1851, Panton graduated from the Academy. Instead of going to India, which had been the original plan, he went to Australia where he had an interesting and varied life (see Chapter 9).

In 1848, after Panton had been staying with the Orrs for a year, John's youngest son, Jack, graduated from the Academy. In the previous prize-giving, he had won first prize for fencing and I have his foils at home. In 1848, he was awarded prizes for the broadsword and for civil engineering. In addition, the directors awarded him an extra prize:

> A special prize was awarded to Mr John William Orr (son of the superintendent) as a mark of the Directors' high approbation of his uniformly correct and exemplary conduct, in every respect, during his five years attendance at the Academy.[15]

In the archive are some small slips of paper which record 19-year-old Jack's expenses on two trips, in 1848, to stay with friends in the west of Scotland. They are detailed and include items such as a brougham to the station 1s 6d (£8), second-class return fare to Glasgow 6s (£32), 'chocolate lozenges 6, cigars 4 – total 10d' (£4.50). (A brougham was a light four-wheeled horse-drawn carriage.) At the end of the slip of paper he has written: 'Due Captain Orr £1.19.6 1/2d.' (£211). Jack had been brought up to understand the value of money and knew that his father would expect him to account for what he had spent. Some of the stories in Chapter 8 illustrate John's frustration with the sons of wealthy parents who did not seem to understand the value of money and constantly overspent.

Jack joined the local Edinburgh Militia for a year and then left for India in 1850 to join the EIC. He had two furloughs back home in Scotland; during the first one, in 1865, he married my great-grandmother Charlotte Cubitt. The Cubitt family had known the Orrs for many years. Colonel Thomas Cubitt and John had served in Dublin at the same time, although they were in different regiments. Charlotte's brother Thomas had studied at the SNMA at the same time as John's eldest son James.

Jack and Charlotte's first child, Fanny, was born during his second furlough in Edinburgh in 1871. John must have been delighted to see one of his grandchildren as a baby, all the rest were born in India. They eventually had three sons and two daughters. One daughter, Annette or Nettie, my grandmother, was born in Madras.

According to his service record, Jack fought in the Burmese Wars of 1852–53, receiving a medal, and in the Indian uprising where he was awarded the medal and clasp. After that he was based in Bangalore and Madras with the 19th Light Infantry and was made commanding officer of that regiment in 1881 with the rank of brevet colonel. He was promoted to major general on his retirement in 1890 aged 62. He and Charlotte settled in Edinburgh at 1 Merchiston Crescent. Charlotte died in 1910 and Jack in 1916. He was buried in Warriston Cemetery and with permission of the military authorities his coffin was draped in the Union Flag. One of the pall bearers was my father, Edward John Campbell Hewitt, then only aged 14.

The census of 1851 lists John Orr 61, Maggie, 26 and Jane Helen 15, six pupils, old Jess and four other servants. One of the six pupils staying was Phillip Bott from Cheshire; he had arrived in October 1848 when he enrolled at the SNMA. I was interested to read Phillip Bott's name in the Roll Book as he is buried in the Orr lair at Warriston Cemetery. In September 1859, when only 25, Phillip died of paralysis, during a return stay with the Orr family. (It could have been as a result of poliomyelitis. Outbreaks occurred from time to time in Scotland. Sir Walter Scott contracted the virus when he was a child.) I wanted to discover why Phillip returned to Edinburgh from his home in Cheshire. It is possible he had travelled north hoping to marry Jane Helen. I discovered that when his father died, he had been left a substantial sum £16,000 (£1,624,000) which he could not inherit until he was 21. The Will was contested and the case was settled in Phillip's favour in August 1857. He was now a wealthy young man. My suspicion may have been confirmed as, when I read John's will, I found he bequeathed to Helen a silver salver given to John by Major Bott. Major Thomas Bott, was Phillip's brother, and had handled Phillip's estate. Major Bott had probably given the salver to John for his kindness in taking care of his ill brother and burying him in the Orr lair.

After Jane died and the children were older, John stopped going on holiday to Fife. On 7 August 1846 he wrote: 'I leave town on Monday morning for Glen Sannox, Arran. I hope to rusticate there for a few weeks.'[16] The only other vacation that I know about is a trip to France in 1853 when John took his two daughters, Maggie and Helen, to Paris and then on to Belgium. I have in the archive his passport which had been issued in London by George William Frederick, Earl of Clarendon who was Secretary of State for Foreign Affairs. It states the following:

> Request and require in the name of Her Majesty all those whom it may to concern to allow Captain John Orr (British subject) accompanied by two daughters travelling on the continent to pass freely without let or hindrance and to afford him every assistance and protection of which he may stand in need. Given at the Foreign Office on 20th day of August 1853.[17]

It is signed by both Lord Clarendon and by John Orr and on the back by the French Consul in Edinburgh dated 29 August 1853.

The passport is attached to a small leather wallet which contains a little notebook and pencil. John has written the address of the Oxford & Cambridge Hotel, 13 Rue d'Alger in this notebook; at the time of writing this is a boutique hotel called the Royal St Honoré. John has noted the names of some places they might visit: Musée d'Artillerie; Pantheon; Saint Chapelle; and Notre Dame. (Musée d'Artillerie was founded after the French Revolution and expanded by Napoleon. It was merged with another military museum in 1905 and is now called the Musée de l'Armée.) A Belgium stamp on the passport may indicate that after leaving Paris, John wanted to show his daughters the site of the Battle of Waterloo.

Before moving on from the Orr family, I would like to mention the mysterious Helen Anderson. When I learnt that John was buried in Warriston Cemetery, I asked Edinburgh Council if they could give me a record of all the people buried in the Orr lair. They sent me a list of nine names. I recognised them all except for one: Helen Anderson. I spoke to Caroline Gerrard of the Friends of Warriston Cemetery to see if she could find out more about this possible interloper; she came back with some interesting information.

We both knew from the burial record that Helen Anderson had lived at 3 Hope Street and had died of apoplexy in 1865. Caroline found that 3 Hope Street was a lodging house. John's Roll Book shows that four SNMA pupils had lodged with Helen Anderson between 1849 and 1854. Caroline discovered Helen Anderson's will and it revealed that John was her executor and that her largest bequest of £40 (£4,069) was to Maggie Orr.

I have no family archival information about Helen Anderson. She must have been a close and trusted friend of John's or she would not have appointed him as her executor. He was prepared to take on this legal duty and arrange for her burial in the Orr family lair. This is another example of John's caring nature.

Chapter 6

Daily Life at the Academy

> The Directors feel highly gratified in stating that the success of the Institution has equalled their most sanguine expectations; and the public may rest assured, that no exertion shall be wanting, on their part, to maintain the confidence they have acquired.[1]
>
> John Orr, Captain and Superintendent on behalf of the Directors.

After parents had decided to send their boy to the SNMA they had to make up their minds which subjects he should study. Here the Prospectus, sent out by John, was a help as it listed the subjects and times of the classes. (The 1833 Prospectus is listed in Appendix 1, Table 2 and **Image 03 monochrome is of the 1843 Prospectus**.) Boys who were planning to have a service career had to take prescribed courses and all were encouraged to do drill, military exercises and gymnastics. John was keen that the pupils should be fully occupied during the Academy day. In a letter in April 1846, he wrote: 'It will be obliging if you will state what branches of study you wish him to attend bearing in mind that it is most desirable that he should not have much idle time.' John was aware that the Academy was in the centre of Edinburgh and there were city temptations on its doorstep.

Apart from its military and educational subjects, the SNMA wanted to teach 'habits of discipline, self-control and gentlemanly behaviour' and to provide a 'liberal system of Education without which no gentleman can properly support his status in society'.[2] A liberal education was one that provided the pupil with a broad-based knowledge to cope with the complexities of the world. In England, however, both at public schools and at Oxford & Cambridge universities, a liberal education meant an emphasis on Classics and mathematics; both were thought essential for the training of the mind.

The Academic session started on 1 October and boys were encouraged to enrol as near as possible to that date. Once they arrived at the Royal Academy Buildings, they had to complete the Roll Book which John had started when he became superintendent. It is a large ledger comprising ten columns which included their names, ages, where they were living in Edinburgh, where they came from, when they arrived and the date they left the Academy. The Roll Book is discussed in detail in Chapter 7.

A course of education at the SNMA would normally last one year; about a quarter of the pupils enrolled for a second year, a few stayed for even longer, like John's sons. One academic year was called a session which was divided into four quarters, each of which started on one of the Quarter Days: 1 October, 15 December, 1 March and 15 May. (Historically, Quarter Days originated from religious festival dates which were then used for hiring of servants and paying of rents: Lady Day, Midsummer Day, Michaelmas and Christmas Day.) It finished at the end of July with examinations and a prize-giving. The only holidays during the session were one week at Christmas, a few days over Easter, the king or queen's birthday and the months of August and September.

By the time John became superintendent, a long list of possible subjects could be studied. Those planning to have a service career had to take military engineering, comprising fortification, military drawing, surveying and levelling. The other subjects on offer were arithmetic, mathematics and natural philosophy (physics), geography, history, elocution and composition. The Academy offered a wide range of languages – Latin, Greek, French, Italian, Spanish, German, Persian, Hindustani and Arabic. In addition, there were classes in landscape and perspective drawing and sketching from nature; fencing; gymnastics; and military exercises with flintlock and broadsword. Civil engineering was added in 1836.

Each class cost a particular fee per quarter which had been agreed between the teacher and the Academy. The total fees for each pupil would be calculated and the parent had to pay this sum in advance to the SNMA who would then remit the individual fees to the various masters minus a small handling charge. There were two small, fixed fees that all pupils had to pay. One was an annual matriculation fee of £1 1s (£101) a year and the other, a quarterly fee of 5 shillings (£24), had to be paid to cover the costs of coal, sergeants, use of arms and mathematical instruments and such like.

John prepared four reports for each pupil during a session which were issued at the end of the months of December, February, May and July. Within the family archive are some of the reports for John's eldest son, James, and a few for his younger son, Jack. All the subjects that could be studied are listed on the left-hand side and columns along the top are for Attendance, Application, Progress, Behaviour, Punishment and Remarks.

James was 14 when he enrolled for his first session in October 1836. That year he studied mathematics, Latin, writing, arithmetic, bookkeeping, history, geography, elocution, and French. The total fees for these classes for a quarter were £9 15s 6d (£979). He was either marked VG or G in the first four columns and had no comments in the last two.

In James's last session, starting in October 1840, he took mathematics, fortification, civil engineering, writing, arithmetic, bookkeeping, Hindustani, military exercises and practical mechanics. The total for a quarter was £10 14s 6d (£1,030). In the May report he received a series of VGs and Gs and remarks of 'very steady' in civil engineering and 'good mechanical talent' in practical mechanics. Over the years in his reports, he had other comments in the Remarks column such as 'improving', 'rather slow but diligent', 'attentive and well behaved' and 'abilities very good'. Parents of today will be familiar with similar comments in their children's school reports.

A pupil, therefore, in 1840 if he enrolled to study eight or nine subjects, would be paying £40 (about £3,842) to £50 (£4,803) per session depending on what subjects he had chosen to study. A possible cost, therefore, for a pupil studying at the SNMA, who required lodgings, might in 1840 be about £100–£150 (£9,606–£14,410) depending on which subjects were being studied and where he was staying.

Most boys were between 14 and 18 years old when they joined. John, unlike Downes, was happy to have younger boys at the Academy and the Roll Book records the enrolment of four 9-year-old boys and fifteen who were 10. At the other end, four enrolled in their late twenties – these latter pupils probably came solely for the military teaching. The masters at the SNMA must have been flexible to be able to teach such a wide age range. In some of the classes, however, such as mathematics, there were junior and senior classes to help cope with the age difference. Pupils had to attend for at least a quarter of a session, which was about ten weeks, and for one whole session before they could receive their final certificate. They were expected to behave in a gentlemanlike fashion and not be late for classes. Bad behaviour would be noted in a book and if this behaviour continued the pupil would be excluded from a receiving a certificate at the end of the session.

The first class of the day started at 9 a.m. From Monday to Friday the last lesson finished at 4 p.m. and on Saturdays they ran from 9 a.m. until 1 p.m. For those who wanted to attend, an hour of fencing or gymnastics took place at 4 p.m. on weekdays. No lunch break took place during the teaching day. In the first half of the nineteenth century, among more affluent classes, only one main meal was eaten each day and it was not taken at midday. Lunch was not normally eaten by men; it was a light meal devised by women who did not want to consume a huge dinner later in the day. The main meal would be around 5 p.m., or later if the family was wealthy.

Curious to know what kind of uniform the pupils wore, I was excited to find out about an unusual set of little-known volumes held in the Edinburgh City Archive called *Old Edinburgh Characters and Costumes* which include drawings of the Academy uniforms.[3] These coloured illustrations were produced in the mid-nineteenth century by a Scotsman called J.C. Howie. Howie started off as an artist and later became a photographer. He worked from different premises in Princes Street ending up with a photographic roof-top studio at number 45.

Old Edinburgh Characters and Costumes is a collection of watercolour sketches which were never published but were bound in 1890. The Edinburgh Archive also holds a further ninety-three unbound paintings by Howie. None of these illustrations, varying from fishwives to the Lord Lyon King of Arms, are portraits; the figures are stylised and the detail is in the clothing that the people wore for their work.

On my visit to the archive, I was able to handle these unusually large books (24x14ins). Howie included illustrations relating to the SNMA, showing the uniform of the superintendent, the sergeant in full dress (front and back), then in undress (uniform worn on non-formal occasions) and a pupil in drill dress and daily uniform (**Illustrations 18, 19, 20 and 21 colour**).

The sergeant was John's right-hand man. He had to preserve law and order, implement John's instructions and carry messages for him. The full dress of the sergeant was a dark blue 'coatee' with red collar and cuffs, grey trousers and black footwear with a cap which was dark blue and had a black leather peak. Howie must have visited in the summer months as in his illustrations the pupils are wearing white trousers – Panton describes the pupils' uniform in detail and mentions that the trousers were grey:

> Our uniform was a very simple Glengarry bonnet with a gold Scotch star on a black silk cockade on the left side, blue drill jacket with gold Academy buttons, black patent leather cross belts, black waist belt with silver Scotch star on gold plate, dark Norfolk grey trousers without side piping, and a thin patent leather stock, as we were not allowed to show any trace of a white collar.[4] [A Glengarry cap or bonnet is a traditional Scottish military cap made from thick woollen material with a cockade on the left side and ribbons hanging behind.]

John wrote to a parent who had enquired about uniform and said that the boy had to wear a jacket, cap and belt which could be bought locally for 25 shillings (£130).[5] It was therefore possible for the pupils who came from far away to buy their uniform when they arrived in Edinburgh. In another letter, John states: 'He will require some white trousers for summer which I will take care are moderate in such a manner to let out as he grows.'[6]

John and the masters had to encourage the pupils to work hard in order to be ready for the examinations during the last week of July. For those intending to join the British army, the possession of the final certificate would help them to obtain their direct commissions. It would also be an advantage for those planning to join the EIC.

If a pupil wanted to become an officer in the British army before 1849, they could either enrol at Sandhurst or Woolwich or they could enter using the Direct Commission system, which meant they paid for their commissions. Most boys at the SNMA who were planning to enter the British army used the Direct Commission system; this was not a simple process. Parents needed to be wealthy and of good social standing.

Purchasing a commission involved some formal requirements as to age, character and health. A certificate of general education had to be produced as well as a recommendation from a person of note. The SNMA would be in a position to fulfil both these requirements. Commissions were scarce and there might be up to twenty applicants for every vacancy. This was due to the government having reduced the size of the army after Waterloo.[7]

Buying an ensigncy in a regiment of foot in 1837 cost £450 (£42,000), but commissions in regiments such as the Guards would cost double that sum. After some time and if you had enough money, you could go on buying promotional commissions up to the rank of lieutenant colonel. Buying a commission would give a man his retirement 'pension' as he would hope to sell it to fund his old age. The government, therefore, was not responsible for a retired officer's pension, if he had bought a direct commission. This is a simplification of the system as other written and unwritten rules applied.

A certificate of good education was supplied by the SNMA and it was then up to each boy's parents to find a regiment that would enrol their son. John made it clear to the family that obtaining a commission in a regiment was their responsibility.[8]

When John himself left school, he wanted to have a military career. His parents had died and he did not have enough money to buy his commission and so he enrolled in the militia. John then became an ensign in the 42nd without having to pay for his commission as the country was under threat of an invasion by the French and more officers were needed quickly. In peacetime, his situation could have been difficult. He might not have succeeded in buying a commission even if his father was alive and had sufficient funds; his father being a jeweller, might not have been regarded as of sufficiently high social status.

John knew that obtaining a final certificate was important for the boys going to India as both his sons, James and Jack, had joined the East India Company as direct cadets. Boys wanting to become officers in Native regiments had to produce proof of a good education and the leaving certificate was perfect in this respect. A direct cadet could go straight to India without further training unless he was planning to join the artillery or wanted to become an engineer, in which case he had to enrol at Addiscombe. It was harder to get boys to join the EIC compared with enrolling in the British army and so recruits were not required to pay for their commissions.

The end of July must have been a nervous time for the boys who were leaving the Academy and hoping to be awarded their leaving certificate. They knew they would have two days of oral examinations. These were held in the Academy building but they were not in private; parents and members of the public could come and observe.

A notice was circulated with the times when each subject would be examined, the one for the 1847 examination is in the family archive. On Monday, 19 July the one-hour examinations started at 11 a.m. with Latin and Greek and German, followed by arithmetic, landscape drawing and French. Finally, at 3 p.m., the military and civil engineering exam took place. The next morning a similar pattern followed with examinations in mathematics, Hindustani, history, and, at 2 p.m., fortification, military drawing and civil engineering.

On show in the Academy building were displays of the military and landscape drawings which the pupils had completed and models constructed in the fortification class. Specimens of writing in Oriental languages could be seen and, in another room, there were examples of English writing and bookkeeping.

The day after the exams had taken place was spent by the masters working out who was going to get each prize. The prize-giving was on the last day of the session and John carefully planned the whole event. It gave him an opportunity to show relatives and guests the military and physical achievements of the boys, as before the actual prize-giving there were military exercises using firelock and broadsword, gymnastic and fencing displays. John kept press cuttings of the reports of the SNMA's public examinations. This large brown-paper looseleaf book (13x17ins) is similar to a scrap book I was given as a child. It appears to be a personal record, not an official one and contains press announcements as well as other cuttings. Most of these reports appeared in the *Caledonian Mercury*.

In the first years after their move to Royal Academy Buildings, the prize-giving days were held in either the Hopetoun Rooms or the Waterloo Rooms. In 1845, it took place in the classical Assembly Rooms in George Street. The following year it moved again and was held next door in the Music Hall, an impressive concert space, which had recently been completed.

Music played a part in the prize-givings and was usually provided by the band of the regiment which was stationed at Edinburgh Castle. The music list for the 1847 prize-giving includes *The Bonnets O'Blue*, which was played as the students marched into the room; a quick step during the broadsword exercise and again when the students marched out. The band could choose the music during the fencing and gymnastics. At the start of the prize-giving they were to play *The Conquering Heroes* and the *Queen's Anthem* at the end. The band then marched at the head of the students leading them from the Music Hall back to the Military Academy.[9]

The annual prize-giving became a well-known event in Edinburgh's social calendar. Many watched the procession of pupils, led by a military band, marching from the Academy, along George Street. The display and ceremony became a popular event which started at 1 p.m., but the doors opened at noon when many arrived. The newspapers over the years describe how many women came to the prize-givings and often reported a 'brilliant assembly of beauty and fashion'. The military band played from the Music Hall gallery.

After the various displays, a speech was given, usually by one of the directors outlining how the Academy was doing. A well-known person then awarded the prizes and a short talk followed by another of the directors who spoke directly to the pupils.

At the prize-giving in July 1833, the reporter for the *Caledonian Mercury* wrote:

> It is impossible to pass unnoticed the Superintendent Captain John Orr to whose admirable conduct, marked as it has throughout been by a rare union of the most conciliating and gentlemanly manners with the utmost firmness of character, this happy result is mainly to be described. The Directors were fortunate indeed in obtaining the services of a gentleman so singularly well qualified for the delicate and difficult situation in which he is placed; and in fact, the institution, under the superintendence of this gallant officer (who *par parenthèse* has bled in the service of his country) has prospered in a degree altogether without example in its previous history.

In 1842, John introduced the 'Superintendent's Prize'. It was to be awarded to the student 'who had distinguished himself in various studies and combined equal excellence in regularity of attendance, gentlemanly deportment and moral conduct'. The first recipient was Charles Watson. He had been born in Llandaff where his grandfather had been the bishop. After he left the SNMA he joined the 71st Regiment (see Chapter 8). In 1846, the Lord Provost of Edinburgh was in the chair and the chief guest was Sir Neil Douglas who was commander-in-chief of Scotland. On this occasion, John asked Lady Douglas to present the superintendent's prize. She made a short speech to James Newell, the recipient and said, 'I cannot doubt that you will for ever remember with gratitude the zeal and kindness of Captain Orr.'[10] (James did not plan to have a military career, according to the Roll Book.)

Fifteen years later, on 25 July 1857, John decided on a change of venue for the military display and the prize-giving. It was held in the Caledonian Horticultural Society's Gardens, next to the Royal Botanic Garden. (In 1864, this garden was amalgamated with the Royal Botanic Garden to form the present Edinburgh Royal Botanic Garden.) The 1857 prize-giving was described in the press as a *fête champêtre.*

The *Caledonian Mercury* reported: 'Though a high wind prevailed, the weather fortunately was fair.' There were manual and platoon exercises then infantry and cavalry sword displays. A field gun was loaded and fired. John devised a realistic mock battle with gunners dropping one by one 'as if picked off by the enemy's rifles' while an ambulance corps took away the wounded. At the end, the V-shaped Redan fort was blown up much to the excitement of all those watching.

A dinner was held in the evening after the prize-giving was over. One of the dinner invitations sent out by John in 1841 is in the family archive. Parents and friends of the pupils could buy tickets; the dinner was not simply for the directors and office bearers:

> The Directors and Masters of this institution will dine in the Waterloo Rooms, after the Examination, on Friday, the 23rd at Six o'clock, when the presence of Subscribers, Parents and Friends of the students, is requested. It will be obliging if those, who propose to Dine, will give notice to

Mr Pringle, at the Adjutant-General's Office, 10 Forrest Street, on or before Wednesday, the 21st instant.

Dinner, 12s 6d, including a bottle of wine. [£60]

Lord Kerr, the chairman, had been ill and could not attend this dinner, so 'he presented to the meeting a haunch of the finest venison ever seen smoking on a festive board.' The reporter in the *Caledonian Mercury* wrote that many toasts were drunk and 'a number of songs from some of the gentlemen present tended to enhance the pleasures of the meeting, which did not separate till a late hour'. The newspaper reports of these post prize-giving dinners speak of the good humour and enjoyment felt by all attending.

In 1845, they started to hold the post prize-giving dinner in the Academy buildings in Lothian Road. That year a guest was Sir Adam Ferguson, a British soldier who had fought in the Peninsular campaign. He was at the Battle of Salamanca and was captured in the retreat from Burgos. (That was the forced march where John was worried that he might be taken prisoner.) Adam Ferguson was imprisoned for nearly two years and was not released until the Peace of 1814. The *Caledonian Mercury* report says that he sang several songs after dinner was over and the evening was spent with great hilarity and good feeling. I have in the family archive a note of the order of toasts at one of these dinners. There are twelve starting with 'The Queen and the Royal Family' followed by the 'Navy and Army' and ending with the 'Guests' and finally the 'Pupils'. It must have been a long evening.

* * *

Being based in the centre of a city with no surrounding land, the SNMA could offer few recreational activities, unlike the RMC. Fencing and gymnastics were in the timetable and pupils were allowed access to the stables of the Royal Academy Buildings. A few cricket matches were arranged. Joseph Panton wrote in his diary that they had cricket occasionally. There is a press report of a cricket match which was played on 21 June 1851 between a joint team from the Edinburgh Academy and the SNMA against the Grange on the Sparkes ground in Edinburgh. The joint Academies won by an innings and two runs.

John planned and was the leader of various outings for the students. Two of these were to islands in the Firth of Forth to mark Queen Victoria's coronation. These trips were a combination of work and pleasure.

The first was on 28 June 1839, a year after the queen's coronation. The boys, some directors and John left the Chain Pier at Newhaven and boarded a steamer for the island of Inchcolm in the Firth of Forth. Those studying military and civil engineering surveyed the island with flagstaffs and theodolites. 'Another detachment was practising at bull's eye and discharging fusillades in honour of her Majesty's coronation.'[11] The SNMA had recently started to teach swimming and those that could swim took to the water, some others went round the island in a small boat. At 4 p.m., 'the superintendent proved to be a remarkable purveyor and had taken care to lay in a liberal stock of cold viands with a competent allowance of sherry, cognac and usquebaugh.' [whisky]. A shower of rain fell, but the 'gudewife' of the island boiled up water from the Monks' Well and a 'comfortable toddy' was produced. (Hot toddy is a traditional Scottish drink made with whisky, water and honey or sugar.) In the evening, they visited the Royal Navy ship, the HMS *Benbow*, and received hospitality from 'the middies and the officers', eventually returning to the Chain Pier in the evening. (*Benbow* was a sailing ship launched in 1813, of 1,773 tons with 74 guns.)

The other expedition took place on 28 June 1844, again to celebrate the anniversary of Queen Victoria's coronation.[12] It was a day trip for all the students and some masters and directors to Inchkeith, another island in the Firth of Forth. The pupils and John mustered at 5.30 a.m. at the Academy building and marched to Granton where they boarded 'three stout pilot boats'. The directors, including Captain Boswell and Sir George Ballingall, left by a steamer from the Chain Pier, accompanied by a piper, fife and drums from Cameronians (26th Regiment of Foot). The pupils conducted a survey of the island and inspected the lighthouse. A display of military exercises took place and the whole party had a cold collation which was 'abundant and excellent'. 'The indefatigable Superintendent seemed for most of the afternoon to be in two places at the same time.' A sudden shower of rain came and 'the hampers grievously diminished in weight, were filled again with empty crockery and bottles'. The report ends by saying how pleasing it was to see the confidence that existed between the students and those in charge. They had achieved the right balance of enthusiasm for their profession yet maintained good discipline.

In June 1852, another day out for the pupils took place, as they all attended the unveiling of the statue of the Duke of Wellington at the east end of Princes Street in Edinburgh. John arranged for the boys to have a prime position for this important event. In 1842, the statue had been commissioned by a committee of Tory landowners, but contributions also came from political opponents – all admired Wellington's military successes and his leadership. The artist was John Steell and this much-loved Edinburgh statue, situated outside New Register House, is locally known as the 'Iron Duke in bronze by Steell'. It shows Wellington, directing a battle, mounted on his horse, Copenhagen, which is rearing up. It is made in fused bronze and is nearly 13ft high, 6ft broad and 12ft long. It sits on a block of red Aberdeen granite and the total height is nearly 26ft. The statue is supported by the horse's tail and back legs which are anchored to the ground. It took eight horses and thirty men to bring the 12½-ton statue from Steell's foundry.

The ceremony took place on 18 June 1852, on the thirty-seventh anniversary of Wellington's victory at Waterloo and the day was declared a public holiday. All the nearby roads were closed, various regiments were stationed along the streets, stands were erected for spectators and two bands played. The report in the *Caledonian Mercury* records that, 'on the pavement in front of the statue were the students of the Naval & Military Academy under the charge of Captain Orr and a number of the directors of that institute.'[13] John is listed in the press as one of the soldiers who had served under Wellington. Those, like John, who had fought at Waterloo wore a sprig of laurel.[14]

The Duke of Buccleuch, who was chairman of the commissioning committee, gave a speech recounting the life of Wellington and praised the statue which was then unveiled. The bands played *See the Conquering Hero Comes* and guns were fired from Edinburgh Castle which were replied to by a battery on Salisbury Crags.

In one of my parents' chest of drawers I found a small linen damask tablecloth showing the Duke of Wellington on horseback **(Illustration 08 monochrome)**. This would have been part of a set of tablecloth and napkins designed in Dunfermline by James Balfour for the Edinburgh drapers, P&R Wright, made to coincide with the statue's unveiling.[15]

Two boys who we know benefited from their education at the SNMA are worthy of mention here. The first is John McDouall Stuart (1815–

1866) who was at the Academy shortly before John became superintendent **(Illustration 09 monochrome)**. He is a famous name in Australia, as in 1862 he was the first European to cross the continent from south to north. The surveying skills he learnt at the Academy helped him to complete this heroic and extremely difficult trip. His journey paved the way for the completion, ten years later, of the Adelaide to Darwin Overland Telegraph line which followed McDouall Stuart's route across the Red Centre. The major road which now runs from Port Augustus in South Australia to Darwin in the Northern Territories is called the Stuart Highway.

Major Charles Nasmyth (1825–1861) is the only student whom I have found who publicly praised his education at the SNMA and said how it enabled him to succeed in his future career. He was described by the writer Alexander Kinglake, who knew him, as 'a man of quiet and gentle manners and so free from vanity … that it seemed as though he were unconscious of having stood as he did in the path of the Czar'.[16] **(Illustration 10 monochrome)**.[17] This drawing was published in *The Illustrated London News* together with his obituary. He was one of the heroes of the Crimean War, as he helped organise the defence of Silistra at the start of that conflict.

Charles was born in Edinburgh in September 1825. His father Robert Nasmyth FRSE (Fellow of the Royal Society of Edinburgh) was Surgeon-Dentist to Queen Victoria. Charles was educated at the SNMA for two years, 1841–1843, and in July 1843 he was awarded the first prize in Hindustani. He is listed in the Remarks column as planning to join the EIC, and did so after attending Addiscombe College; he became a lieutenant with the Bombay Artillery in 1845.

While he was serving in Gujarat with the Bombay Trigonometrical Survey he became ill through the effects of the climate and hard work. He was sent back to the UK on sick leave in 1853. His health did not improve (poor health beset him for the rest of his life) and he was advised to live in a Mediterranean climate and went to stay in Turkey. He joined Omar Pasha's camp at Shumla and became a correspondent for *The London Times*. (Omar Pasha was the commander of the Ottoman forces.) Charles also provided information for the then British Ambassador to the Ottoman Empire, Lord Stratford de Redcliffe.

Various countries became worried about the expansionist policy of Russia. If the Russian army crossed the Danube, Istanbul might fall into their hands and it could then control the Eastern Mediterranean. Britain feared it might lose its maritime supremacy in that area and the trade routes to India might be in jeopardy. Early in May 1854, the Russians did indeed cross the Danube. *The London Times* sent Charles Nasmyth to Silistra, a Turkish town on the south side of the river, to report on the situation. Shortly after he arrived, the town was attacked by the Russians and this action started the Crimean War.

Some other non-Turkish troops were in Silistra, including Captain James Butler who had served with Charles in the EIC. The Russians tried to besiege the town. Captain Butler was hit on the forehead by a bullet and died a few days later, and Musa Pasha, the Turkish commander, was killed by shrapnel. Charles, despite being a civilian at that time, took over command and started to organise the defences. The Turkish officers were inexperienced and the town was expected to fall, but he encouraged the troops to stand firm and defend the town using the fortification principle of retrenchment which he had learnt at the SNMA. ('Retrenchment' is a technical term in fortification where a secondary work or series of works is constructed in rear of existing defences to hinder further progress of the enemy.)

Charles managed to do this without speaking Turkish or understanding Turkish customs. For over six weeks the town held out until, on 22 June, the Russians ordered a retreat as they had received reports of the British and French build-up of troops at Varna (a town on the Black Sea) and they also had learnt that Austria was about to join the Allies. The Russians had lost about 12,000 men, either dead or injured during the attempted siege. The holding of Silistra for these weeks was helpful to the British and French armies as it stopped the Russian advance in that area and allowed the allies to build up their troop numbers in Varna before invading the Crimea. Charles returned to Constantinople in poor health and having lost all his belongings. He was transferred to the British army with the brevet rank of major awarded for his services at the defence of Silistra.

At the SNMA prize-giving in July 1854, Lieutenant Nasmyth's gallantry at Silistra was praised by Sheriff Gordon, one of the ordinary directors, who spoke before the prizes were awarded. Gordon said, 'I might present to you, my young friends, the education, the actions, and the fame of young Nasmyth, as a guide which you may usefully, and as a model, you should strenuously endeavour to follow.'[18]

The following year, in March 1855, Edinburgh Council awarded Charles Nasmyth the Freedom of the City of Edinburgh by making him a burgess and guild brother. In replying he offered 'his most sincere thanks for the very distinguished honour' and went on to say:

> I trust that I shall never be forgetful of what I owe to the happy circumstances in which my early youth was spent, and the ability of those who imparted to me the rudiments of my profession in this my native city.[19]

He was appointed Assistant Quartermaster General at the Headquarters in the Crimean Campaign and received the medal and clasps for Alma, Inkerman and Sevastopol. He was further awarded, by the Turkish Government, the Order of Medjidie and was given a gold medal by them for his achievements in the campaign and for the defence of Silistra.

His ill health continued to trouble him and he was transferred to Ireland and then Australia but eventually he was invalided home in 1859. Charles obtained a Majority in the 4th Foot Regiment on 25 May 1860 and was able to retire the same day by the sale of his commission. He went to live in Pau in France, and, at the tragically early age of 36, Charles died in 1861.[20] There were obituaries in many newspapers and journals. The *Illustrated London News* 'recorded the death of a very estimable man and a gallant soldier'.[21]

Before I finish this chapter, I would like to mention the SNMA's Officers' Club. John was keen to support past military pupils and also to provide a base for old soldiers who lived in or visited Edinburgh. He decided in 1836 to start a club based in the Royal Academy Buildings. He and the directors commissioned the Club's own dinner service and cutlery. Some of these attractive plates, dishes and cutlery were in a box at my parents' house **(Illustration 22 colour)**. The plates have the SNMA emblem in the middle – a of pair of unicorns on either side of a lion rampant surmounted by a crown and swords. Round the edge are two clusters of early weapons and a medallion with the writing *Scot Nav & Mil Acad Club 1836*. When the SNMA closed, the dinner service was divided up amongst the directors and the superintendent. A few of the dishes are on show in the Military Museum at Edinburgh Castle.

Chapter 7

John's Roll Book

We make sense of life by establishing significant facts and by telling revealing stories about them.[1]

Richard Holmes. *The Long Pursuit*.

John started the Roll Book in 1831 when he became superintendent and it is the most important SNMA item in the family archive **(Illustration 11 monochrome)**. Recording the pupils' names was one of the stipulated duties of the superintendent. The Roll Book is much more than that. Thanks to John's meticulous record keeping, a detailed picture emerges of the Academy, the boys, their families and many of the boys' aspirations. It is a rich primary source of information about military education and social history which has never been tapped before and, in addition, it shows its international reputation. From a military point of view, the last column in the Roll Book, headed Remarks, is the most valuable as it contains John's own comments as to the future intentions of pupils who were planning to have an army or naval career. It is a large ledger, 10x16ins, and although nearly 200 years old is still in remarkably good condition with almost all the entries legible.

The SNMA records are valuable as they give more information on each pupil than do the extant records of other military colleges in the UK at that time, albeit for a smaller number of pupils. Up till 1916, the RMC has only a bound register of basic facts where the father is listed as 'military' or 'gentleman' and there is no record of profession or title. Addiscombe had a similar method as the SNMA of recording the details of new cadets but it had no 'Remarks' column. Before 1880, the RMA did not record details about cadets' fathers.

John assigned each pupil a sequential number at the start of the academic year. Every sheet has ten columns, giving such details as name, age, where the pupil lived during the session, who introduced him, where he came from and a note of the date he enrolled at the Academy; lastly, there is John's Remarks column. Some of the entries were not completed at the start, for example the boys' ages were not entered during the first two sessions, but from 1835/36 onwards most of the columns were completed for each student. For the first five years, the entries appear to have been filled in by a member of staff, as they are in the same handwriting. From the session 1836/37 until 1858/59 each entry is in a different script; I assume that the boys were now entering the details themselves. A few of these names were hard to decipher, as some of the boys signed themselves in with a flourish.

The Roll Book covers the period of John's superintendency from October 1831 until July 1864. The enrolment gradually increased until the highest number, 125 boys, joined in 1844. From 1849 onwards, the intake declined and the SNMA closed in July 1858, reopening that October as The Scottish Institute for Civil, Commercial and Military Education. The institution changed little under its new title; in contemporary parlance it was a rebranding. Six pupils overlapped and continued their education at The Scottish Institute of whom only one was planning on a military career. I am therefore treating both establishments as one as far as the Roll Book information is concerned.

The Roll Book records 2,279 enrolments with an average of sixty-nine per year. The overall enrolment figure does not tell you the number of individual boys, as some boys attended for more than one year. I therefore entered each of the records into a spreadsheet, a painstaking task given the difficulty of reading some of the entries. By matching the names and records of boys who attended the Academy for more than one year, I was able to identify recurring students and therefore determine the number of individual pupils.

I wanted to find out how many students overall had studied at the SNMA. By matching the student records in John's Roll Book, I worked out that 1,500 pupils had attended for the 1831 to 1863 sessions. I had no Roll Book for the first six years, but by analysing the entrance fees in the financial accounts for the first four years, I estimated there were around 500 new boys joining. For the sessions 1829 and 1830, I reckoned that no more than another 100 boys joined, as press reports said figures were low. This gives an approximate total of around 2,100 boys who were educated by the SNMA and Scottish Institute combined.

On 8 September 1852, the vice chairman of the Academy, R.S. Seton, announced in an advertisement in *The Scotsman* that the Academy from its inception had prepared over 1,000 pupils for a military career. The Roll Book shows that 600 pupils planned to have service careers. In the early 1830s, there was a larger proportion of military to non-military pupils and it is reasonable to suppose that in the first six years before the Roll Book started that 400 students planned to go into the services. So, Seton's figure of over 1,000 pupils having a military career looks to be accurate. From October 1852 onwards, no more than fifty students joined who were planning to have a service career.

John's notes about the future plans of the 'military boys' in the Remarks column are a valuable historical record. (His writing is recognisable from various letters drafted by him in the archive.) The entry is in some cases an aspiration and not necessarily what happened. The other type of remark that John makes in this column is a brief word or simply initials about the character of the student or his behaviour: VG, very good; VB, very bad; asked to leave; and so on. In a few instances, he simply writes 'dead', where he must have received the news of the death of a pupil.

Some of the comments in the Remarks column are in pencil, these are hard to decipher because they have now faded and some have an ink note written over the pencil remark. The pencil comment could have been written at enrolment when John asked the pupil what he planned to do on leaving the Academy and the ink remark was written when the pupil left and records his more likely future military plans. It is possible that John sometimes entered this information later, when he heard which regiment the boy had actually joined.

Given the SNMA was called a military academy, it is striking that about half of the pupils between 1831 and 1864 have no comment in the Remarks column. Most of these pupils may have been planning to have a civilian career or may not have yet decided on their future plans. (See Table 3 in Appendix 1.) John only noted the boys' future military plans. From 1831 to 1849, 60 per cent of the boys at first enrolment planned to join the services. (In 1849 a sharp decline occurred in the 'military' numbers enrolling which alters the overall figure, this is looked at in detail in Chapter 10.)

I was curious to find out if a pupil's career path, as written down by John in the Remarks column, was fulfilled. Did the education at the SNMA allow a boy to follow the military career that he or his father had planned? In order to do this, I picked a year to see if I could find out what actually had happened to each of the boys who were listed as wanting to become officers in the British army. I chose the session 1844/45 as it had one of the highest enrolments in one year with thirty-nine boys planning to become British officers.

At the end of the 1844/45 session, I found, that thirty-four out the thirty-nine pupils did follow the military path noted in the Remarks column. Two of the pupils changed their minds the following year – one decided to go to Woolwich, instead of Addiscombe and the other did the reverse. Three of the pupils' future careers could not be traced. This analysis suggests there is a strong correlation between the aspiration noted in the Roll Book and what the pupil went on to do. I have come across exceptions, but in most cases John's remark reflects the career path the pupil actually followed.

The enrolment of 1844/45 had not only one of the highest numbers of pupils enrolling who were planning a service career it also had an increase in those wanting a general education. This may have been due to a laudatory press report of the July 1844 prize-giving. This prizegiving was the first to held in the newly built Music Hall and it attracted a big audience. The reporter of the *Caledonian Mercury* on 1 August described 'an unusually large concourse of delighted spectators' attending. He went on to write about the wide range of subjects that could be studied, all taught 'thoroughly'. He mentioned how the Academy was alert to teaching new subjects such as the recent addition of shorthand. He praised the directors for 'adapting their school to the exigencies of the age' while maintaining a high standard in the usual academic subjects. Several people hearing these words in the hall or subsequently reading them in the paper may have been encouraged to enrol their boys in the next session starting in October 1844. The military discipline on offer may have been appealing to parents of wayward teenage sons.

Some boys who had no information recorded about their career aspirations did eventually join regiments. One reason for this could be that when they left the SNMA they had not planned to have a service career and John, therefore, did not list their future plans. A list of the

100 Academy pupils who fought in the Crimean War is in the archive and it was also printed in the press.[2] A small number of SNMA pupils who fought in that war did not have a military aspiration recorded in the Roll Book. An example was William Hope who, after leaving the Academy, went to university and only then started a military career.

I was excited to find that William, when only 21 was awarded one of the first Victoria Crosses. He studied at the SNMA during the 1849/1850 session and was both son and grandson of Scottish judges. After leaving the Academy he went to study at Trinity College, Cambridge and only joined the 7th Regiment (later called the Royal Fusiliers) as a lieutenant in April 1855. In the same month he was awarded the VC for bravery at Sevastopol where according to the citation, on 15 April he 'went out twice under fire to bring in a wounded officer'.[3] This new medal was instituted by Queen Victoria during the Crimean War and William was given his by the queen on 26 June 1857, at the first award ceremony in Hyde Park, London. I gather from a piece on the National Army Museum's website that William was lucky as:

> Apparently the Queen stabbed one of the heroes, Commander Raby, RN, through the chest as she pinned the cross to his uniform. The Commander stood unflinching while the Queen fastened the pin through his flesh![4]

Another SNMA alumnus William Spottiswoode Trevor was awarded a VC. He had been at the SNMA for one year, two years before William Hope. He was awarded his VC for fighting in Bhutan in 1866.

The word 'Scottish' in the title of the SNMA made me think originally that all, or nearly all, of the pupils would have come from Scotland. Yet the Roll Book shows that only a little over half came from there.[5] The majority of these local pupils were using the Academy as a type of further education establishment and had no military plans. Of the over 800 pupils that came from Scotland, about 200 planned to become officers in the British army and about 150 wanted to join the EIC.

As the Academy grew in stature under John's superintendency it began to enrol pupils from further afield. About 12 per cent (nearly 200 out of 1,500 boys) came from England, of whom about half intended to have military careers. Approximately 130 arrived from India with only

Above: **1.** Cabin trunk (23x56x86ins) which has contained the Orr family archive for over a hundred years. *Author's image*

Right: **2.** John Orr's wooden military box, possibly used by him during the Peninsular War. *Author's image*

Above left: **3.** Print of Napoleon Bonaparte by George Baxter (1804–1867), London. Owned by John Orr. *Author's image*

Above right: **4.** Waterloo medal, inscribed to Lieutenant John Orr, 42nd Highlanders, with the original ribbon, buckle and suspender. *Author's image*

Above: **5.** Miniature thought to be of John Orr, painted about 1816. *Courtesy of an owner who would prefer to remain anonymous*

Below left: **6.** Shako badge and brass shoulder plate of the 8th Royal Battalion, part of John Orr's uniform when he served with this Regiment from July 1820 until March 1821 when it was disbanded. *Author's image*

Below right: **7.** Picture of John, Jane, James and Maggie Orr. Painted about 1829. Unknown artist. *Author's image*

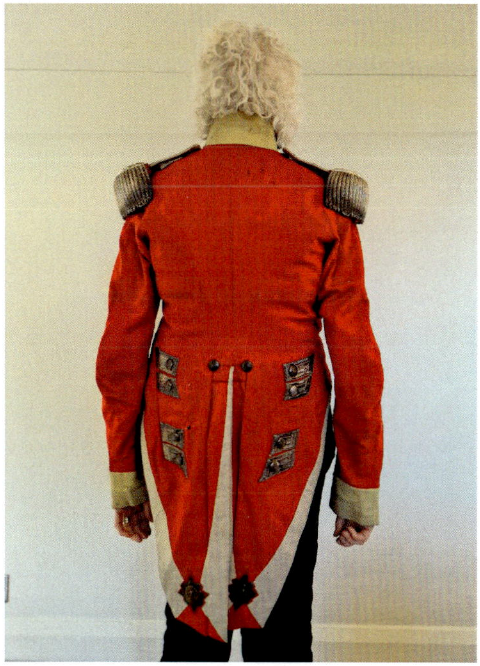

Above left: **8.** John Orr's Edinburgh Militia coatee or jacket, 1831, worn by the author. Scarlet and yellow facings, silver lace, regimental buttons and skirt ornaments with medal pocket. The name 'Orr' is embroidered on the inside collar. Silver bullion epaulettes of the Edinburgh Militia. *Author's image*

Above right: **9.** John Orr's Edinburgh Militia coatee, back view. *Author's image*

Right: **10.** John Orr's infantry officer sword with cipher of King William IV on the guard, complete with lace sword knot, black leather scabbard and leather carrying case. *Author's image*

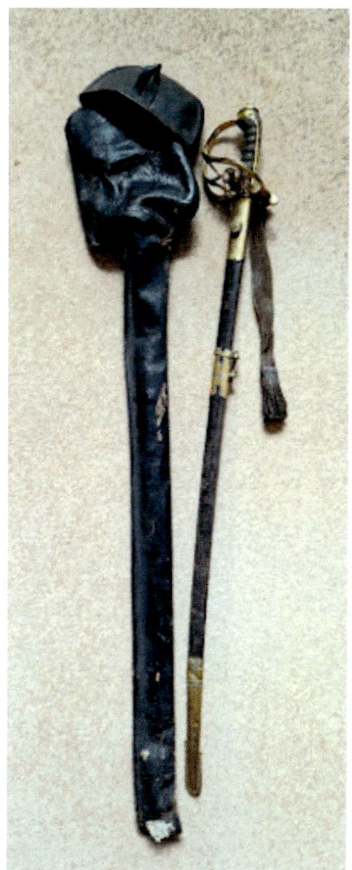

Left: **11.** Preliminary sketch for the portrait of Lord Robert Kerr, given to the Orr family. The official portrait, commissioned by the SNMA was painted by Robert Innes in the early 1830s. *Author's image*

Below left: **12.** John Orr's valentine posted anonymously to his son Johnnie, April 1835. *Author's image*

Below right: **13.** John Orr's valentine posted anonymously to his daughter Maggie, April 1835. *Author's image*

Above left: **14.** Painting of John Orr by Felice Piccioni, 1838. *Author's image*

Above right: **15.** Painting of Jane Orr by Felice Piccioni, 1838. *Author's image*

Below left: **16.** John Orr's crimson silk sash and shoulder crescents, part of his SNMA uniform. *Author's image*

Below right: **17.** Locket with John Orr's miniature portrait inside and his coiled hair under the facing glass. *Author's image*

Above left: **18.** Uniform of the Superintendent of SNMA. One of four coloured sketches by J.C. Howie from *Old Edinburgh Characters and Costumes* Vol 1. Painted in the 1840s. *All four paintings by courtesy of the Edinburgh City Archive*

Above right: **19.** Full dress uniform of the SNMA Sergeant. [refer to Number 18 above for attribution]

Below left: **20.** Pupil at the SNMA in drill dress. [refer to Number 18 above for attribution]

Below right: **21.** Pupil at the SNMA in everyday uniform. [refer to Number 18 above for attribution]

Above: **22.** SNMA Club plates, dishes and cutlery. John Orr started a Club, based in the Royal Academy Buildings for old soldiers and past pupils and commissioned new plates and cutlery. These were distributed among the directors and superintendent when the SNMA closed. *Author's image*

Below left: **23.** Oil portrait of former SNMA pupil Joseph Panton painted in 1904 by Frederick McCubbin. *Courtesy of the National Gallery of Victoria*

Below right: **24.** Portrait of Maggie Orr, John Orr's daughter. Unknown artist. *Author's image*

25. Photograph of a horse-drawn hearse taken in Edinburgh in 2021. John's body was probably taken to the cemetery in a similar hearse. *Author's image*

Above left: **26.** The Orr family gravestone in Warriston Cemetery, Edinburgh. *Author's image*

Above right: **27.** Inscription on the front of the Orr family gravestone. *Author's image*

a third of these boys noting a military aspiration, which was usually to join the EIC. The 100-plus pupils from the rest of the world originated from twenty-four different countries, including eight from Canada, six from Australia and four from the Cape of Good Hope. A number came from places which were not part of the British Empire (e.g., Russia, Mexico, Switzerland). Only a third of these overseas students were recorded as aspiring to have a military career. These figures indicate the general education at the SNMA was highly thought of and its academic reputation recognised outside Scotland.

The Roll Book often gives details about the proposed military careers of the pupils. Nearly two-thirds of these pupils (411 out of 653) planned to join one of the British services and almost all of these boys were wanting to become officers in the British army, with about half listing a particular regiment. Only ten pupils were planning to go on to the RMA for further training and two listed intending to go to the RMC.

The majority of the boys at the Academy who were aspiring to become officers in the British army planned to become foot soldiers, but sixteen chose to enrol with cavalry regiments – a much more expensive option. John often simply writes 'Reg' in the column, but in many cases the regiment is named; surprisingly, eighty different regiments are listed. It is therefore worth noting, during this period, most British army regiments would have had a serving officer who had been educated at the SNMA, assuming their military aspirations were fulfilled. It indicates that the social status and military education at the Academy was considered to be good enough to equip boys for any regiment.

John was interested in and supported the boys who wanted to join the EIC. His two sons followed this path. Between 1831 and 1857, about 15 per cent planned to join the Company. This figure includes those who wanted to go on to Addiscombe for further training before going to India. The SNMA pupils who wanted to join the EIC came from various countries: 147 pupils came from Scotland; 37 from India; 14 from England; 6 from the rest of the world; and 29 where the origin was not listed in the Roll Book.

Once the SNMA was established and a boy gained his certificate, this was accepted by the EIC as proof of his military education. It led to a steady increase in the Academy's enrolment of boys intending to go to India. These young men who went straight to India and had not gone to

Addiscombe were called Direct Cadets. Previously, these cadets had to undergo unpleasant training in India. Sir Ferdinand Mount describes in *The Tears of the Rajas* how his relation John Low went to India in 1805 to join the Company and had received a basic training when he got there at a 'hellhole' college at Tripassur.[6]

Out of 233 aspiring to join the EIC, about 30 listed that they wanted to enrol in its civil service, known as the Company Service (CS). According to my research, the majority of these students in the end joined the military wing of the EIC when they left the SNMA. Only two succeeded in directly joining the Company Service. All CS pupils have, therefore, been included in the EIC military numbers.

It was difficult to join the Company Service, you could not apply, as it was by invitation only. Three of the SNMA pupils who had CS written in the Remarks column originally joined the military wing but were subsequently transferred to the Company Service while they were in India. They, nevertheless, retained their military rank. A former CS official, John Beames, in his book, described this practice and was not happy when it happened, as some of these military officers were less collegiate and held up promotion. Beames wrote:

> We junior Civilians resented the presence of these men, because they stopped our promotion, were harsh and stuck-up and overbearing and introduced military ideas of subordination instead of the genial, brotherly relations which subsisted between numbers of our own service.[7]

Only one SNMA pupil (Frederick Forsyth Grant) is marked as planning to go to Haileybury. After leaving the Academy, however, Frederick decided to join the 3rd Hussars and became aide-de-camp to the Marquis of Lorne who was Governor General of Canada. John had identified him early as a capable boy, one of few students he labelled as 'VG' in the Roll Book. I have subsequently found another pupil who did not have a career listed in the Roll Book but who went on to Haileybury.

The SNMA had a few naval officers as ordinary directors, but little special naval training took place. Only 27 out of the 1,500 pupils planned to join the Royal Navy or marines. The Royal Naval Academy had been founded at Portsmouth in 1733 (later named the Royal Naval

College in 1806). It closed in 1837 and for twenty-five years no naval college existed. The SNMA may have hoped to attract more potential naval cadets. This did not occur probably due to naval prejudice against officers who had been trained in a college, the preferred choice was apprenticeship at sea, often arranged through family connections or patronage. In 1863, the Britannia Royal Naval College opened, more commonly known as Dartmouth College. It was originally sited on board the wooden hulk of HMS *Britannia.* Times changed and this new college proved popular and two years later another hulk, the HMS *Hindustan*, was added as a training ship.

John's column titled 'Introducer' gives us insight into the profession and social standing of over 250 of the pupils' fathers, as their title or profession is indicated before their name. A majority of these fathers were in the army and a few in the navy. Most British army fathers wanted their sons to follow them into the same profession. Some of these boys, however, joined the EIC instead. A reason for this may have been that the father could not afford to pay for their son to enter using the Direct Commission system which would have cost £450 (about 1831 in £43,480 and in 1851 about £52,430).

Before 1830, more than half of young officers were sons of the aristocracy or the landed gentry, but a growing number had middle-class parents.[8] A change was gradually taking place and after 1830, some of the landed gentry could no longer afford to pay for their sons' direct commissions and they were being replaced by middle-class parents who now had the money to do this. These fathers were successful bankers and businessmen; they had to be wealthy, and they knew their son would gain prestige by becoming an officer in the British army. Sir Hew Strachan remarked in his book *Wellington's Legacy*: 'The regimental system, with its ancient lineage and royal connections, and its social and sporting life, bestowed status.'[9]

John's Roll Book shows a mix of fathers from different branches of society, including men who were Members of Parliament and Court of Session Judges. Many were sending their sons to the SNMA for a general education, but a few had decided on a military career for at least one of their boys. Here, John would have been able to give advice to these fathers who knew little about military life. From a cursory look at the Roll Book, I have found five non-military fathers whose boys are recorded with a military aspiration and there are probably many more. Four of them boarded with the Orr family – sons of three wealthy clergymen and one banker (see Chapter 8). The fifth, Sydney Sandford, was the son of an advocate (barrister) in Edinburgh, Daniel Sandford. He joined the Rifle Brigade, but sadly died in Malta when he was only 21 years old.

Pupils were often introduced by a father but not always; sometimes if the father was abroad or dead, the introducer was a colleague who was an army officer or a man who was a friend of the family. For the same reasons, over 200 boys were introduced by women, who were usually the mothers of the boys.

The Introducer column gives various noteworthy parent/son pairings, too many to list here. One of these is an interesting army pairing which involves two remarkable identical twins John James Hood Gordon (1832–1908) and Thomas Edward Gordon (1832–1914), both became generals and both were knighted. John and Thomas enrolled at the SNMA for two years in October 1847, they sat and passed the new army examination in July 1849 (this exam is further discussed in Chapter 10). Thomas in his autobiography, *A Varied Life*, describes how the military surgeon at the army exam told Thomas not to come back to see him again as he had already checked him. Thomas had to explain that it was his twin brother John that he had seen not him. He wrote: 'we were so wonderfully alike in appearance.' Both became officers in the army in August 1849.

The twins came from a large military family; their father Captain William Gordon (1788–1834) had served in 78th Highlanders in the Peninsular War where he had married a young Spanish woman Marianna Carlotta, the daughter of a government official. They were the youngest in the family and their father had died when they were only 2. Captain Gordon had three brothers who were all army officers and so the twins had been put on a special list to apply for commissions without purchase, as the family now had no money to fund direct commissions for them. Only one free commission was available and it was awarded to John. Thomas thought he would be unable to become an officer, but finance was arranged for him to buy his commission, which he was able to repay later in life. They both wanted to serve with British army regiments in India as they 'were without the private income necessary for army life at home'.[10] At Horse Guards, they were introduced to the Military Secretary, Lord FitzRoy Somerset by their guardian, who was their uncle, Major Gordon. Lord FitzRoy Somerset told them that they were too young to go to India and that they should go back to the SNMA and study there for two more terms, which is what they did. (Thomas writes that they looked less than their age of 17.)

They eventually travelled to India in 1850, Thomas was in the 29th and John in the 61st Regiment. John served all his life in India and became a full general in 1894; three years later he was asked to be a member of the Council of India, a position he held for ten years. In 1873, Thomas was appointed as second-in-command to a mission to Kashgar in Central Asia. He later became Military Attaché and Oriental Secretary to the British Legation in Tehran. Afterwards he published a delightful and interesting short book, *Persia Revisited*, and also wrote an article in 1900 in which he referred to Persia and Afghanistan as being the 'Middle East' which was the first time that term was used.[11]

Only two sea-faring fathers are listed in the Roll Book as planning that their sons should go either into the Royal Navy or the marines. (The other sons with naval fathers are not listed as planning to have a service career.) In both cases the aspiration was fulfilled, one became a commander in the Royal Navy and the other enter the Marines. A famous naval father who sent two sons to the SNMA was Vice Admiral Charles James Johnston of Cowhill (1783–1856) who was Commander of the Cornwallis (a three-masted sailing ship with over fifty guns). He enrolled both boys at the SNMA in 1844 and wanted them to join the East India Company. The eldest son, George James (1827–1857), was there for only one year and joined the EIC as a Bengal Cadet in 1845. The younger son, William (1831–1901), who was 14 years old when he enrolled, was at the Academy for four years and went on to Haileybury and joined the Bengal Civil Service.

John and the directors must have been delighted that many members of the nobility and the professions chose to send their sons to the Academy. Some wanted their boys to have military careers, others knew that the teaching at the SNMA was of a sufficiently high standard for their boys to enter university or would equip them for other civilian careers.

An example of a father who was an aristocrat and politician, was Sir John Hope of Pinkie (1781–1853). He was the MP for Midlothian in 1845, 1847 and 1852 and was also a governor of the Royal Bank of Scotland. In 1835, he introduced his 14-year-old son William Hope (a different boy from William Hope VC). John marks him as planning to go into the 71st which was indeed the regiment he joined. He fought in the Battle of Sevastopol during the Crimean War and later commanded a brigade during the Indian uprising. He was knighted and retired as a full general in 1891.

Further evidence indicating that the education at the SNMA was considered of a high standard is that the Principal of Edinburgh University the Very Reverend John Lee (1779–1859) enrolled one of his sons, Alexander Henderson Lee (1828–1901), at the SNMA for two years from October 1841. Alexander has no aspiration listed in the Roll Book, but benefited from the Academy education as he studied civil engineering and became a civil engineer. Principal Lee had a library of 20,000 books and his entry in the *Dictionary of National Biography* mentions that he 'would buy a book of which he had several copies already, and then, not being able to find any of his copies would have to borrow the same book from a friend for a reference'.[12]

It is thanks to John's Roll Book with its ten columns of information that we know so much about some of the boys who went to the SNMA. In addition to the military aspiration of the pupils, John on seventy-one occasions writes a character assessment of the pupil concerned, fifty-six of which are positive. Examples of these are: 'outstanding', 'exemplary', 'VG' (Very Good), 'conduct good', 'talented', and 'a good rifleman' and 'good scholar'. Fifteen pupils have a negative remark such as 'VVB' (very, very, bad), 'VB' (very bad), 'obliged to be withdrawn' and 'left very irregular & bad conduct very lazy.'

Three of the boys with a negative comment have an Indian or overseas home address. As young children, they would have been sent back to the UK and may have had difficult upbringings. I have been unable to track down most of these boys, but I did find some information about two of them. Hugh Cowan came to the academy in 1848 when he was 14 with no career aspiration and John wrote 'VB obliged to be withdrawn'. Hugh's father was a banker in Ayrshire and after Hugh had been asked to leave the Academy, he was sent to have a life at sea. He managed to get his Master's Certificate in the Merchant Service in 1859 but in 1865 was killed in a typhoon in the North China Sea. A sad end for a young man who had managed to turn round his life.

Another student whom John asked to leave was James Horne. He enrolled at the Academy in 1854, his Roll Book entry is 'withdrawn VB'. I have found the family on Ancestry and it would appear that his parents split up, as in the 1851 Census James is living with his father. He died in 1868, when he was 28, and there is an unverified note that his death was due to 'a condition associated with alcoholism'. Two sad stories of young men who died young, but not on the battlefield.

There were eight 'exemplary' remarks. Two of these eight boys have no aspiration listed, which means that John was committed to getting to know and assessing both non-military and military pupils. Charles Glasfurd, one of the 'exemplary' boys, stayed with the Orr family for the one year while he was at the Academy, his story is in Chapter 9.

Another 'exemplary' pupil was Philip Tillbrook (1831–1902) who came from Suffolk. He was 17 when he enrolled at the SNMA in 1847 and was there two years; he did not stay with the Orrs. He was appointed without purchase as ensign to the 75th Foot in 1849 and served in different regiments in both India and the Crimea, retiring on half pay. He and his wife went to live in Belgravia and he became a member of Her Majesty's Body Guard and thereafter a Standard Bearer. These are two civil service appointments with duties on ceremonial occasions.

The only pupil that John marked as 'outstanding' is Henry Blackwood (1818–1865). He enrolled for two years at the Academy in 1834 and stayed with the Orrs. He came from a wealthy aristocratic Irish family and had hitherto been educated at Eton College. (His father was the 3rd Baron of Dufferin and Claneboye.) Henry joined the 17th Lancers in 1836, retiring in 1843 and a few years later he was appointed a Queen's Messenger. He was therefore considered to be both dependable and trustworthy, since Queen's Messengers carried secret and important documents to British embassies and consulates and were often retired army officers.

John's varied remarks regarding many of the boys are an indication of how well he got to know the pupils and how careful he was in assessing them. The number of positive remarks far outweigh the negative ones.

Chapter 8

Pleasures and Pains of Student Boarders

> 'You may rest assured I will do everything in my power for his welfare while he is in my charge.'[1]
>
> John Orr in a letter to a parent.

This quotation is from a letter John wrote to a parent in 1841 and typifies his attitude towards the pupils who boarded with him. He was a strong disciplinarian but believed that everything he did or said was in the boys' best interests. His Roll Book gives the address where a pupil was staying for each of the years they enrolled and this shows that the Orrs had normally five or six boys boarding with them, some staying for more than a year. A remarkable 163 pupils boarded with the Orr family from 1833 to 1863. A little over half of these boys came from Scotland, the rest had mainly travelled from England or Ireland. If they were young and had travelled from a distance, John would try and meet them off the carriage, boat or latterly the train.

I have two primary sources of information about life in the Orr family: these are Joseph Panton's book which gives anecdotes about his life with the Orrs and John's copy letter book. The letter book is a large unlined notebook (13x21ins) with cardboard covers and a brown worn leather spine; the pages are watermarked. It contains letters mainly relating to the Orrs' boarders or prospective boarders and is not an SNMA official letter book. The first letter is dated 31 December 1839 and the last 10 August 1848 and the entries end with a third of the book blank. Between September 1843 and March 1846 no letters are recorded. It may be that Jane became ill before her death in December 1844 and this disrupted the way letters were recorded. There are 140 copied out, mainly in the same handwriting, but some by different people.

The letters to parents and guardians show that John and his family were happy to have the boys staying with them. Many are notifying that fees are due or thanking parents or guardians for settling their accounts and some are replies to parents who are enquiring about sending their son to the SNMA. Two letters were sent to past pupils and there is one to Lord Kerr's son written after his father's death, (see Chapter 4). John may have kept a letter book during the whole period of his superintendency, and it is simply chance that this one copy is in the archive or – with all his other duties – he may not have managed to continue keeping one.

The letters concerning the payment of fees are not, on the whole, interesting. Some, however, give a snapshot of the pleasures and problems the Orr family had with some of the boys who stayed with them. There are insights into John's character and how he looked after the pupils who were boarding.

The charge for the year, comprising four sessions, was 120 guineas (£12,170, as at 1831) for a single room and 100 guineas (about £9,709 as at 1831) for a bed in a room shared with another pupil.[2] This cost covered their accommodation for ten months and two meals a day in the Orr family home.

John had more applications for pupils to stay than he had available accommodation. If he was unable to offer a vacancy, he had a list of other places where they could lodge, some costing as low as £60 (£5,800). A few of the masters took in boarders and they charged £90–£100 (£8,694–£9,660) for boarding for the ten months of the session. John wrote to Mrs Montgomery, the mother of a prospective pupil, in April 1840:

> If I should not be so fortunate as to be able to accommodate your son in my own family when the Academy meets it will afford me pleasure to endeavour to get him lodged where he will be comfortable and where I can have a general superintendence of him.[3]

The 1841 census return shows that John had six pupils boarding: Spenser Vansittart 17, Edward Wickham, 19, Archibald Fergusson 16, Alex

Montgomery 16, Robert Townley Parker 17 and Thomas Ridley, 17. It was a total household of sixteen counting the Orr family and servants. The house must have been crowded!

John had no problems with the majority of the pupils who stayed in their house and most settled easily into the family routine. An example of this was Thomas Ridley; in August 1841, John wrote to Thomas Ridley's guardian, Mr Godson, who lived in Gloucestershire, saying:

> Mrs Orr joins me in offering sincere congratulations on Mr Ridley being appointed to the 54th Regiment. I have heartfelt pleasure in expressing my unqualified approbation of his conduct during his residence here and in assuring you that he has merited the esteem of all his masters. Mrs Orr and myself will at all times be delighted to hear of his welfare with our united compliments to Mrs Ridley and to the young Ensign.[4]

Thomas won the Master's Prize in Latin and the first prize with the Firelock in the July prize-giving of 1841. He became a captain in the Royal Lancashire Regiment, the 54th.

John and his wife, Jane, became fond of many of the boys who stayed with them, even though John was frequently frustrated by their lack of application to their studies. This is part of a letter to Reverend Vansittart written on 15 July 1840 about his son Spencer:

> He [Spencer] is in excellent health and spirits and possesses strict principles, an amiable disposition and good abilities. I only wish that his inclination for study was equal to these.

Spencer was also not good with money (see later).

The first letter in the letter book, dated 31 December 1839, is to James Pedder, a banker from Preston, about his son Thomas who was 18. This relates to Thomas's second and last year at the SNMA and John encloses the masters' reports for the first quarter of the session. John is pleased as the report is 'very satisfactory with the exception of history' but he is worried that Thomas wants to drop the subject as well as practical mechanics and that he will wander about the city when he has extra free time. John goes on:

> his habits I fear are not sufficiently studious to warrant me to expect that he will make any progress in the study of history and geography if he does not return to the class.

In January 1840, John wrote again to James Pedder about Thomas, who was trying to avoid the practical mechanics class. This is one of my favourite letters:

> My dear Sir,
> Since your son's return to us I am sorry to say that his general conduct is anything but satisfactory to me and unless he improves and attends to more of my directions I will be under the necessity of requesting you to remove him from my house. I desired him to occupy his time from 3 to 4 at Practical Mechanics class or join the German class, but he objects on the plea of taking a walk for the benefit of his health. Now you will observe from the arrangement of his classes which I send herewith that he has sufficient exercise in the drill class from 12 to 1 and from 3 to 4 with the Practical Mechanical class, but I have every reason to believe that he has too great a command of money and that his object is to idle along the streets, smoking cigars and drinking cherry brandy. You must be aware that from 3 to past 4 is by no means a desirable time for a young man to idle along Princes Street, and if he is allowed to have time to himself I cannot be responsible for the evil habits he may contract.
>
> If his health were in any way to suffer I should be the first to urge him to walk abroad, but his want of perseverance is what is to be regretted for I am certain if he would apply himself to his various studies that he is more than equal to them and I am not without hope that he would be an honour to us and do credit to himself at our examination.

John is also worried about the amount Thomas spends on his clothes:

> I think him expensive in his wardrobe and will thank you to give me some idea of what you allow him yearly – he is

> not satisfied with the tailor I employ but must get one more expensive.[5]

Matters improved, as in a letter to James Pedder on 30 March John writes:

> Mr Thomas is in good spirits and seems attentive to his classes, I hope he will make a respectable appearance at our examination.

In the July examinations he received the third prize in military history.

Thomas Pedder became an officer in 58th Regiment. (The Remarks column has an entry 'Reg 62' then in different ink 'Reg 58', the latter regiment was his second choice.) He saw service at Wanganui in New Zealand in May 1847. As a captain in the 7th Hussars, he later fought in India where he died in action in 1853.

A letter similar to the one sent to Thomas Pedder's father was sent to Major General Sir Thomas Whitehead, again in Preston, in November 1841, about his son John, aged 18.

> I have reason to believe that your son has written with a view to being relieved from some of his classes at the Academy. I take the liberty of suggesting that he should not be indulged in this wish, for his time I know will be diverted to idleness in the street if not the Billiard Room.[6]

John Whitehead has no written comment in the Remarks column, but he entered the East Kent Militia and became a colonel in that regiment.

Life for the pupils would have been less prescribed in the Orr's house compared with being a cadet at RMC or at Addiscombe. John considered himself *in loco parentis* to the pupils staying with him and was always concerned about their health. None of the pupils during the periods of the letter book became seriously ill, although a number had colds and coughs. The boys were attended to by either of the two ordinary directors who were doctors, Dr Maclagan and Dr Ballingall or sometimes by John's friend Dr Moir.

On one occasion, John was concerned about Charles Watson's health. (This is the pupil who won the first Superintendent's Prize.) Charles started at the SNMA in October 1841, his father was a church minister who now lived in Boulogne-sur-Mer, Saint Omer in France. John wrote to Charles's father:

> In consequence of a slight cold and cough I urged your son on Tuesday 1st to see Dr Maclagan who found him slightly feverish and ordered him to remain in the house. Yesterday though much less fever a blister was applied to his breast owing to the cough continuing. The doctor says this is no cause for alarm but that his cough may be tedious especially at this season when we have so much east wind.[7]

(I was amused to read that Edinburgh's east wind was as unpleasant over 150 years ago as it is today.)

Charles was popular in the Orr household. John wrote to his father in April 1842:

> It affords me great pleasure to say that your son's domestic conduct is everything a parent could wish and I assure you Mrs Orr has very great comfort in his society.[8]

Charles Watson (1824–1894) left the SNMA in July 1843. In the *Caledonian Mercury* of 24 July, he received a glowing endorsement at the prize-giving in the speech made by Dr Maclagan:

> In regard to the other prize, he [Dr Maclagan] had to state that Mr Charles Edward Watson, during the whole period of his career at the Academy, had been so zealous and successful in every department of study, and so exemplary in conduct, that he had exhausted both prizes and panegyric – and the Directors felt themselves compelled to depart from the usual routine, and to present Mr Watson with a sword, in testimony of their admiration and approbation of his eminent success in study, and excellence in conduct.

It was not surprising that Charles was given this eulogy. He received first prizes in civil engineering, architectural drawing, German, firelock exercise and fencing and second prizes in sketching from nature and the broadsword. He joined the 71st Regiment of Foot, as listed in the Remarks column and became an ensign in this regiment in January 1852 while in Dublin. He retired a lieutenant colonel and became a JP in Westmorland. In 1879 he was one of the larger contributors, with a donation of ten guineas (£1,136), to a presentation to John shortly before John died.

John made arrangements for pupils to return to their homes after the session was over. During the period of the letter book there were not yet trains between Edinburgh and England. Those pupils who lived in the Lancashire area usually took a ship from Glasgow to Liverpool. The two options to get to London were by sea or by horse-drawn coach. John wrote to Reverend Richard Tritton:

> It will be obliging if you will inform whether your son will return home by coach or by steamer. The steamboats sail [from Leith] on Saturdays at 3 o'clock and in general arrive at Blackwall on the Monday forenoon.[9]

Reverend Tritton, who was the rector of Morden, Surrey was grateful for John's care and attention in looking after Frederick and sent John and Jane a silver teapot. Frederick (1827–1904) won the second prize in arithmetic and the same in drawing in July 1843, then joined the Welsh Fusiliers. (Here is an example of the Remark's column not indicating the regiment he ultimately enrolled with as he initially was planning to join 'Reg 19 Royal Irish Foot'.) His last military appointment was as lieutenant colonel commanding the 5th Depot Battalion at Parkhurst, Isle of Wight. He obtained his lieutenant colonelcy in May 1869 and retired by selling his commission. He died in Leamington on 23 January 1904, leaving effects worth the huge sum of over £30,000 (£3,439,000). His short obituary in the *Army & Navy Gazette* ends by saying 'He had not the good fortune to see active service' – a comment we would now find wry, but then was made seriously.

❋ ❋ ❋

The SNMA strongly recommended that pupils should only have a small amount of pocket money and reminded parents in the *Rules and Regulations* that in English military colleges the allowance ranged from 1s (£5) to 3s 6d (£17). The implication was that this amount should not be exceeded. It was not possible, however, to make this a mandatory requirement at the SNMA which was a non-residential academy and many pupils were living at home.

A few boys who boarded with John's family were given too much pocket money by their wealthy parents and some even managed to overspend their generous allowance. John was always trying to get parents to support him when he urged the pupils to spend less. Many of the letters involve asking parents to reduce the boys' pocket money, or not to increase it. John tried to insist that he should have control over dispensing the pocket money, he could then withhold it as a sanction. Simply advising some of the pupils who were about 18 years old to spend less and study more, did not work. Withholding pocket money was a helpful tool to get the pupils to apply themselves to their studies.

At the RMC the amount of pocket money that cadets could receive was stipulated:

> No cadet was allowed to join the College with more than a guinea in his pocket and was not permitted to receive any money whilst at the College except a weekly allowance from his parents limited to 3s 6d [£16] for an Under-Officer, 2s 6d [£12] for an upper school cadet and 2s [£9] for a lower school cadet.[10]

The RMC was in the country and the nearby village was out of bounds. It offered various outdoor activities. The SNMA, by contrast, was a day school in the centre of a capital city and an attempt to exert control over some of the boys would have been difficult.

Another connected problem was that pupils who did not have enough pocket money to buy what they wanted simply charged the items to John Orr's account. John tried to insist that the boys should first ask him for permission to do this. He would often only find out about the item when he received the account. He then had to ask the boy to countersign the bill before sending it to the parents who would settle the account.

If a pupil abused the system, John ordered the shop to no longer accept orders from that particular boy.

An example of this happening is in a letter to Anthony Wilkinson about his son, also named Anthony. Young Anthony had enrolled in 1846 when he was 17 years old, his father was a magistrate and deputy lieutenant, living in Durham:

> My dear Sir,
> I now beg leave to enclose my account for your son, I regret that his expenses are so great. I have done and am doing all in my power to restrain his expenses and to induce him to put greater value on money. Those bills which I have marked with an X were incurred without my sanction. I have warned him seriously and also the different tradesmen that no article is to be got or paid for by me that I do not previously give a written order for.[11]

Anthony Wilkinson left the SNMA in July 1847 having been awarded the Master's Prize in fortification.

Spencer Vansittart was a problem both with pocket money and with the running up of bills. Spencer was the son of yet another Church of England clergyman, Reverend William Vansittart who lived in Maidenhead, Berkshire. Spencer was at the SNMA for three years starting in October 1838. Reverend Vansittart wrote to John in August 1840 and asked him to increase his son's pocket money for the following year. John was not happy with this request as Spencer had already run up a bill of £60 3s 6d (£5,821) for various items between 1 March to the end of July. John agreed to increase the pocket money but he asked that he, John, should be in control of its disbursement and he ordered the shopkeepers and tailors not to accept further orders from Spencer.

The Orr family liked Spencer and John wrote:

> It is impossible to know him as we now do without being attached to him and I would wish him to understand that any indulgence is to depend on his exertions at his studies and general good conduct.[12]

This remark is an example of John's paternalistic feeling to many of the young men who boarded with him; nonetheless, he was determined that Spencer should try and achieve the best possible results academically. John's last letter to Spencer's father ends up:

> indeed he is a favourite with us all and we will at all times feel delight to hear of his promotion and welfare, with our united compliments to Mrs Vansittart, the ladies and not forgetting the ensign.

Spencer received the fourth prize in Military History at the prize-giving in July 1840 and first prize in the same subject in July 1841. He joined the Royal Regiment of Foot and retired with the rank of captain. (His aspiration in the Remarks column was fulfilled.) He spent most of his life in Ireland and became a Justice of the Peace for Limerick. He died in Castle Connell in 1902 leaving £32,404 2s 8d (£3,135,000). A notice in one of the local papers after his death stated:

> The high regard in which the deceased was held in the locality in which he spent a great part of his life was evinced by the exceedingly large proportions of the cortege which was representative of all classes. His quiet and dignified manner and the sincere and hearty interest which he evinced in the welfare of his neighbourhood, endeared him to the people.[13]

Sometimes, it was clear a pupil did not fit in with John's regime and he would then politely request of the parent or guardian that if the young man was coming back to the Academy the following year he should stay elsewhere. One of the pupils whom John did not want back was Mr R. Rintoul, who was aged 17 – this was because 'his habits were such and his want of firmness to abide by good advice'. He was a pupil for only one year: 1839–40. John wrote to his guardian, Mr Hamilton Rowan, in Downpatrick, Ireland on 11 August 1840 saying:

> As I stated to Mr Rintoul before he left us, I do not think it would be for his advantage to return to my house – should he wish to continue at the Academy where he acquitted himself

> very creditably. He might reside in lodgings where he would not be subject to the restraints which I find it necessary to impose on the young gentlemen under my control. I should on all occasions afford him my advice and assistance.[14]

Mr Rintoul did not return to the SNMA. He is listed as joining the 50th Regiment.

I was surprised to find only two comments in letters about possible girlfriends. In the letter to Anthony Wilkinson about his son Anthony, John went on to say:

> Since you left, I am happy to say that he is giving me more satisfaction both at home and at the Academy and I have no reason to suppose that there has been any attempt to renew his acquaintance with the young lady or her family.[15]

The only other remark comes in a letter to Edward Bligh in Lancashire in 1847. His son Frederick was two years at the SNMA starting in October 1845. He was 16 when he first enrolled and John wrote in March 1847:

> I am sorry that his expenses should be so great as they are. I have done and am doing all in my power to restrain his habits of extravagance and to induce him to put a greater value on money. One item which you will observe in the account – a charge of £1 16s 9d (£178) for a garnet ring has given me uneasiness. I did not know of it until the bill was presented and on questioning your son regarding it, he tells me that he gave it away but declined to say to whom.[16]

It cannot have been a major problem as John goes on to write: 'His conduct otherwise is much more to my satisfaction than it formerly was and the report by the masters of his studies during the last quarter is good.' In 1847, Frederick won the Master's Prizes for military drawing and for German. He also won other prizes for fencing, history and geography and an extra prize in landscape drawing.

During the period of the letter book, John had the most problems with Edward Wickham who stayed with the Orrs for two years from October

1840 until July 1842. John wrote a series of letters to his father John Wickham, who was the justice of the peace and local deputy lieutenant in Somerset. Edward was 18 years old and was the oldest pupil staying in the Orr house that year and caused John a great deal of heartache. The first incident is reported in a letter in April 1842 when John wrote to Edward's father:

> without my knowledge he lately went on a Saturday after classes with some young friends into the country and the party I regret to say got into a foolish scrape for which they were each fined by the magistrate £10 [£1,000].[17]

On 5 June in another letter where John wrote describing a fine of £6 (£600) relating to the injury of a horse.

The worst incident had yet to come and was described at length in a letter to Edward's father. Edward had come back extremely late one night. He knew the house rule that the doors were locked at 11p.m. and no one was allowed to come in later, unless by prior arrangement. John wrote:

> On Friday last I sat up expecting him till one o'clock in the morning. When he was not appearing, I ordered the door not to be opened without my permission. Your son came to the door after 2 o'clock and made such a noise demanding admission stating that he had a right to come in at any time he thought proper.[18]

Afterwards, John confined him to his room until he heard back from his father. He told Mr Wickham what a poor example this was to the younger pupils staying in his house. With behaviour like this, 'I cannot maintain discipline and respectability so essential to an establishment of this kind.'

John then received two letters from Mr Wickham, which I do not have. In a letter towards the end of July, John replied saying that he was gratified to receive these letters:

> I do assure you I am sincerely anxious to make the youthful follies of your son as little injurious to him as possible.

> We are now friends and I trust will continue so during the remainder of his stay here. I propose to pay him 5 shillings (£25) weekly to prevent his getting further into debt while he remains in Edinburgh.[19]

If the boy had shown signs of changing, it is remarkable how forgiving John is of past bad behaviour. Edward Wickham won the second prize in the Broadsword in July 1841. He left the SNMA in 1842 and joined the 61st Regiment of Foot. (Aspiration in the Remark's column is correct.) He attained the rank of major and retired on half pay in 1866.

Panton writes about how some of the older pupils would ask 'the Old Captain' to join them if they were going out in the evening. He tells us about a night when some of the boys and John went to Mother Clark's restaurant in Newhaven, for a fish dinner. The favourite dish was 'crappit heid' which was often eaten with haggis. (Crappit heid was the stuffed head of a cod or similar fish. The stuffing was made with oatmeal, onion, suet, fish liver and seasoning and a walnut-sized piece was stuffed behind the eye sockets. It was originally cooked in sea water and was a popular Scottish dish.) Before they went into Mother Clark's, John said to Joseph and his friend Tom, 'Panton, and you Tom Leith, remember gentlemen, that it is your duty to keep sober tonight, in order, if necessary, to carry me home on a shutter.'[20]

The students might also ask John and some masters to join them for a 'beef-steak dinner at the Flesh Market Close'. (Flesh Market Close is an old narrow street in Edinburgh. It leads from the High Street down to Market Street. There used to be a slaughter house near the foot of this street, beside the old Nor Loch.) Joseph writes:

> Here door-mat upon door-mat of reeking steak, hot from the grill, would be served up one after the other, garnished according to taste with onions or oysters, and a theatre entertainment usually followed.

John preferred the boys to stay with the Orrs over Christmas, but he was happy to let some of the older pupils to take a trip away at Easter. Parental permission would be required for these trips. The most popular break was a walking holiday in Stirlingshire. John advanced the necessary money and would have it refunded by the parents. A Loch Lomond visit is briefly mentioned in some of the letters in the letter book and is described in detail in Joseph Panton's diary.

During the Easter break in 1850 Panton, Jack Finley, Phillip Bott and Richard Rycroft (all pupils staying with the Orrs) went on a walking holiday in the Trossachs, an area of Scotland east of Loch Lomond and west of Stirling renowned for its beauty. John had advised them to go and stay in the schoolmaster's house. When they arrived at the village of Brig-o-Turk they found the house was only a 'But and Ben' which is a Scottish description of a small two-roomed cottage. Panton and Finley had to share a bed which was in a cupboard recess. Bott and Rycroft found a room in another cottage. (Three years later, in 1853, Brig-o-Turk was the village which was the site of the love triangle involving John Ruskin and his wife Effie Grey and John Everett Millais.)

They managed to get hold of a fiddler and organised a dance that evening in Panton and Finley's little room, having put all the furniture outside. Many of the villagers joined them and it did not finish till midnight. Panton describes the start of the evening:

> A box was brought in for the fiddler to stand on: refreshments in the form of oatcakes and whisky were provided in the next room and we opened the ball with some of the ladies of the district, old and young, in a mad reel, just to show we were not knocked up with the day's march.[21]

John was a good judge of character and he was happy for responsible boys to go off on a trip like this, knowing they would behave themselves.

❋ ❋ ❋

There are two unusual copies of letters in the letter book which were written to pupils who had recently left the Academy. One is to Edward Tomkinson (see Chapter 9), the other is to Thomas Gardiner which was sent in September 1847 while John was on holiday with his family in Elie, Fife. (John may well have copied it himself in haste into the letter book. The writing is poor and difficult to transcribe.)

Thomas Gardiner enrolled for two sessions at the SNMA starting in October 1845 and while staying with the Orrs became a friend of John's son Jack. He received his certificate in July 1847 and joined the 40th Regiment. (He was another pupil whose aspiration in the Remark's column was fulfilled.) Thomas had been awarded several prizes at the end of the session including the Master's Prize in English and others in landscape drawing, history, geography, and firelock and broadsword. John wants to encourage him to do well in his regiment:

> My dear Gardiner
> Your note of the 23rd reached me here at the home where I rest. I was on the ramble visiting St Andrews and could not think of taking a pen in my hand until now. I really feel ashamed at my delay.
>
> I imagine you are by this time feeling a little excited at the idea of joining your corps. Let me tell you that much depends on your first start. Do let me, my dear fellow, remind you of my old advice to be heeded don't allow yourself to be in the habit of sitting late at mess. Being steadiness of conduct and diligent in application to your formal duties will gain the estimation of your brother officers and best addressed when an opportunity does occur your commanding officer will have pleasure in selecting you for the adjutancy or any other staff appointment.

John goes on to tell Thomas that his son Jack has been spending three weeks in the Lake District and they are expecting him back soon. He asks Thomas to send him a report as to how he is getting on. He says his daughters send their best regards and finishes the letter 'Your sincere friend'. This is a touching letter which demonstrates how John cared about his students even after they left school. He wants to support a young officer at the beginning of his career.

Thomas Gardiner served with his regiment, 40th Foot, in both the East Indies and India. He retired with the rank of colonel and died a wealthy man, aged 80, in England.

As mentioned previously, at many of the prize-givings there were comments about how caring John was towards the pupils,. It would be a natural formality on these occasions to compliment the superintendent, yet these comments seem to be heartfelt and are mentioned by both directors and masters. In 1840, Sir Henry Jardine gave a speech after the prizes had been awarded and mentions John. It is interesting how well he was received by the pupils.

Sir Henry alluded in very flattering terms to the valuable and efficient services of Captain Orr, the superintendent to whose exertions he justly attributed the growing prosperity of the Institution. It was gratifying to witness the enthusiasm with which the pupils responded to this compliment showing at once their sense of its justice and their high regard for the superintendent.[22]

This is further reflected in a speech by John Bowie, a prominent lawyer and ordinary director who spoke before the prizes were awarded in July 1847. The press report says: 'Mr Bowie then alluded to the watchfulness with which Captain Orr superintended the progress of the pupils, and the parental solicitude he entertained towards them even after they had left the institution.'[23]

After reading the letters in the letter book and Joseph Panton's diaries, I began to feel I was getting to know John as a person. It was a joy to understand how well he got on with many of the boys and reading the stories about his going out for dinner with them made me smile. Many of the pupils found him a good companion, but he felt he had a responsibility to make sure that they all behaved well and therefore treated them as he would his own children. An example of this, is when he was having trouble with Edmund Hardy he wrote in a letter to his father: 'I often spoke to him very seriously indeed had he been my own son I could not have been more open and candid with him.'[24] A few of the boys, particularly the older ones, resented his discipline and when this happened, John found the situation awkward to handle. Many of the other 18-year-olds, however, such as Joseph Panton and Charles Watson, got on well with John and enjoyed a very good relationship with him.

Chapter 9

Future Lives of Four of John's Boarders

> A biography is a chronical of facts and a portrait, one without the other won't work.[1]
>
> Ruth Scurr. *Goya.*

John had affection for the pupils who stayed with his family and spent much time cajoling and motivating them to study so that they could achieve the best for themselves after they left the SNMA. Some of these boys went on to have noteworthy and varied lives and I have chosen to write in more detail about four of them: Colonel Edward Tomkinson, Major General Charles Glasfurd, Lieutenant Colonel Stuart-Wortley and Joseph Panton.

Colonel Edward Tomkinson (1825–1870)

Apart from Joseph Panton, I have found out more about Edward Tomkinson than most of the other pupils, as there are several letters from John to Edward's mother in the letter book. Edward joined the 8th Hussars and served them later in the Crimean War.

John always invited parents to visit the Academy, either when the pupil enrolled or to attend the annual prize-giving. For parents living outside Scotland, often their only contact with the Academy was by letter and it is interesting to see how John builds up a closer relationship with some parents than with others through the number and length of the letters in the letter book. The longest correspondence is with Mrs Tomkinson, Edward's widowed mother. Edward was born on 11 July 1825 in Reaseheath Hall near Nantwich in Cheshire and was baptised by his father who was a vicar. He attended Rugby School before enrolling at the SNMA in October 1840 when he 15 years old, and studied there for three years. Edward's father, Reverend Henry Tomkinson, had been the vicar at St Mary's Church, Acton, near Nantwich but had died in 1838.

John wrote fourteen letters to Mrs Tomkinson which show both Edward's development and how fond John and Jane had become of him. His first year was uneventful and in August 1841 John wrote to Mrs Tomkinson to assure her that all had gone well 'that amiable conduct while here gained him the esteem of all his masters'.[2]

In April 1842, Mrs Tomkinson asked John to increase Edward's pocket money to 6 shillings (£30) weekly. John agreed but with the proviso that issuing will depend on 'his good behaviour and application to study'. He went on to say he would like to see 'a greater degree of application', but was pleased to have reports that his French and drawing were improving. He ends up by saying, 'I am happy to say he is in excellent health and a favourite with us all.'

At the end of the session, John wrote that he had worked 'better at his studies' though there is 'still room for further exertion on the part of Mr Edward'. John arranged for him to return home by sea from Glasgow to Liverpool and wrote to Mrs Tomkinson: 'I feel deeply interested in him and pray for his future welfare.'

In August 1843, Mrs Tomkinson asked John's advice as to whether Edward should take up his commission or come back to the SNMA for another session. John replied that he was sure that Edward would never regret passing another year at the Academy but 'much depends on Mr Edward' and 'his own exertions', meaning it was pointless his coming back if he was not prepared to study. John added that if he did return 'there must not be a single debt contracted without my previous knowledge.' John mentioned a confectioner's bill that had recently come in for 9s 6d (£49)! Edward must have had a sweet tooth or was generously sharing the confectionary with others.

Mrs Tomkinson sent Edward back to the SNMA for a further year and she asked if he could do drill only on alternate days. John welcomed him back but said it was not possible to do drill on alternate days as it 'would throw him behind his companions'. She hoped that John would let him have enough pocket money so that he could enjoy life in Edinburgh and John replied that Edward would be given enough so that he may 'partake of good society when it does not too much interfere with his studies'. Mrs Tomkinson was grateful for all John's support and sent the Orr family a Cheshire cheese. John and Jane were delighted with the gift.

John was pleased to hear on 12 May 1843 that Edward's appointment as a cornet in the cavalry regiment 8th Hussars had been announced in the official *Gazette*; this matched his aspiration in the Remarks column. John wrote to Mrs Tomkinson saying, if possible, Edward should stay until the middle of June so that he could finish the military drawing class. They were now working outside 'with practical work in surveying, a knowledge of which is of consequence to every officer, more especially to one in the cavalry'. At the end of the letter he said, 'Mrs Orr and I will for ever feel a deep interest in his welfare and I don't doubt he will do honour to his profession.' He thanked her for enquiring after his own health and replied that he, John, 'is now much recovered'.[3] (It is unknown what had been wrong with him.) Later in May, John wrote that, 'Mr Edward has, since the first burst of excitement, conducted himself with great good feeling and judgement.'

After the session finished, towards the end of July 1843 John received two bills for transport which Edward had charged to John's account. John wrote to Edward who was now with the 8th Hussars in York:

> Watt has rendered an account against you for a landau gig on 24 May 16/- [£83] and on 27th same month an Indian dogcart 18/6d [£97]. In all £1 14s 6d [£180]. Please let me know by return if the same is correct. I hope you got the two boxes safe which I forwarded for you, in the hurry of packing I find that Johnnie's boot jack was put in by mistake.
>
> How do you like the riding school and your new line of life? Watson is still with us and leaves tomorrow. I am as usual in a great bustle clearing up accounts to be off to the country. Mrs Orr writes best regards.[4]

John then forwarded the bills to Edward's mother on 3 August. He ended by saying to Mrs Tomkinson: 'I observe with pleasure the compliments you pay to this city which should you be induced to visit it would give Mrs Orr and myself sincere pleasure to become personally acquainted with you and to be of any use in my power to you.'

I enjoyed reading these letters and they helped me understand the care that John took over the pupils staying with him. Over the three years, John had been coaxing Edward to work harder and learn as much as he could before becoming an officer. The 1851 census shows he was a lieutenant with this regiment and was based at the Preston Cavalry Barracks, Steyning in Sussex.

A few years later, in February 1854, war had been declared on Russia and on 24 April, Edward, aged 29, sailed in the *Shooting Star* from Plymouth to Constantinople (known as Istanbul after 1920) with the third troop of the 8th Hussars. Sailing with him was Captain Henry Duberly and his wife Fanny; during the time she was in the Crimea, she kept a diary and published it after the war.[5] Edward appears from time to time in her diary and she shows that he was a caring person as well as a keen soldier.

Fanny Duberly was a strongminded and vivacious woman; she was also an excellent and intrepid rider. She was happier in the company of men, although she was devoted to her husband and often worried about him. Henry was the paymaster for the regiment and so did not take part in the battles. Fanny's diary gives us a day-to-day understanding of the privations and difficulties that the cavalry division had to face during the Crimean War.

On board Edward's ship, the *Shooting Star*, there were sixty-two horses, fifty-two for troops and ten for officers. The horses had a miserable journey as they were not properly supported, the ship's hold was intensely hot and they did not have enough water. Bad weather was encountered in the Bay of Biscay and the horses were thrown about resulting in the deaths of some of them. The ship eventually arrived in Constantinople on 22 May 1854.

The regiment stayed in the city for a few days and then sailed on to Varna, a Bulgarian port on the Black Sea, arriving on 1 June. Shortly afterwards the regiment was ordered inland to make camp at Devna about 19 miles away. On Monday, 5 June the troop was woken by reveille at 2.30 a.m. and was ready to leave by 5.30. Fanny said that her breakfast was a 'a stale egg and a mouthful of brandy'. She described a long tiring ride of eight hours in extreme heat. Eventually, they arrived at the place where they were going to camp, but although a stream was nearby there were no trees to provide shelter. She wrote:

> Captain Tomkinson made me a bed of his cloak and sheepskin; and drawing my hat over my eyes, I lay down under a bush, close to Bob [her horse] and slept till far towards evening.[6]

On another occasion, Edward was sent off to reconnoitre where the Russians were positioned. He returned with a bunch of flowers for Fanny. She wrote in her diary: 'Captain Tomkinson returned today from Basarardchick, bringing me a handful of roses from the ruined village, observing as he gave them to me, that I now possessed roses from nearer the enemy than anyone else.'[7]

In August 1854, the 8th Hussars were still in Devna. Fanny wrote to her sister Selina describing how in the evening after dinner she and her husband and other officers often went into Edward's tent and while the officers were smoking, she would sit on the ground and 'surreptitiously drink their rum and water and coffee'.[8] These diary excerpts show Edward's affection for Fanny Duberly and his sociable nature as he was happy for his tent to be used regularly for the evening get-together.

The 8th Hussars embarked for the Crimea on 1 September. About two weeks later, the troops and horses went ashore about 30 miles from Sevastopol. Roger Fenton, the first wartime photographer and correspondent, took a photograph of the 'cooking house' of the 8th Hussars which shows the basic conditions for providing food in a war zone at that time **(Illustration 12 monochrome)**.[9]

Edward fought in the Battle of Alma and was then involved in the Battle of Balaclava where the 8th Hussars took part in the infamous Charge of the Light Brigade. This disastrous charge was mainly the result of antagonism between the two cavalry commanders who were brothers-in-law: Lord Lucan, Commander of the Cavalry Division, and Lord Cardigan, who was Brigadier-General in command of the Light Brigade.

During the Battle of Balaclava, Lord Raglan, Commander of the British troops, delivered a series of orders to Lord Lucan. These orders continue to be debated by historians, but all agree they were not precise enough. Raglan wanted the Light Cavalry to prevent the Russians from removing guns that they had captured in some redoubts. Raglan was on a high vantage point and his view of the battle area was not the samc as that of Lord Lucan, who could not see the redoubts.

The third order was:

> Cavalry to advance and take advantage of any opportunity to recover the Heights. They will be supported by infantry which have been ordered to advance on two fronts.

Lord Lucan did not understand the order. He waited to see the infantry advance, but none came. He thought that Lord Raglan was asking for a cavalry unit to charge Russian artillery, which he knew was absurd. Captain Nolan then delivered the last order. Nolan hated Lucan and was impatient for action and simply repeated the final order 'Lord Raglan's orders are that the cavalry is to attack immediately.' Nolan gave a wild gesture that to Lord Lucan seemed to be in the direction of the North Valley and was not in the direction of the redoubts that Raglan had intended should be attacked. The North Valley was where Russian cavalry had gone after being routed by William Ainslie and the Highland Brigade. Lord Lucan, upset by Nolan's brashness, was determined to obey the order and rode over and directed Lord Cardigan to attack the Russian position on the far side of the valley. The misunderstanding of the last two orders set in motion the Charge of the Light Brigade.

It was a disastrous attack. Edward survived but he had his horse shot from under him. The *London Evening Standard* of 5 September 1857 reported that Edward 'led the squadron he commanded with courage and steadiness'. There are some reports he was injured, but if so, the damage was not serious enough to be noted in an official list of those wounded in the battle. Fanny mentions that his horse was killed, but not that he was injured.

The Light Brigade, under the command of Lord Cardigan, was an easy target for the Russian cavalry and Nolan was killed almost immediately. The valley was a dead-end. Fire rained down on horses and men and those who survived the advance had to turn round to come back and were fired on again. The Charge lasted twenty minutes. Six hundred and seventy took part, 110 officers and men were killed and

160 wounded, but Lord Cardigan was uninjured. Five hundred horses were also killed. Dreadful though these losses were, it is now thought remarkable they were not even larger, bearing in mind it was an artillery attack on a cavalry unit.

Those riders whose horses had fallen, like Edward, had to walk back a mile. Lord George Paget who was one of the last to return, later wrote: 'What a scene of havoc was this last mile – strewn with the dead and dying and all friends!'[10] The Charge was immortalised in the poem by Tennyson, but in reality, it was a serious blunder which decimated the British cavalry.

For his service in the Crimea, Edward received the brevet rank of major, the English medal and four clasps, together with several other medals. He became a full major in 1857 and the commanding officer of the Cavalry Northgate Barracks in Canterbury. In December 1866, Edward, aged 41, retired on half pay having served seventeen years with his regiment. On 1 May 1869, the *Army and Navy Gazette* listed his appointment as an aide-de-camp to Queen Victoria with the rank of colonel. Only eleven months later, on 14 May 1870, he died, aged 45, at his London home in Lower Seymour Street; he had never married. Edward's obituary in the *Nantwich Guardian* of 21 May gives the cause of his death being 'a long-standing tumour of the brain'. The obituary adds that, 'since his return to Nantwich has devoted himself as far as his health would permit to his duties as a magistrate and chairman of the Highways Board.' His body was taken home to Cheshire and was buried in St Mary's Churchyard at Acton.

Edward was popular with the Orrs; they found him a genial person to have in their house and he later fulfilled John's military expectations of him. His three years at the SNMA gave him the grounding for his success with the 8th Hussars. Fanny Duberly's descriptions of Edward show him to be a kind and caring man.

Major General Charles L.R. Glasfurd (1831–1887)

Charles Glasfurd was one of only eight pupils whom John noted as 'Exemplary' in his Remarks column of the Roll Book. He was born in India while his father John was serving with the EIC. His mother had died when he was 3 and he was sent back to the Glasfurd home in Inverness when he was 6, where he started his education. In 1848, when he was 17, he enrolled at the SNMA and was there for one year, staying with the Orr family. Charles did well at the Academy and at the end of the year prize-giving in July 1849 was awarded first prize in firelock and artillery exercise, second prize in broadsword and third prize in landscape drawing.

He obtained a direct cadetship into the EIC's army and departed for Bombay in 1849. (He is listed in the Roll Book as planning to go to India.) He sailed through the Mediterranean to Alexandria and then made his way by land to the Red Sea, and continued the journey by ship. The whole trip to India only took him thirty-eight days using this route. (His father's journey, purely by sea, in 1828 took 147 days.) Though both he and his father were serving in India at the same time over an eight-year period, they never met up. They corresponded but his father married again twice (his second wife also dying young) and father and son become estranged.[11]

After a few years in Bombay, during which time Charles became a good linguist, he was transferred from the army to the Revenue Survey. He briefly rejoined his regiment during the uprising in 1856–57 and saw service in Multan in the Punjab. In 1858, he was transferred back to the Survey, which was a civilian occupation, yet he retained his military rank and finished up as a major general.

In 1860, a new treaty between the British government and the Nazim of Hyderabad was signed. (Nazim was the title given to the ruler of the state of Hyderabad.) In this treaty, a narrow strip of land running along the Pranhita River to the Godavari Basin was ceded by the Nazim; it was in the district controlled by the Madras Presidency. Charles was offered a new post involving land-value assessment and mapping this area. (His mapping and drawing skills would have been learnt at the SNMA.) The territory had not yet been explored by the EIC.

His diaries were lodged at Cambridge University; they reveal his interest in Indian life and concern for the welfare of the Indians who lived in the Godavari basin where he worked for several years. (The Godavari is a long river which runs across central India from west to east.) I was excited to be able to look at and handle Charles's diaries. Three were written between 1860 and 1863 and the fourth in 1868.

In addition to his surveying work, Charles was the magistrate, judge and collector of revenue for this strip of land about 200 miles long by 40 miles in breadth. A few villages were situated along the river with some cultivation but the rest of the land consisted of large tracts of jungle and only a few hamlets.

Charles started to use *palkee* also known as palanquins. (These were large covered box litters for one person, carried on two poles by four or six people.) He had not travelled this way previously as he 'considered it so effeminate'. He now, however, started to use them for overnight journeys, sleeping while he was being carried and noted how good it was leaving in the evening and 'finding yourself in the morning about 30 miles further than where you started'. He was shocked by the dirt and lack of water in some of the hamlets and carried beads and handkerchiefs to give as presents to villagers. He was interested in the terrain, sometimes making drawings of the type of rocks and hills he saw.

A suitable site for a new station had to be found and Charles organised its construction. He chose a place called Sironcha and lived there for eight years. Charles was lucky, as a physician called Doctor Cameron had been seconded to the area; he became a close friend and was able to look after Charles during his frequent bouts of fever. After the basic station had been constructed, he had a substantial house built for himself – until then he had been living in a small, thatched building. He wrote in his diary that it cost him the large sum of £1,500 (£152,000) to build the house and he describes how his home in Sironcha was 'his little oasis'. He enjoyed hunting and frequently mentioned in his diaries the killing of bull bison and tigers within a mile of his house. Charles also founded the village of Glasfurdhapeta, which was named after him. It was 7½ miles north of Sironcha.

He remained in India for nineteen years before he took a furlough, an indication of how much he liked and was committed to his work there, since a furlough was normally taken after eight years of service. In 1868, he returned to Scotland and in 1870, aged 41, he married Jane Cunningham Cornwall in Edinburgh. Two months later they sailed for India. He was posted as deputy commissioner in Betul, a town in Madhya Pradesh in central India. Their first son, Alexander, was born there in December 1870, and a second, Duncan John, in 1873. Later,

1. Engraving by Thomas Dick of John Orr's portrait by Malcolm Innes in 1850. The original oil painting belonged to the Orr family, but was lost when in storage. *Author's image*

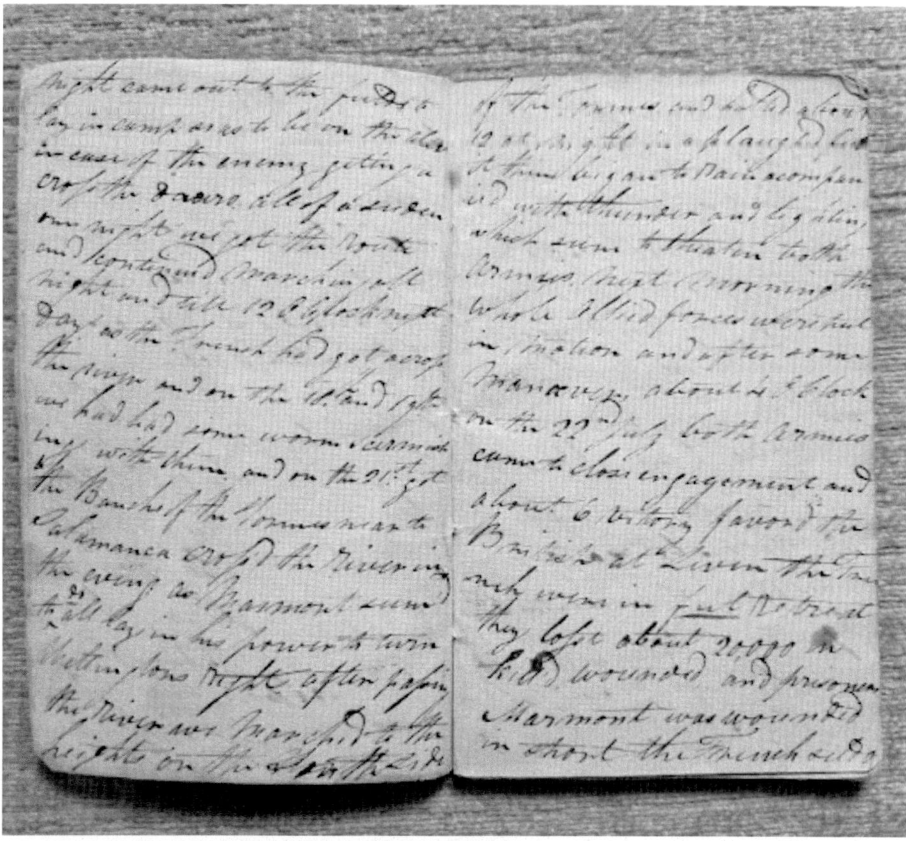

night came out to the pickets
lay in camp so as to be on the alert
in case of the enemy geting a
cross the Douro till of a sudden
one night we got the route
and continued marching all
night and till 12 o'clock next
day as the French had got across
the river and on the 18th and 19th
we had had some warm scrimmish
ing with them and on the 21st got
the Banks of the Tormes near to
Salamanca crossd the river in
the evening as Marmont seemed
to all lay in his power to turn
Wellingtons Right after passing
the River we marched to the
heights on the South side

of the Tormes and halted about
10 o'clock at night in a plough'd field
it then began to Rain accompan
ied with thunder and lightning
which seem to threaten both
Armies. Next morning the
Whole Allied forces were put
in motion and after some
manoevers about 4 o'clock
on the 22nd July both Armies
came to close engagement and
about 6 victory favord the
British at Liven the French
were in full Retreat
they lost about 20000 in
killd wounded and prisoners
Marmont was wounded
in short the French side

Above: **2.** Pages from John Orr's Peninsular War Diary, describing the days before the Battle of Salamanca. *Author's image*

Left: **3.** Scotch Brigade goblet given to John Orr when the regiment was disbanded in December 1818. He joined the regiment in Dublin in August 1817. *Author's image*

Scottish Naval and Military Academy.

PATRON.

Field-Marshal his Royal Highness Prince Albert, K.G., K.T., K.P., &c. &c.

PRESIDENT.

Field-Marshal His Grace the Duke of Wellington, K. G., &c.

VICE-PRESIDENTS.

His Grace the Duke of Buccleuch and Queensberry, K.G.
His Grace the Duke of Argyll.
His Grace the Duke of Leeds.
The Right Honourable the Earl of Dalhousie.
The Right Honournble the Earl of Morton.
General the Right Hon. Sir G. Murray, G.C.B., &c., Master-General of the Ordnance.
Major-Gen. Sir William M. Gomm, K.C.B., Governor and Commander-in-Chief of the Mauritius, &c. &c.
Major-Gen. Sir Neil Douglas, K.C.B., and K.C.H., Commanding Her Majesty's Forces in Scotland.

ORDINARY DIRECTORS.

Right Honourable Lord Robert Kerr, K. H., *Chairman.*
Sir Henry Jardine, *Deputy Chairman.*

Captain J. D. Boswall, R.N.
James L'Amy, Esq., Advocate.
Lt.-Colonel Wm. Macdonald.
Sir George Ballingal, M.D.
Dr David M'Lagan.
Rear-Admiral Stoddart.
Sir Alex. M. Gibson, Bart.
Lt.-Col. Robertson Macdonald.
Rear-Admiral J. H. Tait.
Lt.-Col. Johnston, K.T.S., late 99th Regt.
Lt.-Col. Cadell, Hon. East India Co.'s Serv.
Captain Grove, R.N.
Harry Maxwell Inglis, Esq., *Treasurer.*
Thomas Scott, Esq., *Auditor of Accounts.*

Captain Orr, *Superintendent.*

THE FOLLOWING ARE THE BRANCHES OF STUDY PURSUED AT THIS INSTITUTION:—

Branches of Study.	Teachers' Names.	Hours of Instruction.	Days of Teaching.	Teachers' Fee for each Class per Quarter.
				£. s. d.
Military Engineering, Fortification, *Military Engineering, Military Drawing, Surveying and Levelling,*	Mr Thos. Compton, late of the Royal Military Academy Woolwich,	10 to 11, 11 to 12, 12 to 1, 1 to 2, or two hours every second day,	— Daily, — — Daily, —	2 2 0 2 2 0 £3. 3s. only, if taken at the same time.
Architectural Drawing,		— 1 to 2 —	Daily, except Saturday,	1 11 6 If attending Civil Engineering, £1. 1s.
Do. and Civil Engineering,		— 2 to 4 —	Mondays, Wednesdays, and Fridays,	3 3 0
Civil Engineering,		— 2 to 4 —	— Ditto, —	2 12 6 £2. 2s. to those attending Military Engineering.
Landscape, Perspective Drawing, and Sketching from Nature, *Water Colours,*	Mr George Simson, R. S. A	— 10 to 11 — — 11 to 12 —	Mondays, Wednesdays, and Fridays,	1 1 0 1 11 6
Higher Mathematics and Navigation, *Algebra, Geometry, Trigonometry, and Theory of Fractional Arithmetic,* *Lectures on Natural Philosophy,*	George Lees, A.M.	— 9 to 10 — — 10 to 11 — — 12 to 1 —	Daily, except Saturday, Saturday,	1 1 0
Do. on Chemistry,	Dr Fyfe,	— 12 to 1 —	— Ditto, —	
Latin, *Greek,*	Rev. S. M'Moline,	— 11 to 12 — — 12 to 1 —	Daily, except Saturday,	1 1 0
Arithmetic, Writing and Book Keeping,	Mr James Trotter,	— 9 to 10 — — 10 to 11 —	— Ditto, —	0 15 0
Geography, Ancient & Modern History, *Elocution & Composition,*	Mr Wm. Graham,	— 1 to 2 —	Mondays, Wednesdays, and Fridays, Tuesdays & Thursdays, ...	1 1 0
Hindustani and Persian, (also, if required, Arabic, Bengali, Mahratta, and the Elements of Sanskrit,	Mr Ballantyne,	— 3 to 4 —	Daily, except Saturday,	2 12 6
French ... *Elementary* *French* ... *Composition*	Mons. Senebier,	— 3 to 4 — — 2 to 3 —	— Ditto, —	1 1 0
Italian, *Spanish,* *Portuguese,*	Sign. G. Rabagliati,	— 9 to 10 — — 3 to 4 — — 9 to 10 —	— Ditto, —	1 11 6
German,	Dr Nachot,	— 3 to 4 —	— Ditto, —	1 11 6
Fencing,	Mr Roland,	— 11 to 12 —	Tuesdays, Thursdays, and Saturdays,	1 11 6
Practical Mechanics and Modelling,	Mr Drummond,	— 6 to 6 —	— Daily, —	According to time.
Gymnastics, and other Athletic Exercises,	Mr G. Roland, Jun.,	— 1 to 2 —	Three days in the week,	1 1 0 Or £3. 3s. only, if taken for the Session.
Military Exercises with the Firelock and Broad Sword, &c.,	Sergt. Webster, late R. A.	— 12 to 1 — — 2 to 3 —	Daily, except Thursday and Saturday,	1 2 6
Lectures on Military History,	Mons. Surenne, F. A. S. E.	— 12 to 1 —	Thursdays,	0 7 6

Students to produce Certificates of Conduct from their last Master, if required.

N. B.—Students attending the Academy are admitted Gratis to Mr Surenne's Quarterly Lectures on Military Antiquities.—A Specimen or Specimens of their Drawings, to be delivered to the Directors, for the purpose of being deposited in the Academy, by each of the Gentlemen attending the Drawing Classes.

Young Gentlemen may attend the Gymnastic Class from 8 to 9 in the morning, from 1st March to end of July, without matriculating.

Matriculation or General Entry Fee, £1. 1s. per Annum for the first Three Years, and thereafter to cease.—Officers belonging to the Army or Navy are admitted without payment of Entrance Fee.

Quarterly Fee for each Class, for Expense of Academy, 5s. where only four Classes are taken; 4s. where five are taken; 3s. 6d. where six are taken, and 3s. when more than six.—*Note.* Pupils provide their own Foils.

Quarter-Days 1st October, 15th December, 1st March, and 15th May, or the first lawful day thereafter, on which days the Fees are payable in advance. Students are requested to give notice to the Superintendent when they are appointed to the Army, Navy, or Honourable East India Company's Service.

It is desirable that the Parent or Guardian should attend when tickets are taken out, especially at first, or when a change of Class is to be made.

Holidays.—Four days at the times appointed for the administration of the Sacrament in Edinburgh, in May and November; a week at Christmas; Good Friday; and the Queen's Birth-day; vacation from beginning of August to 1st of October.

Absence.—When Students are unavoidably *late* or *absent*, notice in writing, *signed by the Parent or Guardian*, must be sent to the Superintendent.

N. B.—Arms or Instruments, Furniture and Walls, destroyed or damaged by Pupils, to be replaced or repaired at their expense. No presents or gratuities by Students permitted.—*No Student is entitled to a Director's Certificate unless he has attended one Session at least, and, been present at the Examinations.*

By order of the Directors,

JOHN ORR, *Captain and Superintendent.*

Royal Academy Buildings,
Lothian Road, Edinburgh,
April 1843.

4. SNMA Prospectus dated 1843. *Author's image*

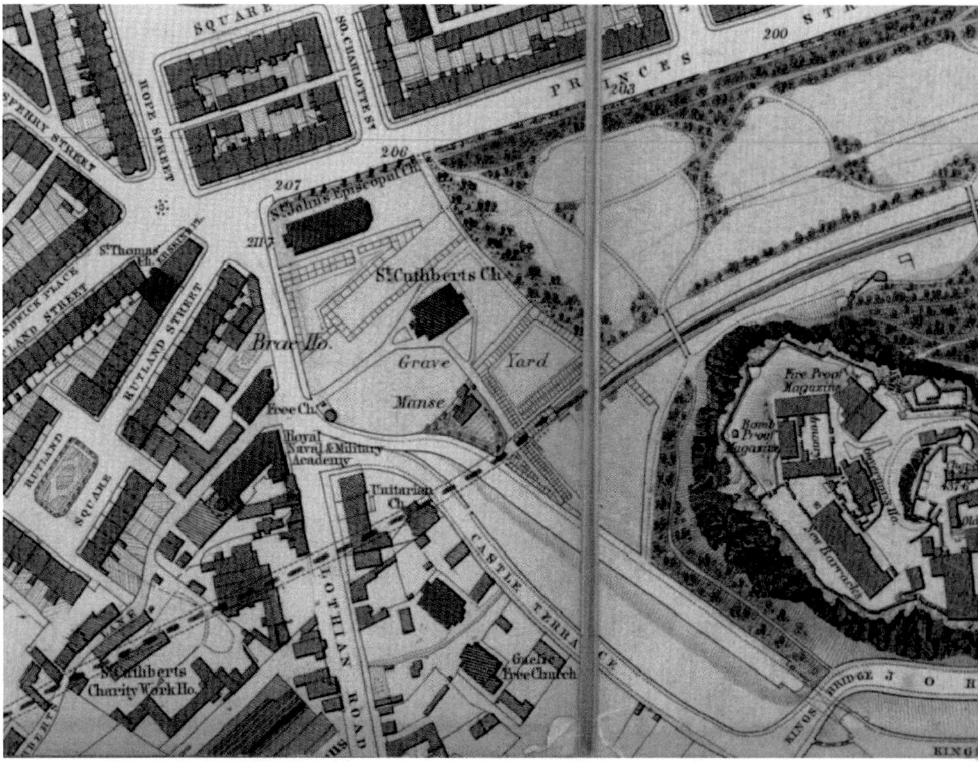

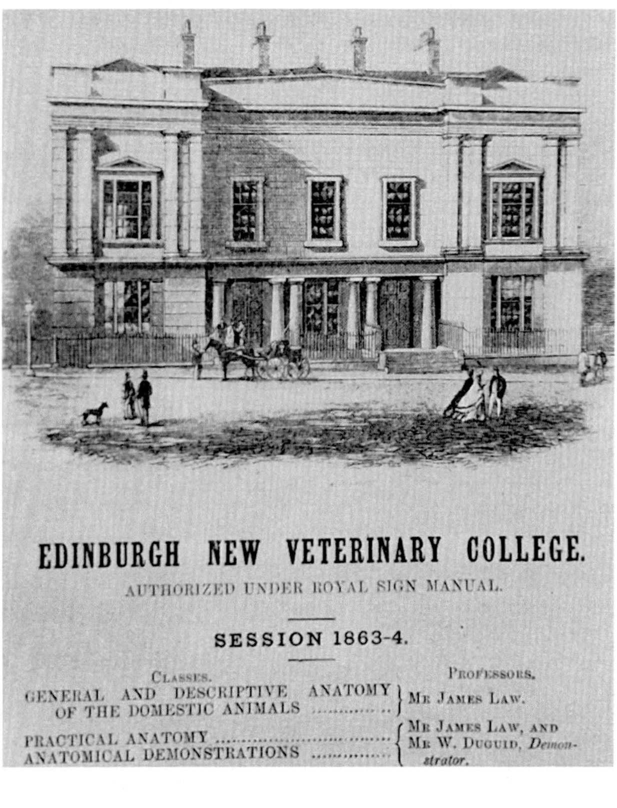

EDINBURGH NEW VETERINARY COLLEGE.

AUTHORIZED UNDER ROYAL SIGN MANUAL.

SESSION 1863-4.

CLASSES.	PROFESSORS.
GENERAL AND DESCRIPTIVE ANATOMY OF THE DOMESTIC ANIMALS	MR JAMES LAW.
PRACTICAL ANATOMY .... ANATOMICAL DEMONSTRATIONS	MR JAMES LAW, AND MR W. DUGUID, *Demonstrator.*

Above: **5.** Map showing position of the Royal Academy Buildings on Lothian Road, Edinburgh. Detail from the plan of the City of Edinburgh by W. & A.K. Johnston. Drawn by Alfred Lancefield, 1851. *Courtesy of the National Library of Scotland*

Left: **6.** Drawing of the front of the Royal Academy Buildings which were used by the SNMA until 1862 when it was taken over by a veterinary college. *Illustration from the Prospectus of the Edinburgh New Veterinary College Session 1863–64*

Above left: **7.** Photograph of Sir Henry Yule by George Shaw. He was a polymath who wrote a number of books including *Hobson-Jobson*. After studying at the SNMA he joined the EIC but returned some years later to teach at the Academy. *Courtesy of the Scottish National Gallery*

Above right: **8.** Small tablecloth made of linen damask, showing the Duke of Wellington on his horse Copenhagen. Produced in Scotland to celebrate the unveiling of the Wellington statue in Edinburgh on 18 June 1852. *Author's image*

Below left: **9.** Photograph of John McDouall Stuart taken about 1860. He was a pupil at the SNMA and later was the first European to cross Australia from south to north. Unknown photographer. *Courtesy of the State Library of South Australia*

Below right: **10.** Engraving of Major Charles Nasmyth who was an SNMA pupil who became the hero of the siege of Silestra, at the start of the Crimean War. The portrait was published in the *Illustrated London News* together with his obituary on 13 July 1861. *Courtesy of the Antiqua Print Gallery*

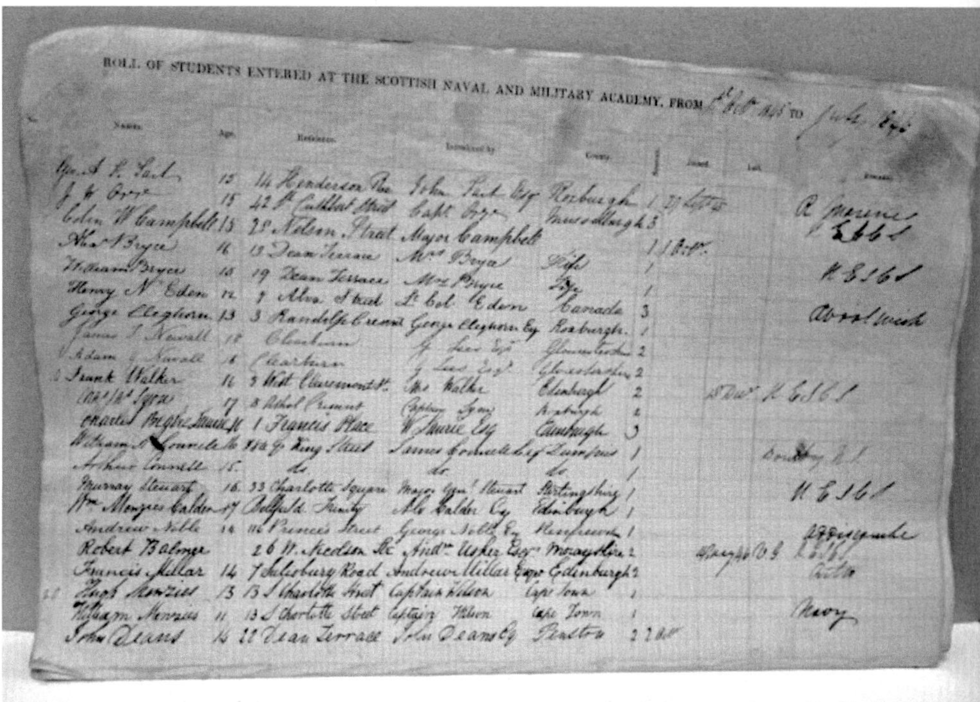

11. A page from the SNMA Roll Book, showing an extract of the enrolments for the 1846–47 session. *Author's image*

Above: **12.** Photograph of the 8th Hussars field kitchen in the Crimean War taken by Roger Fenton. Colonel Edward Tomkinson, an SNMA pupil, was in the 8th Hussars and would have had his food prepared in this 'cooking house'. *Courtesy of the Royal Collections Trust*

Below: **13.** Photograph of the Bay of Naples taken by Lieutenant Colonel Stuart-Wortley who was a pupil at the SNMA. *Shrimp Catchers at Sunrise*. 1851. *Courtesy of Alamy*

Above left: **14.** Photograph of John Orr wearing a plaid, probably taken about 1870. *Courtesy of the Black Watch Museum, Perth*

Above right: **15.** Photograph of John Orr taken when he was in his mid-eighties. *Author's image*

Below left: **16.** Photograph of John Orr taken when he was in his late eighties. *Author's image*

Below right: **17.** Silver-plated vase given to John Orr on 15 October 1879, shortly before he died. It was one of a pair presented to him with a purse of 300 guineas by friends and colleagues and many of the past SNMA pupils who boarded with the Orr family. *Author's image*

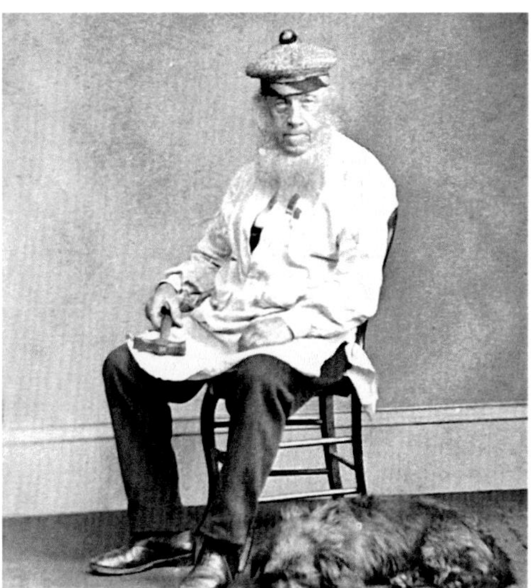

Charles became Commissioner of Survey and Settlement at Hyderabad. He retired in 1884, and, as his health was poor, they went to live in Algiers to avoid the Edinburgh winters; he died there in 1887 when he was 56.

In November 2018, two of Charles's great-grandchildren, Peter aged 87, with his wife Jennifer, 83, and Peter's sister Susan Glasfurd, aged 77, travelled to India to see where their great-grandfather had lived. They wanted to visit Glasfurdhapeta and Sironcha. It was a big undertaking; they were elderly, and were living in Western Australia. This journey was written up in *The Times of India* and in another Indian publication, the *Business Standard*. Peter said he had heard family stories of the love and affection the villagers felt for Lieutenant Charles and he had read his great-grandfather's diaries and was determined to go and see the place for himself.[12, 13]

After they arrived in India, they had an internal flight and a long car journey through the jungle to arrive at the village. Susan said, 'when we reached Glasfurdhapeta the welcome we received was beyond description.' All the inhabitants turned out to meet them as they had heard stories about Charles. He had inaugurated the village and rescued villagers from wild animals on many occasions. They were moved to meet his descendants and, on each side, there were tears. The family travelled on to Sironcha and found that the house Charles built 'was in all its glory still standing' and was now a government guest house.

Susan's comments before they left India are touching and they will resonate with many people trying to piece together their family story:

> We were here to find history from fragments of historical notes, here to piece them together and create a story for our family history; and it was here that we discovered why our ancestors had such emotionally strong ties to India. This is a holiday that will remain in our hearts for all time.

John's classification of Charles as being 'exemplary' is shown by his care, interest and support for the Indian villagers with whom he lived for many years. This is shown in a sentence Charles wrote in his diary – he wanted 'to make myself a name, if not for abilities as brilliant as some, at least for kindness and consideration for my Ryots and their welfare, and for my zeal in whatever conduces to their wellbeing and comfort'. (Ryot comes from the Hindi word 'raiyat' who is a person who holds land and cultivates the soil.)

Lieutenant Colonel Archibald Henry Plantagenet Stuart-Wortley (1832–1890)

Henry Stuart-Wortley had a remarkable career. I came across his name online in an article about a photographic exhibition held in 1994 at the Huntington Gallery in California. The report showed examples of some of his photographs and I was struck by their beauty. I was intrigued to find out more about this pupil from the SNMA who had had a retrospective photographic exhibition in California nearly 100 years after his death.

Henry was born in Wortley, Yorkshire to wealthy parents. He was the son of Charles Stuart-Wortley and his grandparents were Baron of Wharncliffe and Lady Emmeline Manners. He had served as a page of honour to Queen Victoria before coming to the SNMA in 1847 and was there for one year, when he stayed with the Orr family. Henry entered the army in 1848 and joined the 1st (The Kings) Regiment of Dragoon Guards, not his aspiration in the Roll Book where John has written 'Reg C Guards'. He served as a Cape Mounted Rifleman in the Cape Border Wars against the Xhosa between 1850 and 1853.[14] It was while he was in Africa that he first became interested in photography and when he later fought in the Crimea, he met Roger Fenton who took an informal photograph of Wortley with Colonel Wood and Colonel Colborne in front of an old stone building, which can be seen online. Henry was in the Crimea from 1854 to 1855 and was a deputy assistant quarter master with the rank of brevet major.

After the Crimea, in 1856 he was retired on half pay, aged 24. In 1858 and 1859 he became one of two Tory Members of Parliament for Honiton. From 1860 onwards, photography became his passion. Henry started to travel, firstly with a trip to India, and in 1861 he visited Naples where he took some beautiful photographs of the sea, many at dusk or dawn. Some of these photographs were later exhibited in London in 1862, and were much praised, which resulted in his being made a member of the Photographic Society of London. Two of these photographs were shown online in a selling exhibition in London in 2018.[15] Of these, the one I liked best was called

Shrimp Catchers at Sunrise, Naples 1861 **(Illustration 13 monochrome)**. Its sale price was £5,000. It shows the rising sun casting a shaft of light across the Bay of Naples. In silhouette, a small group of fishermen are standing in the water, their two small boats in the foreground. The shore is black and, in the distance, Vesuvius has a slight plume of smoke rising to mix with the clouds which are caught in the early morning light.

Henry continued to exhibit regularly in the Photographic Society's exhibitions and became their vice president. He finally retired from the army in February 1862, having sold his commission; he had been granted the honorary rank of lieutenant colonel. In 1864, Henry opened a studio in London and founded the United Association of Photographers. He wrote extensively both on the technical and the artistic aspects of photography. He invented three different photographic appliances: a printing frame for making combination prints; a field developer's box; and a mechanical shuttle, and founded two commercial enterprises – the United Association of Photography and the Uranium Dry Plate Company.[16]

Henry loved travelling and visited Turkey, India, Greece and Ceylon. In 1880, he went on a world tour with this second wife which took him via Australia and New Zealand to Tahiti. A book on his Tahitian photographs was published in 1882. He exhibited his photographs until the mid-1880s, when his health began to deteriorate, and he died in London 1890.

The exhibition of his photographs at the Huntington Gallery, California, in May 1994 was the first showing of his work since a retrospective one in London after he died. Everything on view came from the collections of Henry and Arabella Huntington and John Paul Getty. In the catalogue, Katherine DiGiulio wrote that his moonlight scenes 'established him as one of the most romantic seascape photographers in the history of the medium'.[17] The *Los Angeles Times* published a review by William Wilson. He wrote: 'Wortley had turned photography into art.' He went on to describe his later pictures:

> In these works thin bands of landscape take on the role of calm rationality, while the skies become the brooding, capricious creatures of emotion, now black with anger, now as wise and elegiac as a peaceful death. One sky shows clouds scudding apart like shiny pearls vaporizing. It feels like an instant of solemn ecstasy.[18]

Joseph Panton (1831–1913)

Of all the pupils at the SNMA, I feel I know Joseph Panton best and his entertaining diaries show him to be a straightforward man who enjoyed life and had many interests. I was lucky to come across an online reference to his edited diaries, *Strength in Battle*, and managed to obtain a copy. Panton also has a write-up in the *Australian Dictionary of Biography*.[19] There is a fine oil portrait of him by Frederick McCubbin, a well-known Australian artist, executed in 1904, which is owned by the National Gallery of Victoria **(Illustration 23 colour)**.

Joseph was born on a farm in Aberdeenshire. His early education in Aberdeen was poor and the tawse was used frequently. (The tawse was a thong of leather that was used in some Scottish schools to beat children who misbehaved.) He was pleased when, aged 16, he started his education at the SNMA. He studied there for three years, boarding with the Orr family, and was happy in their household (as detailed in previous chapters).

He was taught civil and military engineering by Thomas Compton who had hitherto been an instructor at Woolwich College. Joseph was a good pupil and he mentions in his memoir that on one occasion when Compton was unable to teach the class, he put Panton in charge of it. Joseph much enjoyed military reconnoitring, a skill he used in later life. Towards the end of his stay at the SNMA, he was often asked to take out two or three other students and survey an area either in the country or the suburbs. He enjoyed this and said, 'It came easy to me, that without assistance I could walk or ride over a district, make a few notes, then sit down and make a good plan of it by sketching in the principal features of the country to be seen *en route*.' He used a prismatic compass and field book.[20]

At the prize-giving in 1849, Joseph was awarded the first prize in both civil engineering and in mathematics. In addition, he received the Master's Prizes in fortification, architectural drawing and painting. He left the SNMA in July 1850:

> When we broke up at midsummer, I carried home my medal and prizes. Thus ended my third and last Session at the dear old Scottish Naval & Military Academy.[21]

The plan had been that Joseph should go to India and join the EIC, although that is not listed in the Remarks column. About this time, he received a letter from his uncle, Colonel Joseph Anderson. Anderson had retired from the EIC and was now living near Melbourne. He urged Joseph to come to Australia; it was a beautiful country and there were great opportunities to make money. His uncle told him 'there was nothing doing in the service [EIC] at the present time'.[22] Others confirmed this and told him that 'the Service at that time offered such poor chances of preferment, that in fact anything was better than garrison life and slow promotion.'

Joseph boarded the *Thomas Arbuthnot* in Portsmouth towards the end of 1850 and arrived in Sydney in March 1851. The journey, which lasted 106 days, went via Trinidad and Tristan de Cunha, and was uneventful apart from 'a shake up in the Bay of Biscay'. He moved on to Melbourne where he met his uncle Colonel Anderson and they rode north out of the city into the bush to his uncle's estate of about 40,000 acres at Mangalore. It was mainly a sheep farm, with only a few head of cattle for milk and meat.

In that same year, readily available gold was discovered at Ballarat in the same state, Victoria, and Joseph set off with two friends to see what it was all about. When they came home, they arranged for others to manage the farm as they wanted to go back to the goldfields. He applied for the position of a mounted semi-military escort between the goldfields and Melbourne. Governor La Trobe considered he was 'a bit too heavy to be an Escort, it would be too severe on the horses'. (Panton was 6ft 4in in height.) Instead, the governor appointed him as a police commissioner. He was to be based in the goldfields and one of his jobs was to issue prospecting licences; his record was issuing 1,800 in one day. While he was there, Joseph made drawings of life in the goldfields and he bought some prize-winning vineyards. He encouraged the cultivation of vines when the gold became scarce.

In 1858, Joseph returned to Europe and married in 1860. After returning to Australia, he travelled all around the continent and held a series of official appointments. He eventually became the magistrate of Heidelberg, now a northern suburb of Melbourne, and while he was there, he mapped the Yarra Valley. The small town of Panton Hill, about 30 miles north east of Melbourne, is named after him. He later became the senior magistrate in Melbourne from 1874 until 1907 when he retired, aged 75.

He was an enthusiastic supporter of the arts, and regularly attended music festivals, but above all painting was his first love. While he was at the SNMA, he had enjoyed the drawing classes, taught by George Simson, and often won the prize. He sketched wherever he travelled, later working up his drawings into oil paintings. These were shown in various exhibitions, sometimes with mixed acclaim; he was often criticised for his use of bright colours. He was a commissioner for the 1880 Melbourne International Exhibition, a fellow of the Royal Geographical Society in London and vice president of the Victoria branch of the Royal Geographical Society of Australasia. He was elected president of the Victorian Artists' Society in 1888. He died in St Kilda, a suburb of Melbourne, in 1913.

While I was visiting my daughter in Australia, we made an appointment to go to the Victorian State Library in Melbourne to see the Panton archive. It was exciting to handle some of Panton's actual writings and we were surprised and delighted to discover in a box some of the books he had won as prizes at the SNMA. His time at the Academy must have been important to him to have brought these books to Australia and kept them throughout his life.

On reading these biographies, it seems that some of the boys overlapped while staying with the Orrs. In 1847–48 Joseph Panton and Henry Stuart-Wortley were staying with the Orrs and when Stuart-Wortley left, Charles Glasfurd arrived. One can imagine dinner time in the Orr's home with these bright boys sitting round the table being encouraged by John to make the most of their lives after they left the Academy. The biographies brought to life some more of the names in John's Roll Book.

Chapter 10

The Directors' and John's Failure to Prevent the Academy's Decline

> I may remind you that this is rather an eventful period in the existence of the Academy.[1]
>
> Captain Charles Hope,
> RN at the Prize-giving July 1850.

During the first eighteen years of John's superintendency, the SNMA's enrolment grew and the college gained in prestige. When he became superintendent the total enrolment was only sixty-seven pupils. Apart from a drop in 1835, a steady growth took place in the number of boys coming to the Academy and in 1844, 125 enrolled, nearly double the number compared with 1831. The enrolment was made up of three types of boys, those that were planning a career in the British army, those wanting to join the EIC and the rest who were presumably intending to have a civilian career. Up until 1849, the combined service numbers were always more than the boys planning on a civilian career, but after 1849 the situation was reversed. In October of that year a sharp drop occurred in those wanting to become officers in the British army and from 1850 there was also a decrease in the number of boys planning to go to India.

I first looked into possible reasons for the drop in numbers in those hoping to join the EIC. There were always fewer boys planning to go to India compared with those wanting to become officers the British army. Overall, only 233 out of 1,500 pupils planned to go to India, fewer than some historians thought. This is not surprising as without the Roll Book (given it was sitting in my cabin trunk!) they did not have access the figures. After a high point in the mid-1830s the numbers declined until in 1851 only three new pupils are listed with an aspiration to join the EIC.

The EIC had originally been a trading company, but this part of its operations was stopped in 1813 and it had become a managing agency for the British government. Its role was to exert control in India, using its administrative and its military wings. The historian John Keay wrote:

> Stripped of its commercial assets the Company's surviving function was mainly as a political front and a military scapegoat. London's ignorance and India's distance might commend the Company's continuance, but so did the fiction of its being less accountable than a government department; 'Company mismanagement' after all sound better than 'official maladministration'.[2]

The majority of the SNMA pupils who planned to join the Company came from Scotland – these, of course, included John's two sons. SNMA always had at least one ordinary director who had served with the EIC. There had been a strong Scottish connection with India ever since the Company had been established and a family tradition of going there persisted into the nineteenth century. For many young men from moderately wealthy families, it could mean the quality of their lives was improved. Officers as they rose in rank could afford larger houses and employ more servants than would have been the case in Scotland. They would come home at the end of their period of service with a pension. John's Roll Book, however, shows this tradition was beginning to wane. Here the figures indicate that during the 1840s a growing number of India-based parents did not plan for their sons to join the EIC and return to India.

A life in India had many problems. The cost of being kitted out to join the Company was high (although it was considerably cheaper than buying a commission into the British army). Either the cadet or his family had to pay for this before he left, or money had to be borrowed and repayment could take a long time. Mess life was also expensive as once he got to India, a third of a young officer's pay went on mess bills.[3] Once he had joined a regiment there were possible ways to mitigate the problem, as an officer could be seconded to other regional duties, although still retaining his military rank. This happened to two pupils that I have mentioned: Sir Henry Yule who was for a time in charge of parts of the Indian railway system and Charles Glasfurd who spent most of his working life seconded to the Regional Survey.

Illness was a constant worry. John's two sons and their families were lucky as none of them died in India; indeed, both sons and their wives, returned to Scotland and lived into old age. Many men, women and children were not so lucky and died of cholera, dysentery, yellow fever or malaria. Leave back to the UK was not permitted for eight years unless the officer became ill and was invalided home. As there were few unmarried young European women in the sub-continent, officers were under pressure during the first furlough to find a British wife who was happy to make the journey to India. Once children were born, they were normally sent home to the UK to be educated and might not be seen again for many years.

Sir David Gilmour in *The British in India* comments on the boredom of both officers and men. After having breakfast, the problem was 'what to do for the next dozen hours or so until evening came'.[4] He writes: 'officers whiled away the hours in the Mess, also reading, eating, playing cards and trying to sleep.' Neither officers nor men felt well in hot weather and there were frequent complaints of feeling 'languid and peevish'. Many resorted to alcohol.

As the nineteenth century progressed these reasons began to make India less attractive. The way of life for officers and men had not changed over the years. What had become an issue was the rate of promotion, which in the Native army wing of the EIC was solely on length of service; ability was not relevant and there had always been fewer high-ranking officers than in the British army. A keen and intelligent young officer might wait several years before he reached a senior rank; although he could be awarded a brevet rank this would mean no increase pay.

A similar seniority promotion problem existed in the British army but officers could buy their commissions up to the rank of major general. This was not an official option for officers enrolled with the EIC. In some places, an unofficial 'step process' took place where junior officers paid into a fund to give to an officer near retirement an incentive to go.[5] The delay in getting promotion was increasing. A mess toast was 'A bloody war or a sickly season', these being the only means of promotion.[6]

As I have mentioned, Joseph Panton was warned about the slow promotion and boredom and he therefore did not go to India. This was a general feeling, which helps to explain why the numbers enrolling at the SNMA were falling. In 1856, no student is recorded as having an interest in a career in the East India Company. In 1857, the Indian Rebellion took place and by 1858 the EIC had been disbanded. After the Rebellion, the Company's Native regiments stayed in India and became known as the British Army in India.

Now to look at reasons for the decline in numbers planning to join the British army. The SNMA had never been given authority to award free commissions, but this cannot explain the sudden reduction in numbers enrolling as this had been the situation while the enrolment had been growing during most of the 1840s. I would need to look for another cause for the decline.

In July 1849, the government brought in a new compulsory army examination for young men planning to join the British army by buying their commissions. Most of the boys enrolling with the SNMA who wanted to become officers in the British army would have to sit this exam. Could its introduction be a reason for the decline in numbers enrolling at the SNMA? The timing seemed right. Was there a high failure rate? I needed to find out more about the exam and the commissioning system.

In the mid-nineteenth century only 20 per cent of officers in the British army had been trained at the RMC.[7] Most officers, therefore, were the product of the Direct Commission system. Some in the military were growing dissatisfied with their education and were thinking of bringing in some kind of assessment. Sir Hew Strachan describes some of these officers as the 'well-born incompetent'.[8] A problem was that the Duke of Wellington who was commander-in-chief for a second time from 1842 to 1852 did not consider that change was necessary as he had a firm belief that officers did not require high academic knowledge or military education. It was more important that they should come from the higher echelons in society. As Strachan explains in another article, for Wellington the ideal army imitated the old social system and should be composed of officers from the nobility or landed classes and privates who were farm labourers.[9] In 1840, Sir John Macdonald, the adjutant general declared: 'It is the proud characteristic of the British army that its officers are gentlemen by education, manners and habit.'[10]

The government, eventually, persuaded Wellington that something had to be done and it was agreed that there should be an examination for all young men wanting to enter the army with a direct commission. It was a radical change for many of the SNMA pupils and for all other young men hoping to join the British army in this way. John and the masters had little foreknowledge as the announcement was made in March 1849 with the new examination starting three months later, in July.

A memorandum giving details of the exam was published in several newspapers and there are two copies of it in John's press cuttings book.[11] The pupil had to be able to read English correctly, take dictation and know the basic rules of arithmetic, logarithms and algebra. Either Latin prose and poetry was to be translated or the pupils had to show an advanced knowledge of French or German. They would be examined in the history of Ancient Rome and Greece. A thorough understanding was required of both of ancient and modern geography as well as the physical geography of Great Britain and the empire. The exam would only have one military question which was on basic fortification and the drawing of simple forts. A medical examination and confirmation of the young man's religious affiliation were required.

Books were listed at the end of the memorandum. These included volumes on geometry, arithmetic and algebra; various histories of England, Europe and Classical Rome and Greece; a book on ancient and modern geography; and Latin, French and German dictionaries. Some of the textbooks in mathematics and history had been written by the professors at the RMC.

The government instructed the masters at RMC to devise the examination. (The results of the exam had no relevance to the college as none of the cadets sitting it were planning to go to Sandhurst. The examination was only for those young men intending to buy their commissions.) The remit was to test the academic rather than the military knowledge of recruits. The major part of the exam had a heavy emphasis on mathematics and Classical subjects. It was mainly an oral exam and was to be held at Sandhurst initially; the examiners were the masters at the RMC. They would decide whether a pupil had passed or failed and would send the result to Horse Guards, who officially announced who had passed.

There were various problems with how the examination was drawn up. The masters at Sandhurst had usually studied at Oxford and Cambridge universities and were used to dealing with applicants for the RMC who were well versed in mathematics and the Classics. The memorandum gave no information about the type of questions the boys would be asked, nor the academic level of knowledge they expected them to possess. John and the staff at the SNMA would, therefore, not know whether the present teaching at the Academy would prepare boys adequately for the exam.

To find out more about this examination and particularly its failure rate, I visited the Royal Military Academy, Sandhurst (RMAS), as it is now called, and met the Assistant Curator of the Sandhurst Collection, Dr Sebastian Puncher.[12] The RMAS is housed in a grand, elegant classical building with a large, pillared portico surrounded by acres of lawn stretching down to a lake. Outside is a row of impressive old cannons. It must have been daunting for the young candidates to arrive at this imposing building to face what they knew would be a critical examination. Some would have travelled from all over England, Scotland and Ireland and would have had to arrange accommodation and then transport to arrive at this place in rural Berkshire, 40 miles from London.

Sebastian Puncher was helpful and looked out several articles and documents for me to read. He had completed a thesis on education at Sandhurst and Woolwich, a copy of which can be read online: 'The Victorian Army and the Cadet Colleges: Woolwich and Sandhurst *c.*1840–1902'. He told me that at first there had been problems with the new 1849 examination and many pupils had failed.

Among the documents was a copy of the notes written by a young man called Owen Tudor Burne, aged 18, who had taken the exam on 3 May 1855. He was not a SNMA pupil but had been educated by his father who was a clergyman and had managed to obtain a commission for his son in the 20th East Devonshire Regiment. Owen, however, needed to pass the army examination before he could accept his commission.

Owen Tudor Burne's experience was six years after the inauguration of the examination. I have, however, included, his story – it provides background as to what it was like to going to the RMC to take this exam. The news of the numbers failing after its inception in July 1849 would have quickly spread to military people and to families intending that their sons should become officers. It was beginning to look as if this might indeed be a reason for the decline in enrolment at the SNMA.

The night before the exam, Owen stayed at an inn in the village of Black Water about a mile from the railway station. There were twenty-nine other young men called up for the exam that day. He says that 'five being affected with nervousness stayed outside'. At 10 a.m., the twenty-four-remaining walked 'in a body up the long avenue shivering with cold (alias "funk"), myself at the head'.[13] The 150 Sandhurst cadets, in their red coats, watched them walk up the drive. After they arrived, the boys had a medical inspection and then they drew lots to see in which order they would be examined. Each person's examination lasted between three to five hours, depending on how nervous the person was and how difficult he was finding the examination. The exam was partly viva voce and did not have standard questions. In 1855, a Select Committee of the House of Commons led an investigation into the RMC, which included asking questions about the new army examination. The committee interviewed the lieutenant governor and various professors. Reverend Chepmell, one of the professors, said examiners had the freedom to ask different questions to each student and that if he felt the pupil was nervous, he would give a series of easier questions to answer first.[14]

Owen's description reflects this format, and that outlined in the Memorandum. In his notes, written afterwards, he says he was most nervous during the French examination. He at first was failed because he mistranslated a French passage due to the poor writing of the professor. Owen, being 18 and already a confident young man, complained. He told the professor:

> I had come a long way and was not coming again and that his writing was very bad; to which he answered that his was better than mine. After chaffing for some little time, he gave me another paper which I did right and then read a little and got a good mark, as I think he wanted to go and get his dinner.

Another young man, who was nervous, might not have been so forthright. In a later memoir, Owen, by then a major general, says, 'I passed my examination, coming top of the list.' Only twelve of the twenty-four who took the exam that day passed. Sir Hew Strachan writes that, 'between May 1852 and April 1855 there were 456 failures to 1,444 passes. Until May 1854, when pressure on the reduced numbers of officers lowered standards, the failure rate averaged about half the candidates, and on occasion rose to two-thirds.'[15]

The Sandhurst Select Committee also interviewed Colonel Prosser, the lieutenant governor of RMC from 1854 to 1856. A member of the committee asked Colonel Prosser about how difficult the examination was. The colonel replied, 'It is rather less strict than it was two or three years ago, in consequence of the great pressure by the parents and friends complaining of our being so severe.'[16] Colonel Prosser's remarks confirm that the examination had been difficult for the cadets who sat it in the early years. Even six years later, in 1855, when Owen sat the exam, half of those in his group failed. The failure rate between 1849 and 1854 varied between a half and two-thirds.[17]

After my visit to Sandhurst, I felt sure that the introduction of the army examination had an effect on the numbers enrolling at the Academy. News will have spread quickly about the failure rate and I now wanted to find out what action the SNMA took to try and mitigate the situation.

Before the new army examination was instituted, John and the directors felt they were providing a high standard of education for whatever career the boys wanted to follow. The 1848 Prospectus says that the courses they offered were a good preparation for 'the Government and East India Colleges of England'. Pupils who had gone to these colleges from the SNMA had done well. It went on to remark that because the Academy offered such a variety of subjects many were coming for a general education and 'have no views of entering either the Navy or Army'.[18]

At first sight, the army examination should not have been a problem for pupils at the SNMA. From further investigation this was not the case. The Academy provided a good all-round education, but it was not set up like an English private school, which emphasised mathematics and the Classics. At the SNMA prize-giving in July 1849 the speech was given by Sheriff Gordon, stating, among other things:

> Now, it is certainly not for me to compare the Scottish Naval & Military Academy to the more profound schools

> of learning. No such hope was ever held out, and no such intention animated the minds of those gentlemen who originated this Academy. They did not intend that all branches should be embraced in it, but that it should contain essentially the elements of a school for the education of young men intended for the navy or army and undoubtedly, we do nothing here which is inconsistent with its original character when we mingle with those mental studies.[19]

This paragraph accurately sums up the ethos of the SNMA. It was there to provide the core academic requirements of a young man who intended to have a military or civilian career. This new examination involved mainly academic subjects and had an emphasis not simply on mathematics but on Classical studies which included both Classical languages, history and geography. The SNMA would now be competing with other schools which specialised in these subjects.

Soon after the results of the first examination were known, schools all over the UK complained about how difficult it was to pass the new army exam. Some parents must have reconsidered their sons' further education and decided not to send their boys to the SNMA, which would explain the drop in numbers at the start of the 1849/50 session. John and the directors realised that they had to take positive action. On 27 October 1849, three weeks after their session had started, with its low enrolment, John on behalf of the directors issued this notice in *The Edinburgh Evening Courant*:

> The Directors have the satisfaction to state, the Course of Study pursued at the Academy embraces *every Branch of Military Education* and is well fitted to qualify their students for the prescribed Examination. To afford the greater security in this respect, the Directors have resolved (in addition to the present Quarterly and Annual Examination) to institute *Special Examinations* for such of their pupils as are destined for the Army.[20]

The italics of '*every Branch of Military Education*' are surprising. Apart from the one question on fortification, no military knowledge was needed to sit this new exam. It would appear that neither John nor the directors understood why so many candidates were failing. They should actually have been increasing the teaching of Classical subjects and mathematics.

I wondered what options parents had to prepare their sons for the exam. Using the British Newspaper Archive, I started to find notices advertising military teaching courses. This was the rise of the specialist crammers. These were men who saw that money could be made instructing boys in a crash course aimed only at passing the army exam. The advertisements appeared in many of the regional newspapers and it would therefore have been easy for a parent to find such a person to teach their son in their own area.

The following is an example:

> TO CANDIDATES FOR COMMISIONS IN THE ARMY
> MILITARY EDUCATION
> A gentleman possessing considerable and successful experience in preparing Gentlemen for the requisite Examination for Commissions in the Army will be glad to Read with any Gentlemen who may be desirous to pass this Examination. The highest references given. Terms may be known on application to C.H.B., Hamilton Lodge, Portobello, Edinburgh.[21]

The masters at Sandhurst became worried at the number of pupils who were presenting for the army examination who had been to crammers. They did not like the idea of young men being taught in this way. After a few years, Lord Raglan instructed that the listing of books at the end of the Memorandum should be removed.[22] After this the professors at the RMC were asked several times by tutors and teachers to please supply a list of books which would indicate the ground that would be covered by the examination. Due to Lord Raglan's instructions, they were unable to supply such a list. This decision must have made it difficult to prepare for the exam and will not have helped the pass rate.

Some parents kept their sons at school instead of sending them to crammers or to the SNMA for their last year or two. This was a reasonable decision especially if the school had a good Classics department.

Edinburgh Academy prided itself on having 'a higher standard of classical instruction than was common in Scottish Seminaries'.[23] It is interesting that between 1848 and 1850, the annual pupil numbers at the Edinburgh Academy rose from 84 to 117. More institutions were requiring entrants to take examinations, many of them with an emphasis on mathematics and Classics. Schools such as the Edinburgh Academy benefited from this, whereas colleges like the SNMA with a broader type of education were the losers.

Before the start of the next session on 7 September 1850, John issued a new notice, not just in *The Scotsman* but in English newspapers as well. It stated: 'The Course Studies in Mathematics, Fortification, Civil and Military Engineering, Languages &c, is eminently well calculated to enable Young Gentlemen to pass the requisite examination at the Horse Guards.' John and the directors still did not understand that the education they offered would need to be at a higher level in mathematics and in Classical studies to pass the British army exam and they continued to talk about fortification and military engineering. In these advertisements, John listed the names of eighteen pupils who had obtained commissions and fourteen who had joined the EIC in the last session. I have verified that they did indeed receive their commissions during the 1849–50 session. This confirms that some SNMA pupils were able to pass the examination. It is possible they had been previously attended schools with a Classics-based syllabus.

On 11 August 1851, their vice chairman, Sir Henry Jardine, died. He was a great loss to the Academy as he had been a director and vice chairman since it was founded in 1825. Major R.S. Seton from the EIC, one of the ordinary directors, became the next vice chairman. He had become an ordinary director in 1845; there were several directors more senior, and with no background information as to Seton's character, it is a mystery as to why he chosen for the position. He was in post by December 1851. Seton was born in North Berwick where his father was a tenant farmer. After he left Addiscombe in 1811, he served twenty-seven years in the Madras Artillery retiring from the EIC in October 1838 as a major.

An odd thing then happens. From December 1851, all the normal press notices issued by the SNMA go out either under the name of Major R.S. Seton on behalf of the directors or no person's name is listed. Up until then these notices had been issued by John as superintendent on behalf of the directors. Indeed, Article 17 of the 1834 *Rules & Regulations* states that, 'All notices or advertisements connected with the studies of the Academy, shall be signed by the Superintendent.'

It is not clear why this happened. Was it because that the Academy was in such a serious position with the enrolment going down that the directors considered announcements should be issued by the vice chairman? Another possible reason could be that Seton wanted to exercise power in his own name and he did not have the same trusting relationship with John as John had had with Sir Henry Jardine. The result is that after the appointment of Seton as vice president, John is sidelined.

He now disappears from the decision making at the SNMA, as far as reports in the press are concerned. Those who are keen to find out more about the Academy are told to write to the secretary to receive a prospectus, not to John. (According the SNMA regulations the secretary kept the books and prepared agenda for meetings, wrote the minutes and prepared the draft annual report.) I have found only one notice in 1855 when John's name creeps back as the second choice for getting a prospectus. John is not ill as he continues to organise the prize-givings, but he does not appear to have any involvement in the running of the Academy.

On 16 December 1851, Seton issued a notice in *The Edinburgh Evening Courant*, trying to promote the SNMA as being well equipped to prepare pupils for the army entrance examination. The directors must have been concerned as only two out of twenty-two pupils were planning to become officers in the British army; they joined twenty-five who had the same future plan and were having a further year's instruction.

> The Course of Instruction pursued by this Institution is specially designed to qualify Young Gentlemen to pass the Examinations prescribed by the Horse Guards, the Admiralty and the Honourable East India Company and forms also an excellent preparation for the Universities and for Government.

On 13 September 1852, the usual press notification of the beginning of the new SNMA Session was printed in the *Caledonian Mercury*. Seton announced on behalf of the directors that they were going to start a three-year programme of study for those intending to sit the army examination. The Academy was having to rethink the education of future cadets due to the numbers that were failing the army exam and the low numbers enrolling at the Academy who were planning to join the British army. No details were issued as to what would be studied in this new course. From a future letter it appears doubtful that they increased the teaching of mathematics and Classical studies. The SNMA announced the fees for this three-year military course which were 25 guineas (£3,034) for each of the first two years and 15 guineas (£1,821) for the final year. A paragraph was added:

> The Scottish Naval & Military Academy was founded in 1825. The Institution has been eminently successful. No fewer than a thousand Officers have already been trained within its walls. It is gratifying the Directors to know that many of them are now filling offices of high rank and responsibility with credit to themselves and with honour to the Academy.

The announcement made no difference. Two weeks later, only three pupils enrolled who planned to have a career in the British army, supplemented by five whom John noted as aiming for EIC.

On 1 September 1853, the SNMA chairman, Sir Neil Douglas died. Seton gained more power as he immediately took over as chairman. A little over a year later, Seton was awarded the brevet rank of lieutenant colonel in order to bring him up to the rank of recently retired EIC officers. From 1855 onwards, John is listed as 'Military Superintendent', the implication being that he is no longer superintendent of the whole Academy. Seton remained as chairman until 1856 when he was replaced by Major General Viscount Melville, a more senior military figure.

During the 1850s, while the military intake was declining, the number of pupils who were enrolling for a general education remained approximately the same each year. Seton and the directors did nothing special to attract more pupils who were interested in a non-military career. Prize-giving day still centred around military, gymnastic and fencing displays. Many of the speeches concentrated on those who were leaving to go into the services. Those who had done well academically received their prizes, but the main emphasis that day was always on the military side of the Academy.

The lack of emphasis on the academic achievements of the boys at nearly all the prize-givings had started to be mentioned in the mid-1840s. The *Caledonian Mercury* on 30 July 1846 said the non-military aspects of the Academy should be emphasised. If the examinations in academic subjects were given more emphasis 'it would then be discovered that its classes are admirably adapted to form the education of a gentleman whatever his profession may be'. The reporter would like the 'Directors to take measures next session by which the intellectual classes of the Academy would be brought more prominently at the Examinations'.[24]

Nothing changed. At the following year's prize-giving on 22 July 1847, Mr John Bowie, an ordinary director made a similar point. He wanted to tell those who might be thinking of sending a son to the Academy and might be worried about them being 'induced to enter either service' that this is not so:

> From one end of the year to the other this was the only occasion which partook of a military parade – that neither drum, fife nor bugle was to be heard within its walls – that the pupils even assembled at the sober and unpretending sound of the gong. (Greeted with applause.)[25]

John was an old soldier and it is understandable that he found difficulty in emphasising the non-military aspects of the institution. Prize-giving day was the great showpiece of the Military Academy. As John's influence in the running of the Academy was eclipsed by Seton, he put his all energy into the military displays at the prize-giving. These showed with a bit of theatrical flair the achievements of those who had been at the Academy whether they were intending to have a military career or not, as all pupils were encouraged to do military exercises and many did gymnastics and fencing. An example was the prize-giving of 1857 which took place in the Botanic Garden in Edinburgh, described in Chapter 6.

No new 'military' pupils enrolled in October 1857. Two boys with military aspirations joined that October for their second year of study, the other twenty-six pupils enrolling have no comment in John's

Remark column. No major prize-giving event was held in July 1858. *The Edinburgh Evening Courant* simply reported a list of the prize winners.

As the numbers enrolling for a military career decreased, the SNMA would have been well advised to make more emphasis on its good academical credentials. It should have considered teaching in greater depth Classical subjects and mathematics, both required for the army examination. John and then later Seton and the directors, however, simply inserted small advertisements in Scottish and English regional papers giving the dates when its session opened. The Academy attracted various pupils from England, but with more publicity this number could have increased. Between 1831 and 1864, 181 pupils came from England (12 per cent out of 1,500) and 56 from Ireland (4 per cent.) A newspaper report of the prize-giving in 1849 mentions that, 'it was truly said by several gentlemen from England, who attended on this occasion that were the merits of the Institution more widely known, its sphere of influence would be much extended and that England itself would send many of their sons to profit from its excellent system.'[26]

In October 1855, thirty-three new pupils enrolled of whom only four wanted to join the British army and one the EIC. A year later, in October 1856, although the new enrolment was marginally higher only one boy wanted the join the British army and one the EIC. The Institute was worried and Major Mair, one of the ordinary directors, had an interview in London with Lord Palmerston, Lord Panmure (Secretary of State for War) and the Commander-in-Chief to find out again if the Academy would be allowed to award a few commissions in a similar way to Sandhurst. Nothing came of this meeting.

Early in 1857, the directors tried another approach. They sent a delegation to meet the Lord Advocate (Senior Scottish law officer). It comprised of the Lord Provost, two MPs, Colonel Seton and three other army directors and the secretary. Surprisingly, John, as Military Superintendent, was not included in this group. It is possible he was ill, but excluding him would fit into the pattern of his no longer being involved with running of the Academy. The group put their case to the Lord Advocate who said he was friendly to the Academy's cause and would take the matter further. Again, there was no positive result.

Only twelve new boys enrolled in October 1857, none of whom planned a service career. They joined sixteen who were having their second year. The SNMA was no longer sustainable. On Saturday, 10 July 1858, a few days before the end-of-term prize-giving, a notice appeared in the press of the formation of The Scottish Institute for Civil, Commercial and Military Education which would replace the SNMA in the autumn.[27] In essence, it would be the same organisation but with a slightly different curriculum and the teaching staff would not change. The formation of the Institute is discussed in Chapter 11.

I reached the conclusion that the main reason for the SNMA's decline in enrolling of pupils planning to go into the British army was the introduction of the army examination and resultant rise of the specialist crammer. The SNMA offered a wide range of subjects but not in enough depth for some of their students to pass the army examination.

This was confirmed by an article in *The Edinburgh Evening Courant* of 28 August 1858, which gave verbatim the contents of a letter written the previous month on 17 July 1858 by Colonel Seton. It indicated that the SNMA directors believed that the rise of crammers was to blame for the decline in enrolment of 'military' pupils. It is an emotional letter written by Seton to the Prince Consort, who was the SNMA Patron, the day after the end of term examinations had taken place.[28] (The letter in full is in Appendix 6.) Seton outlined the reasons for the 'break-up of the institution'. He wrote:

> The Institution continued to prosper till the introduction of the new system of Competitive Examinations by the Horse Guards, and it was then hoped that the sound and practical course of Education pursued by the Pupils of the Scottish Naval and Military Academy would prove their passport for obtaining the necessary certificate of qualifications for Commissions. These expectations, however, have been entirely disappointed. The Examinations alluded to have completely ignored all Professional Education, whilst the acquisition of knowledge by the slow process inseparable from sound education has been quite superseded by a class of Seminaries, where, the mere exercise of memory, three months of close application will suffice to enable a Pupil to

> pass the prescribed ordeal. The directors of the Institution, under the patronage of your Royal Highness, could not lend themselves to a course so delusive and superficial, and the consequence has been such a diminution of the number of their Pupils, as has compelled the directors to resolve to discontinue at the close of the present session the Scottish Naval and Military Academy.

This letter, both defensive and arrogant, supports my supposition that the content of the examination, the resulting failure rate and the rise in crammers had had a direct effect on the enrolment at the SNMA. Seton wrote that it was 'hoped' their own type of education would enable boys to pass the exam. The Academy had, it would appear, not raised the level of their teaching in mathematics and Classical studies. The SNMA directors could see that their education was not preparing pupils to pass this examination, yet they were not willing to change. They considered they were supplying the best general tuition for pupils, though many who wanted to go into the British army were not passing the army examination.

Would the end result have been different had John not been sidelined? On reflection, probably not, because John was also keen to emphasise the military side as demonstrated by the prize-givings. After the SNMA closed, the new Scottish Institute opened in October 1858.

Chapter 11

The Scottish Institute and John's Retirement

> The object of The Scottish Institute is to afford instruction in these departments of Literature, Science and the Arts which are usually included in a liberal education.[1]

The renaming of the Academy in October 1858 as The Scottish Institute for Civil, Commercial and Military Education was a desperate measure to try to attract more pupils. Certainly, in its first year the total enrolment had doubled from twenty-eight to sixty-two. The sixty-two pupils included five boys who had studied at the last year of the SNMA, only one of whom planned to join the British army. John must have found it depressing as no new pupils enrolled who wanted to have a service career. It managed to struggle on for some years and closed in around July 1865. The Roll Book in the family archive does not list the pupils who enrolled for the 1864–65 session.

When it opened, the Institute still had 'Military' in its title and listed military classes. John was entitled simply superintendent and was again sending out the prospectuses. He and those in charge must have had a lingering hope that it might continue to attract young men planning to go into the British army. (Direct commissions could be purchased until November 1871.) It was, in essence, a similar establishment to the old SNMA, but when the Edinburgh Almanack eventually named the directors, they were the teaching staff – gone are all the office bearers of high social rank.

Little had changed regarding the main subjects taught, which were English, mathematics, history and geography. As well as the usual foreign languages, they continued to provide teaching in Hindustani, Persian,

Arabic and Sanskrit. Fortification, civil engineering, surveying, military drawing, mining engineering and mechanical drawing were still listed. The only new subjects were photography, singing, and the elements of political economy.[2] (Perhaps news of Stuart-Wortley's enthusiasm for picture-taking had encouraged the addition of photography.)

For the first time, the Institute offered a first course fee of £2 2s (£224) per quarter which included English, grammar, dictation, history, geography, writing, arithmetic, and Latin or French. These lessons would occupy the pupils for five hours daily. The second course fee was £2 12s 6d. (£279) per quarter which included much the same subjects with the addition of social economics. Gymnastics 10s 6d (£56) and a matriculation fee of 5s (£27) were both charged per quarter. Should parents want to add or deduct classes this could be arranged and a new fee would be calculated. The prize-givings, organised by John, still had military aspects and the person giving away the prizes was sometimes a retired serviceman. John was probably unhappy with the formation and trajectory of the Institute as there were now no military pupils and little prospect of this changing. Some of the Institute students stayed for two years, some for longer. A few of the boys during these years were younger at first enrolment than when it was the SNMA. For instance, nineteen 9- and 10-year-olds enrolled during this period whereas only three in this age range had joined from 1831 to 1857. Most boys were 15 or 16 when they enrolled.

Important changes were taking place in the way commissions were awarded. In 1858, the army examination became solely a written one. The questions continued to be set by the professors at the RMC but the written exam was taken in Burlington House, London and, according to Brigadier John Smyth in his history of Sandhurst:

> After 1858 all Sandhurst cadets were given priority of appointments to commissions (by or without purchase) over those who avoided the Sandhurst course and comforted themselves in passing a qualifying examination and then waiting for a Direct Commission.[3]

The Scottish Institute had the same sessions as the SNMA and its first prize-giving took place in July 1859. Instead of using the Music Hall in George Street, the ceremony was held more modestly in the Royal

Academy Buildings and it was no longer the big social occasion with a march along George Street to the accompaniment of a military band. *The Edinburgh Evening Courant* of 26 July 1859 reported that The Scottish Institute was 'The successor of the Scottish Military Academy, somewhat enlarged in its design and scope, but under the same Superintendent and Masters'. The report remarked favourably on all the academic examinations and said that 'special attention had been given to the improvement of the military department by the introduction of the newest modes of drill, and the discipline and exercise adapted to the use of the most modern best weapons'. These included the new short Enfield rifle. No sociable dinner in the evening seems to have taken place.

During the session, 1859–1860, John Orr's son, Jack is listed on the staff as Lieutenant Orr teaching fortification and civil engineering. (He was back in Scotland on furlough from India.) A further contraction in format occurred that year as the examinations and prize-giving only lasted one day and were again in the Royal Academy Buildings. At the prize-giving in July 1860, Reverend R.H. Stevens who presided, remarked to the pupils, 'I am glad to find that much of the military element has been preserved in it. It is right that there should be incorporated with it a course of study which is more strictly civil and mercantile.' He went on to give some unusual and enlightened comments about the Indian uprising:

> At the time of the late mutiny in India, we had more than mere insinuations that, if not the mutiny itself, at least some of its aggravating circumstances might be traced to a want of sympathy which lately subsisted between Sepoys and their officers, and to, it maybe, the cold and haughty and sometimes cruel treatment of the men by those in command. I trust that you will cultivate now a different spirit from that which is alleged to have existed in the East. I do not say there is sufficient proof of this, but it is deeply to be regretted that it should have been possible for competent observers and judges to make such statements … I trust that you will cultivate now a different spirit from that which is alleged to have existed in the East.[4]

The ironical fact was that no students that year wanted to enrol in any military regiment.

A problem must have arisen in the spring of 1862, as in May the Institute left the Royal Academy Buildings and moved to 13 Hill Street for the final part of the session. Much of the property in that part of Lothian Road where the Royal Academy Buildings were situated was in the process of being bought up by the Caledonian Railway which was planning to extend the line up to the west end of Princes Street. The directors of The Scottish Institute would have known they needed to move at some stage. For some time after the Institute left, the Royal Academy building was used as a veterinary school and so the forthcoming railway acquisition cannot have been the main reason for the Institute leaving. Royal Academy Buildings were probably now too large and too expensive. There were only thirty-three new enrolments and none were intending to have a service career. The property at 13 Hill Street was much smaller. (The premises at the time of writing are in use as a small business centre.)

In July 1862, a further cutback occurred, no public examinations were reported and only a simple prize-giving was held. The prizes this year were given away by Mr Robert Nasmyth, the father of Major Charles Nasmyth, the hero of Silistra. He concluded his speech by saying that he had heard from Dr William Graham, the English master, 'of the general good conduct of the school, and that was owing to the management of Captain Orr that gallant gentleman who was differently engaged that day fifty-one years ago when he distinguished himself at the Battle of Salamanca (loud cheers)'.[5] It is confirmation that John was back as the functioning superintendent.

The press notice for the start of the new term in October 1862, in *The Edinburgh Evening Courant* of 4 September, listed the usual core subjects and military exercises. Fortification, civil engineering, fencing, drawing, surveying and Hindustani were still included. 'Dancing' was added to the subjects being taught and it was listed above 'military exercises'. (John cannot have been happy about that.)

In October 1863, only twenty-two new pupils enrolled joining twenty-three who were there the previous year. The Institute was no longer viable. On 30 December, an announcement in *The Scotsman* showed that the Institute had changed its name. It was now listed as

'The Scottish Institute for Languages, Mathematics and Commerce', the words 'Civil, Commercial' and 'Military Education' had been removed from its previous name. It was the first time that 'Military' was not in the Institute's title. The same announcement appeared in different papers in the early months of 1864. I felt for John, he must have been deeply unhappy about how the SNMA had been transformed into a small college with few pupils which no longer taught any military subjects.

An announcement in the *Daily Review* of 16 July 1864 advertised the start of the next session on 3 October. It listed the subjects that the Institute would be teaching which confirmed there would be no military classes. John, now aged 74, was not named as superintendent; instead James Kilgour, the Classics master, was listed as managing director. What had happened to John?

The first public reference that John was no longer superintendent appeared a week later in a press report of the prize-giving on 23 July 1864.[6] The Reverend Thomas McLauchlan was the chairman that year. At the start of his speech, he referred 'to the long and faithful services of Captain Orr, whom we understand has retired from the office of Superintendent'. The chairman went on to say that the Institute would no longer be teaching military subjects: 'It was just such a school where ordinary branches of a liberal education were given.'

There is no record in the archive as to when and why John ceased to be superintendent; it must have happened early in 1864 and well before 16 July. I do not know whether he resigned or whether the directors told him that as the Institute would no longer be teaching military matters, they had no need of a superintendent. It cannot have been a happy parting of the ways or his retirement would have occurred with a eulogy at the end of session prize-giving.

When John left, he either took or was given the Roll Book. I, therefore, have no pupil records for The Scottish Institute for the session October 1864/65. It may have been their last year. There is one report in the *Caledonian Mercury* of 5 October 1865 indicating that the Institute opened on the 2nd.[7] There appear to be no reports about the Institute after this and it may not have even opened for that new session.

James Grant, John's old friend, in 1883, his book *Old & New Edinburgh* Volume II, remarked:

> The next edifice of any importance demolished at that time was the Riding School, with the old Scottish Naval & Military Academy so long run by an old officer of the Black Watch and well-known citizen, Captain John Orr, who carried one of the colours at Waterloo.
>
> It was a plain, although rather attractive, Grecian edifice; however, just about the time its site was required by the railway, the introduction of a certain amount of competitive examinations at military colleges elsewhere rendered the institution unnecessary. Prior to its extinction the academy sufficed to send more than a thousand young men as officers into the army, many of whom have risen to distinction in every quarter of the globe.[8]

The Institute failed as it was not prepared to increase its Classical and mathematical education, but to its credit, it did not want to become a cramming institution. Once that decision was made, there was no hope of increasing pupil numbers who were planning on a military career. It was then competing for general pupils with all the other well-established academic schools in Edinburgh. It now, however, had nothing special to offer and so pupil numbers declined until it was no longer viable.

Chapter 12

John's Old Age and Death

> 'The deceased officer was held in high esteem and respect by all who knew him.'[1]
>
> Obituary of John Orr.
> *Greenock Advertiser.*

After leaving The Scottish Institute in 1864, John, aged 74, continued to live at 42 St Cuthbert Street with his two daughters Maggie aged 39 and Helen 29. The Black Watch Museum in Perth has a photograph of John taken about this time which shows him wearing a plaid **(Illustration 14 monochrome)**. According to a letter, he was one of the last people in Edinburgh to do this. (A plaid is a long piece of tartan cloth, typically made of wool, worn over the shoulder as part of Scottish Highland dress.)

It would have been a cause for celebration in 1870 when John's daughter Helen, aged 35, married Colonel Archibald Goldie Young. He was a widower, nearly twenty years older than her, who had known the Orrs for many years and had been a trustee of John and Jane's Marriage Contract. Goldie Young was, by all accounts, a kind and generous man. He died a few weeks after Helen's death, in 1893, and as he had no children from either marriage he made provision for Maggie, John's eldest daughter, in his will. He gave her an annuity of £100 (£11,800) and allowed her to live rent free in what had been his and Helen's house. Maggie stayed there until she died in 1910.

John was still hosting boarders into his eighties. The 1871 census reveals that he and Maggie had four boys aged 19, 17, 15, and 12 living with them. The eldest is listed as an apprenticed chartered accountant and the other three were scholars. There were four servants – a housekeeper, a cook, a table maid and one other. Jess Eddington continued to be housekeeper until she died in 1876. Running a big town house with four servants would have been expensive and therefore it seems strange that John and Maggie wanted to stay on in this large property. John may have been reluctant to sell and move away from the house which he and his wife Jane had bought many years before with the money from their Marriage Contract.

As John aged, he got into financial difficulty. In Maggie's death papers there is a small piece of paper (8x3ins) dated January 1869. It was a type of informal promissory note with an embossed stamp. On the paper is written:

> Edinburgh 6 January 1869
>
> At six days sight I promise to pay to Margaret M Orr or her order the sum of three hundred pounds sterling have received. [£29,480]
>
> John Orr. [His signature.]

On the back there is:

> £50 [£4,914] repaid December 1874. 50 paid January. MMO. [Margaret Mather Orr]
>
> Edinburgh 18 March 1880 received from the executors of the late Captain John Orr the sum of two hundred pounds being the balance remaining unpaid of the sum contained within the Bill.
>
> Margaret M. Orr.

This describes how John had to borrow £300 from Maggie when he could no longer pay the household bills. The last sentence was written by Maggie after John's death when she was repaid the sum of £200 (£21,630) that was still outstanding. There is no indication in the family archive of when and how John started to have money problems. He was lucky as he retired from the army with a full pension of about £134 (£13,170) paid in quarterly instalments. Living in such a large house was probably beyond his means as he no longer was receiving his salary as superintendent. The only additions to his pension were the fees from the boarders. If he continued to have guests for meals as he had done when he was the superintendent, this would have been expensive.

Joseph Panton's diary described the social life in the Orrs' house when John was superintendent and it may have been difficult for John to give up this kind of life.

How did Maggie have £300 to lend to her father? The most likely explanation is that she had been left money by a relation. The only bequest I have found was the £40 (£4,069) left to her by Helen Anderson (see Chapter 5). The note on the back of the promissory note shows John was only able to repay £100 [£9,827] of the loan. It must have been a difficult family situation. Maggie clearly knew that there might be a problem with either John repaying the money or her receiving a settlement from his estate. She, therefore, asked him to formally sign the loan note. This situation made me look in more detail into Maggie's life.

Maggie was John's companion and support during his old age, but she was an interesting person in her own right and appears to have had a strong character. In 1844, aged 19, she had taken over as the female head of the household when her mother died. I have a small painting of Maggie in which she is looking out with a self-assured determination and it is easy to believe she was successful in this new role **(Illustration 24 colour)**. Her fashionable ringlets frame her face and she wears an attractive, but plain, off-the-shoulder flesh-coloured dress. The archive includes a photograph where she is slightly more relaxed. As mentioned in Chapter 5, Joseph Panton said he and his fellow students had all fallen in love with Maggie. Despite her formidable appearance in the portrait, Maggie must have been an engaging person who could charm others.

Her obituary in *The Scotsman* of 16 November 1910 indicates that Maggie was a woman of note. It reveals she had interests outside the home and that she worshipped at the Barclay Church, which belonged to the Free Church of Scotland. (It was an evangelical sect which broke away at The Disruption in 1843.) She was keen on mission work and was particularly concerned about the lack of women doctors in India. This situation was mainly in the north where, in wealthy or middle-class Indian homes, fathers or husbands refused healthcare for women in their household from male western doctors. Maggie would have heard about this when her brothers and their wives returned to Scotland during furloughs.

The matriculation records of Edinburgh University show that in November 1871 Maggie enrolled as a mature student to study medicine, but only for one year. Like several other women who joined at the same time, she was not planning to take a degree. She was part of a group of forty who enrolled to support seven women who were trying to get a medical degree from Edinburgh University.[2] These women were known as '*Septum contra Edinam*' (The Seven against Edinburgh).[3] They had to endure much vilification and obstruction and, despite completing the course, were not allowed to graduate with a degree. Maggie's support of 'The Seven' shows her commitment to their cause. To honour the memory of the 'Septum', in 2019 seven current female medical students accepted posthumous degrees on behalf of these ground-breaking women.[4]

Another concern Maggie had was supporting the working tailors of Edinburgh. Her obituary notes:

> She superintended a large staff of lady readers, who once a week read for an hour or more in any workshop that welcomed them. Miss Orr lived to see the harvest of much of her labour in the improved conditions of the workshops and the brightening of the workmen's homes.

As well as having these outside interests, Maggie would have spent time running the household and looking after John as his health declined. I have no record of how John viewed Maggie's outside concerns, although it seems she had inherited her father's public-spirited interest in the education of others.

The family archive has a photograph of John when he was in his mid-eighties. He has a long white beard and is sitting upright in a chair, looking strongly at the camera, wearing a three-piece suit with his two medals on a lapel **(Illustration 15 monochrome)**. His gloves are on his knee, an umbrella beside him and he has an air of calm authority. There is perhaps a tinge of sadness or resignation in his expression, but he looks alert and well.

I have a copy or draft of a letter written by John in May 1874 to the Right Honourable Secretary of War, Horse Guards, London. He hoped that his pension might be increased. John lists his war record and goes on to talk about his time as superintendent of the SNMA from 1831 until it closed:

> Being now in my 85th year I hope you will pardon me in requesting you kindly to lay my case before His Royal Highness the Duke of Cambridge in the hope that he may

> grant me a good service pension as one of two survivors of the Old Black Watch, who fought at Waterloo.[5]

I have no confirmation that this letter was sent nor whether he received an additional pension. The pension sheet I have in the archive covers 1865–1868. It shows that during this period he was paid over £33 (£3,357) quarterly. From 1875 to 1877 there were maintenance expenses associated with his house. In the family archive is an invoice listing window repairs, repair work to floors, a wall and a roof hatch and a mention of a complicated legal action to recover over £101 (£10,120) as half the share for damage to a mutual gable wall which involved both a neighbouring property and bad workmanship by a builder. There is only a lawyer's list of letters, but not the actual letters in the archive. I notice the solicitor has addressed these to Maggie and not to John. The maintenance costs of such a large town house would have been challenging for John to pay with limited resources and on-going financial difficulties.

The second photograph from the archive is of John in his late eighties **(Illustration 16 monochrome)**. He has aged and is wearing a long white shirt over his trousers; his medals are pinned to his shirt. He wears a Glengarry cap, his beard is much longer, his hair is unkempt and he has a dog at his feet. He no longer sits upright and is slightly hunched in the chair. He has a hammer in his hand which reminded me that woodworking had been a hobby when he was younger. In Maggie's death papers there is a note about 'a work box made by my father the late Captain Orr'. On looking at this photograph, I remember that senility is one of the words on his death certificate.

In 1879, old colleagues and previous pupils of the SNMA were concerned about John and Maggie's situation. A committee was set up to gather funds for a presentation and advertisements were posted in *The Times* and in the *United Services Gazette.* William Maughan was the secretary of the Presentation Group. He was the son of an EIC officer and had been a pupil for two years at the SNMA, starting in October 1851; after he left he qualified as a chartered accountant. The advertisement in the *United Services Gazette* of 11 October is headed 'Testimonial to Captain John Orr, late of the Forty-Second Highlanders: Sometime Superintendent of the Scottish Naval and Military Academy'. It goes on: 'Captain Orr is in his ninetieth year. He is one of the very few survivors of the Peninsular and Waterloo and he is the last of the officers of the 42nd who fought at Waterloo, where he was injured.' The names of some of those who had already subscribed are listed and the sum so far raised was £250 [£27,040].

On 14 October 1879, some seven weeks before John died, Colonel Aitchison of Drummore (whose older brother – since deceased – had been at the Academy) and other dignitaries came to 24 Torphican Street with a touching present for John which reflected the respect and love they had for him.[6] Maggie, Helen, and Helen's husband, Colonel Goldie Young, were there. The gift, handed over by Colonel Aitchison, was a pair of handsome silver-plated vases and a purse of 300 guineas (£34,070). I am lucky to have one of the vases **(Illustration 17 monochrome)**.

The inscription on the vase is:

> PRESENTATION
> To
> CAPTAIN JOHN ORR
> Late of the 42nd Regiment.
> Sometime Superintendent of
> The Scottish Naval & Military Academy, Edinburgh.
> Along with a Purse of Three hundred guineas.
> By some of the old pupils and other friends
> as a
> token of their regard and affection.
> 15 October 1879

On the back there are the words 'PENINSULAR' and 'WATERLOO'.

In the family archive is a folded piece of paper on which are printed the names of the ninety-six people who contributed to the sum raised to pay for the vases and the purse.[7] The names on the list confirm the inscription that many of the subscribers were past pupils who had stayed with the Orr family; others were directors, teachers and friends. The paper lists their individual contributions – about two-thirds gave a donation between a pound (£108) to three guineas (£340) and a third gave over £5 (£540).

The biggest contribution was from J.A.S. Freeland who donated £25 (£2,704). This is a remarkable sum of money. Freeland was a retired lieutenant in the Royal Horse Artillery but was not educated at the SNMA and I have not managed to find his connection to either John or to the Academy.[8] The Duke of Buccleuch, a vice president, gave £20 (£2,163). Lieutenant Colonel Charles Watson contributed 10 guineas (£1,136). Watson was at the SNMA from 1841 to 1843 and stayed with the Orrs (see Chapter 8).

Dr David Maclagan, a long-time ordinary director, subscribed, as did his son William who was by then the Bishop of Litchfield. He had studied at the Academy for two years starting in October 1841. (Three sons of David Maclagan went to the SNMA.) Another contribution came from Colonel Yule (see Chapter 4). Many of the students were by then lieutenant colonels and colonels.

The speech was given by William Maughan. It was printed as an illuminated address, which was presented to John, together with a list of the subscribers. (I have this list, although the illuminated address is not in the family archive.) William Maughan's words sum up John's character and attributes.

> Dear Captain Orr – We, your friends, whose names are subjoined, beg to ask your acceptance of the accompanying testimonial as a slight expression of our regard and affection, and of our appreciation of those qualities which, throughout a long and honourable carer, have commanded the respect and esteem of everyone who has had the privilege of knowing you. You are the only survivor of the officers who were with the gallant 42nd Regiment when it achieved such high distinction at Waterloo, and you are among a very few who survive of all the splendid army which fought in the Peninsular War, and subsequently gained that great battle. Brave in the field, and faithful and judicious in the important trust committed to you as superintendent of the Scottish Naval & Military Academy for so many years, you have ever shown an example of firmness and true discipline, combined with all that is attractive and lovable in social intercourse. That you may still for some time be spared for us, and that every comfort and blessing may attend you, is the wish of all your friends.[9]

A reply, on behalf of John Orr, was given, by his son-in-law Colonel Goldie Young.[10]

On 7 December 1879, John died at his home, Maggie was with him. He was 89 and his death certificate lists senility and exhaustion. He was interred at Warriston Cemetery three days later. The invoice from William Veitch, undertaker, shows the total sum of the account was for £21 5s 6d, (£2,301) which included the cemetery dues.[11] As had happened to Jane, the coffin had been taken straight from the family home to the cemetery. There was no church funeral, simply an interment. (The involvement of the church in a funeral did not return to Scotland until the late nineteenth century.)[12] The undertaker's account lists the 'best hearse and pair' with four assistants. The coffin was described as follows:

> Strong coffin with wax cloth and calico lining covered with black cloth, double rail mounting, registered inscription plate and handles with silk tassel ropes. Black cushion for the top of the coffin.

A few years ago, I saw in Edinburgh a horse-drawn hearse which was probably similar to the one used to take John to Warriston Cemetery **(Illustration 25 colour)**.

A large number of mourners assembled to witness the interment, as the undertaker's account lists twelve carriages and pairs. The cortege left from 24 Torphican Street, where they had gathered. The carriages followed the hearse from there to the graveside in Warriston Cemetery.[13] The Orr family plot is in the middle section of the cemetery, below the grave of Sir James Young Simpson, the pioneer of anaesthetics. Each year, I plant more daffodils on the gentle slope in front of the gravestone **(Illustration 26 colour)**. Various Orr family members are also buried in this lair. The front of the stone notes the deaths of Jane and John **(Illustration 27 colour)**.

In the archive are the executory papers. When John died, £4 10s (£486) is listed as the cash in the house, and some money was in a deposit account. Only £27 13s (£2,991) was left of the presentation sum of 300 guineas. Most must have gone to pay outstanding debts. The Probate Register dated 2 January 1880 recorded that John left an estate valued £1,421 7s (£153,700). This sum, however, was mainly made up of a life policy of £1,114 (£120,500) which matured on his death.

In his will, John left everything in trust for his daughter Maggie. On her death, the residue was to be divided into thirds. One third was to go the children of his son James. Another third was for Jack, his other son and his family, and the final third would be life rent to his daughter Helen. When Helen died her share was to be divided into two, one half going to James's children and the other half to Jack's.

Death notices were in most of the Scottish papers and some English ones as well. The longest was in the *Greenock Telegraph and Clyde Shipping Gazette*.[14] It gave a brief history of his career and mentioned the recent presentation of the vases and the purse of 300 guineas. It ended by saying 'the deceased officer was held in high esteem and respect by all who knew him'.

It is not surprising that the longest obituary was in a paper from John's small home town. He had been born there nearly ninety years earlier and was the longest surviving officer of his regiment to have fought at Waterloo. Instead of living quietly on his pension after he was retired from the army, he had gone on to have a full and busy later life, turning around the SNMA after the Downes saga and tirelessly encouraging the boys to make the best of themselves. It has been a privilege to share his story.

In Retrospect

The family archive, although broad ranging, is fragmentary and I have spent many years of research trying to fill in the gaps in John Orr's life from additional sources. Looking back on those days when my mother and I rummaged in the cabin trunk, I reflect on how I knew so little about John. He was a presence in our home with his portrait in the hall and the other paintings around the house, but I was not aware of what he was like as a person. I do feel now that I understand him better, having followed him as a young man during the Peninsular War, the Battles of Quatre Bras and Waterloo and on to his time as superintendent. His letter book displayed the care and concern he had for the pupils staying in the family home. The enthusiastic and grateful comments by directors and teachers show that John was a good and effective superintendent who pulled the Academy up from its decline under Downes. He was a disciplinarian but he had affection for the pupils and was committed to ensuring they went on to have successful lives. Panton's diaries reveal John's sense of humour and what life was like in the Orr household. He was a sociable person, with a warm personality, a kind man who enjoyed life.

Looking back over the years of research another thing that has given me pleasure has been uncovering the lives of some of the pupils and those that ran the SNMA. I know if I had delved further, I would have found more interesting characters but then there would have been the danger of the book never being finished!

As I reach the end of John's story, I have a deep feeling of sadness as the last thirty years which followed the decline of the SNMA were such a contrast to his earlier life. Aged 89 and struggling with the problems of senility, it must have been moving for him to receive the presentation and good wishes from all those who had contributed to the vases and the purse. It was a reminder of the time when he was the much-loved and admired superintendent of a successful military academy.

Richard Holmes wrote that, 'the dead call to us out of the past, like owls calling out of the dark. They ask to be heard, remembered, understood.'[1] I am delighted that John's life and the story of the Scottish Naval & Military Academy have been uncovered and are now in the public domain.

Author's Note and Acknowledgements

I have many people to thank without whom this book would probably not have been started and certainly would never have been finished. I did not plan to write a book initially, it emerged from my casual research, after sifting through the family archive.

The research trail starts after my mother died, I found in the cellar a metal uniform box, full of old army uniform. I was not sure to whom it all belonged, as several ancestors had been in the army. A friend put me in touch with Dr Stuart Allan who at that time was in charge of the Military Museum at Edinburgh Castle. He kindly came to see me and looked at the uniforms. He said the best person to work out the provenance of the items would be a colleague, Allan Carswell, now working freelance. Allan made a list of all the items and managed to approximately date most of them and in some cases named the regiment. In the box were items that belonged to John including his militia jacket with his name in it, from when John had rejoined the Edinburgh Militia in 1831. Allan has continued to help over the years answering my questions and reading parts of the text.

Stuart Allan told me that the Military Museum had some SNMA artefacts. I arranged a visit. Stuart had kindly looked out all the papers for me and I found an article which said that Edinburgh Council held in their archive an interesting series of large books which contained coloured drawings of some of the staff and pupils at the Academy. These were the Howie drawings which I mention in the book and are pictured on the cover.

I made an appointment to go to the Edinburgh Archive where they allowed me to look at and handle the bound volumes of Howie's sketches. (The staff at the Archive have been helpful on many occasions since then.) The only other visitor that day was Dr John McGowan, a retired police superintendent who was writing the history of the Edinburgh police. We chatted and exchanged emails. John was extremely supportive of my initial tentative research and encouraged me to think of putting them together as a book. He explained that self-publishing was not difficult and he would send me online one of his earlier books. I could delete the text and cut and paste my own into it; it would then give my writing the appearance of a proper book. At a critical time, this was an enormous encouragement, as although I had written informal articles before, I had never written a book. Despite being occupied with his own research John offered to read some of my earlier chapters which was hugely helpful.

On Ancestry.com I discovered an Orr family tree which included John's name. I left a message and found the website had been created by Professor Roger Jeffery and Heuke Weiber. They were looking into connections between Edinburgh and India in the nineteenth century and had found that certain pupils at Edinburgh Academy went on to study at the SNMA before going to join the East India Company. I met them and explained about my research. Roger volunteered to read my chapters. He is not a specialist in military history, although he knows a great deal about India and it was encouraging to have an academic reading my work. He was at that time the Director of the Centre for South Asian Studies for the University of Edinburgh.

In 2014, I noticed on Google a small piece about John on the Inverclyde Heritage Group website. It had been posted by Isobel McCully, one of the volunteers who ran the site. She had spotted John's obituary in the *Greenock Telegraph* of 8 December 1879. Pamela McLean at Inverclyde Council arranged for me to give a talk in the Watt Library where I met Isobel. She drove me round Greenock and showed me the church where John had been baptised. The event in Greenock resulted in my giving a talk to the Renfrewshire Family History Society about John and the SNMA.

I visited the Royal Military Academy, Sandhurst where Dr Sebastian Puncher kindly gave up time to show me many interesting papers, and suggested his doctoral thesis would be helpful, which indeed it has been. Over the years he has been prepared to take time to answer the questions I have sent to him.

After finishing the text, I knew that some of the narrative needed to be checked by historians. I am deeply grateful to Sir Hew Strachan, Victoria

Schofield and John Harding-Edgar who have read passages and chapters from my book, flagging up errors and making helpful comments.

Andrew McMillan, the Honorary Archivist for the Edinburgh Academy, has always been happy to answer the questions that I have thrown at him. Caroline Gerrard who runs the Friends of Warriston Cemetery where John is buried has supplied me with helpful research information. I am grateful to both of them.

I am particularly grateful to my friend Dr Patricia Maitland who has carefully reviewed one of the final versions of the book and has given me some excellent suggestions. I also appreciate many other friends who, over the years, have either read particular chapters or the whole book. These include Ralph Eccleston, Jean Hewitt, Dorothy Leeming, Major General Euan Loudon, Moragh Reid, Timothy South and Christopher Williams.

I would like to thank Harriet Fielding, my Commissioning Editor at Pen & Sword, for her encouragement and advice. Maggie Hamlyn informally read my initial contract and I am grateful for her wise comments. In addition, I would like to thank Elizabeth Haylett Clark from the Society of Authors who also read my contract with Pen & Sword and who has given me guidance whenever I needed it.

I have had the support of my family throughout. My son David and his wife Rebecca are delighted that all the years of research have paid off. My daughter Melissa has spent many hours, over many years, reading, reviewing and making suggestions. Her partner, Annie South, helped to structure the information in the Roll Book spreadsheet which enabled many valuable statistics to be extracted. I thank them both for their support and the time they have spent living with John Orr.

Without the help, support and contributions from all these people, this book would not have been completed. I owe them all a deep debt of gratitude. It should be noted that any errors in the text are my responsibility.

Appendix 1

Tables

Table 1: Approximate number of students enrolling each year (page 35).

Year	Entrance money	Number of students enrolled*
1825–26	£181 13s [£15,860]	173
1826–27	£164 17s [£14,740]	157
1827–28	£129 13s 6d [£11,940]	129
1828–29	£99 15s 6d [£9,091]	95

*Estimated figures based on total entrance money divided by the entrance fee of one guinea. I do not have the accounts for the years 1829/30 and 1830/31.

Table 2: Subjects, masters, hours and fees from 1833 Prospectus issued by Captain John Orr.

Branches of Study	Teacher's name	Hours of instruction	Teacher's fee for each class per Quarter
Fortification	Lieutenant Shaw	10–12 or 12–2 Monday Wednesday and Friday	£1 11s 6d [£159]
Military Drawing, surveying, levelling	Lieutenant Shaw	10–12 or 12 to 2 Tuesday, Thursday, Saturday	£2 2s 0d [£212]
Landscape and Perspective drawing	Mr Humble	10 to 11 and 11 to 12	£1 11s 6d
Sketching from nature	Mr Humble	Twelve lessons	£1 1s 0d [£106]
Arithmetic, algebra, geometry	George Lees	One class 9–10 daily not Saturday	£1 1s 0d

Branches of Study	Teacher's name	Hours of instruction	Teacher's fee for each class per Quarter
Higher mathematics and navigation	George Lees	One class daily 10–11 not Saturday	£1 1s 0d
Lectures on Natural Philosophy	George Lees	Class from 12–1 Tuesday and Saturday	£1 1s 0d
Latin and Greek	Reverend J.C. Shepherd	Classes 11–12 daily except Saturday	£1 1s 0d
Elementary Arithmetic and Book keeping	Mr James Trotter	One class daily 10–11 except Saturday	15s 0d [£76]
Elocution, composition, geography, Ancient & Modern history	Mr William Graham	One class daily 1–2 except Saturday	£1 1s 0d
Persian and Hindoostanee for beginners	Mr Ballantyne	One class daily 12–1 except Saturday	£2 12s 6d [£265]
Persian and Hindoostanee more advanced	Mr Ballantyne	One class daily 9–10 except Saturday	£2 2s 0d
Arabic	Mr Ballantyne	One class 3–4 daily except Saturday	£2 2s 0d
French elementary	Mons C.P. Buquet	One class daily 3–4 except Saturdays	£1 1s 0d
French composition	Mons C.P. Buquet	One class 2–3 daily except Saturdays	£1 1s 0d
Italian	Sig G. Rabagliati	One class 9–10 daily except Saturdays	£1 11s 6d
Spanish	Dr Llacayo	One class 3–4 daily except Saturdays	£1 11s 6d
Portuguese	Dr Llacayo	One class 9–10 daily except Saturdays	£1 11s 6d
German	Dr Cantor	One class 9–10 daily except Saturdays	£1 11s 6d
Fencing	Mr Roland	Classes 9–10, 10–11 and 11–12. Mondays, Wednesdays and Fridays	£1 11s 6d

(Cont'd)

Table 2: *(Cont'd)*

Branches of Study	**Teacher's name**	**Hours of instruction**	**Teacher's fee for each class per Quarter**
Gymnastics	Mr Roland and Sergeant Major Mercer	One class 8–9 and 1–2 daily except Saturday	£1 1s 0d
Military exercises with firelock, broad sword etc.	Sergeant Major Mercer	One class 12–1 and 2–3 daily except Saturday	£1 1s 0d

Table 3: Aspirations of pupils when they first enrolled at the SNMA, in 1831/32 and 1863/64 (page 82).

Destination	**Count of pupils**	**Proportion of total pupils**
No aspiration recorded	847	56%
British army, navy or militia	411	27%
EIC	233	16%
Other military organisations*	9	1%
Total	**1,500**	**100%**

* This includes one pupil was planning to go into each of the following services: Austrian, Spanish and Persian.

Table 4: Table showing the country of origin for each pupil in 1831/32 and 1863/64 according to their first enrolment record (page 84).

(For the first five years no country of origin was recorded in the Roll Book.)

Country of origin	**Count of pupils**	**Proportion of total pupils**
Scotland	843	56%
Not recorded	234	16%
England	181	12%
India	133	9%
Rest of the World	109	7%
Total	**1,500**	**100%**

Appendix 2

General Rules to be adopted as a basis for the formation of the SNMA. Listed in the Prospectus

The Scotsman on 24 August 1825.

1. That the same and designation of the Establishment shall be the Scottish Military Academy.
2. That with a view to commence the Establishment on a respectable footing, a sum of £3,000 [£262,000] shall be raised by Subscription, in 300 shares of £10 [£873] each.
3. That no Subscriber shall hold more than two shares, nor be liable for more than his subscription; the amount of the shares to be exigible [demandable] at such periods and by such instalments, as may be fixed by the Directors and the instalments to bear interest from the period of being called up.
4. That for paying annual dividends on the said shares, and meeting the ordinary Expenses of the Establishment, each student shall contribute towards the Academy Fund, such Entry Money, or Annual Sum, as may be fixed by the Directors.
5. That every branch of Military and Gymnastic Exercises shall be taught at the Academy; also the Modern Languages, viz. French, Italian, German, Spanish, Hindoostanee, Persian etc.; likewise Fortification, Gunnery, Surveying, Navigation, Mathematics, Military Landscape and Perspective Drawing, History, Geography, and every other branch of Education that the Committee may progressively deem useful and expedient.

6. That the Class Fees for each Branch shall be moderate, and fixed by the Directors.
7. That the Establishment shall have a Patron, a President, five Vice Presidents, Honorary Directors, twenty-five Extraordinary Directors, and fifteen Ordinary Directors.
8. That the Patron, President, Vice Presidents, and Honorary Directors, shall not be required to be Shareholders.
9. That one Share shall qualify for an Extraordinary and Ordinary Director.
10. That the Management of the Establishment shall be in the Extraordinary and Ordinary Directors, as General and Ordinary Committees.
11. That the Establishment shall have a Superintendent and such other Teachers as the Directors may deem necessary.
12. That three or more Trustees shall be appointed, in whose names all deed in favour of the institution shall be taken.
13. That a regular Contract shall be drawn up on the above principles, and shall contain such further Rules and Regulations as the General Committee of Directors shall afterwards think proper to adopt, under the sanction of the Shareholder.

Appendix 3

Office Bearers of SNMA 1831/32

(The year that John joined the SNMA.) *Edinburgh Almanack* 1832

Patron His Majesty King William the Fourth
Presidents Field Marshal His Grace the Duke of Wellington
General His Grace the Duke of Gordon
Vice Presidents His Grace the Duke of Buccleuch and Queensberry
His Grace the Duke of Argyll
The Most Noble the Marquis of Lothian
The Right Honourable the Earl of Dalhousie
Lieutenant General Sir Herbert Taylor
Major General the Hon. Patrick Stuart
Extraordinary Directors
The Right Honourable Lord Provost
The Right Honourable the Earl of Roseberry
The Right Honourable the Earl of Glasgow
The Right Honourable the Lord Forbes
The Right Honourable the Lord Abercromby
Sir William Hamilton
Major General Sir J. Malcolm
Admiral Sir P.C.H. Durham
Admiral Sir David Milne
Lieutenant General Sir John Hope
Lieutenant General Mackenzie
Lieutenant General Hughes
Lieutenant General Robertson
Lieutenant Colonel Sir Robert Mowbray
Lieutenant Colonel Leatham
Lieutenant Colonel Harvey of Castle Semple

Adam Duff, Esq Sheriff-Dep. Edinburgh
Wm Burn, Callander
Captain Robert Deans
James Nairne, Esq. WS
Ranald Macdonald, Esq. of Staffa
Eagle Henderson, Esq.
Colonel Loraine
Captain Fyffe RN
John Swinton, Esq.

Ordinary Directors.

Right Honourable Lord R. Kerr, **Chairman**
Sir J. Hope, Bart of Pink
General Campbell of Lochnell
Sir Henry Jardine
Colonel Spens
Colonel McBean
Captain J.D. Boswell RN
R. James L'Amy, Esq. Advocate
Lieutenant Colonel William Macdonald
Sir George Ballingall, MD
G.L. Finlay, Esq. WS
William Douglas, Esq.
Dr McLagan
Captain Stoddart, RN

Trustees

Lord Robert Kerr
Sir Robert Keith Dick
Sir Patrick Walker
Sir Henry Jardine
Captain J.D. Boswell RN
Sir Patrick Walker **Secretary**
M. Pringle **Assistant Secretary**
Captain R. Deans **Treasurer**
Thomas Scott, Accountant **Auditor of Accounts**
The Reverend James Chapman, **Chaplain**
The Royal Bank of Scotland, **Bankers**
Captain John Orr, **Superintendent**

Appendix 4

Rules & Regulations 1834

The Role of the Superintendent

1. The Superintendent is to be considered as the organ of the Directors, and the person next in authority to them; it being his duty to carry their intentions as to the management of the Establishment into effect, and to enforce such regulations as they may from time to time consider necessary to enact for the government of the Institution.
2. At all meetings of the Directors or of their Committees, he shall lay before them a report of what has occurred since their former meeting, and shall be in attendance to give any information which may be required from him.
3. He shall take care that the Pupils are quiet and orderly in going to and from their different classes.
4. He shall visit the class-rooms during the hours of teaching whenever he may think proper, and shall receive from Masters their reports as to the absence or irregularity of the Pupils, should such occur, taking care to enter the same in his report-book.
5. When parents and guardians or others call at the Academy, it is the duty of the Superintendent to attend them, and to furnish any information wanted.
6. He shall direct the despatch of intimations of meetings of Directors, Committees, and all other necessary notices.
7. When Pupils apply for certificates of their attendance, conduct, and progress, it shall be the duty of the Superintendent to prepare them; but he shall not deliver the same without the special authority of the Directors. Such certificates to be signed by the Chairman, and countersigned by the Superintendent.

8. He shall receive the class-fees, issue the class-tickets, and insert the names of the Pupils in the entrance-book.
9. He shall keep a cash-book, in which he shall enter all his receipts and disbursements on account of the Academy.
10. In the absence of the Treasurer he shall grant receipts for subscriptions and donations, and also for class-fees if required.
11. He shall make up a general quarterly state of the attendance, conduct and progress of each Pupil from the report-books of the Masters, and from his own observation, and shall make extracts therefrom, to be sent quarterly to parents or guardians.
12. He shall take particular care that the masters are not interrupted during the hours of study, unless upon the business of the Academy.
13. The Superintendent shall receive all communications from the Masters and Pupils to the Directors, and shall lay the same before their first meeting.
14. He shall have the general charge of the Library, whole Stores, Furniture, and other property belonging to the Academy, of which an inventory shall be made and entered in a book to be kept for that purpose by the Secretary, and to be subscribed by the Superintendent. When an article is lent, the Superintendent shall take a receipt for the same, and shall not allow anything to be lent to any person not belonging to the Academy, or to be applied to any other purpose than for the use of the Institution.
15. When articles are required to be furnished or repaired, the requisition for them must be made through the Superintendent; and he shall keep a book, in which shall be inserted a list of such articles, and the order of the Directors thereupon.
16. He shall enter in his orderly-book all the appointments that take place from the Academy, whether in the King's or in the Honourable East India Company's service.
17. All notices or advertisements connected with the studies of the Academy, shall be signed by the Superintendent.
18. Although the responsibility of the duties above detailed is laid upon the Superintendent, he shall be entitled to call on the Assistant Secretary to aid him with his services when he considers them necessary.

19. While the special duties of the Superintendent are thus detailed, it is to be expressly understood, that these are stated without prejudice to his general powers, in virtue of which he will act in every case not here specified, and upon every emergency not provided for by the rules, but which may require prompt attention, according to his own judgment and discretion; in all such cases, however, taking care to make an immediate report of the same to the Weekly Committee of Directors.

Appendix 5

Army Examination Memorandum issued in 1849

Examinations for Direct Commissions into the British Army.

The following is the Official Memorandum of the points upon which candidates are to be examined before they are recommended for commissions.

1. Candidates had to be able to read English correctly and write it from dictation.
2. In arithmetic he should be acquainted with the four first rules (simple and compound), proportion, fractions, the use of logarithms, with a competent knowledge of algebra.
3. In languages he should be able to translate into English some Latin author in prose or poetry; at the same time, he should parse and show his knowledge of grammar, syntax and prosody.

   The candidate will be required to construct an extract from a French work into English, and to state, in writing, the exact meaning of the French author.

   If not master of the Latin grammar, and he should not have received a good classical education, he must in lieu thereof, thoroughly understand the French and German grammar.

   He should, therefore, be able to translate an extract from an English work into French or German, and to state, in writing, (in French or German), the exact meaning of the English author.
4. In History, he should have read Hume's History of England, with Smollett's continuation; a History of Rome and Greece, and a History

of Modern Europe; and be prepared to answer such questions as the examiners may propose on the above subject.

5. In Geography, he should possess a competent knowledge of ancient geography; of the modern divisions of the world; the principal rivers, sea-ports, and military posts in Great Britain and Ireland; of her Majesty's dominions in every part of the world.
6. In Fortification, he should have read some easy work on the subject, and have received some instruction in drawing.
7. If the candidate be a member of the Church of England, he will have to produce a certificate of having been confirmed; if not a member of the Church of England, he will be required to produce a certificate from a minister or priest, stating that he has been well instructed in the principles of the religion in which he has been brought up.
8. A medical examination will take place, to ascertain that the candidate is in every point of view fit for military service.

List of the works which are likely to facilitate the studies of the candidates: Narrien's Geometry, which includes practical geometry on the ground, and the tract on proportion and the circle; Scott's Arithmetic and Algebra; Keightley's History of Greece and Rome; Hume's History of England, with Smollett's continuation; Russell's History of Modern Europe, with the continuation to 1832; the Rev H.L.M. Chepmell's Abridgement of the Histories of Greece, Rome and England; Samuel Butler's Sketch of Ancient and Modern Geography; Captain Macauley's Field Fortification; the Eton Latin Grammar; the Valpy or Dophin editions of Caesar, Virgil and Live; Tarver's French Grammar; Demmler's German Grammar.

Appendix 6

Letter to the Prince Consort, Patron of SNMA from the Vice Chairman informing him of the closure of the Academy. 17 July 1858. *The Edinburgh Evening Courant* 28 August 1858

The Directors of the Scottish Naval & Military Academy having found it necessary to break up and discontinue that Establishment, have explained their reasons for doing so in the following letter, addressed to his Royal Highness the Prince Consort, the Patron of the Academy:

> TO HIS ROYAL HIGHNESS THE PRINCE CONSORT,
> &c &c.
> May it please your Royal Highness,
>
> The Directors of the Scottish Naval and Military Academy, having found it necessary to break up the Institution of which your Royal Highness has been so long the Patron, beg respectfully to forward to your Royal Highness a statement of the circumstances which have compelled them to take this step.
>
> The Scottish Naval and Military Academy – the only School of that description in Scotland – was established in Edinburgh, thirty-three years ago, by private subscription, for the purpose of affording to young men intended for the Naval and Military Services that Professional Education and Training, which hitherto could only be obtained by

attendance at the Government Institutions in England, and which necessarily involved a comparatively heavy expense, and separation from their homes and families.

Another object of the Institution was to afford gratuitous Education to the Sons of Officers whose circumstances called for consideration.

Your Royal Highness was graciously pleased to mark your approbation of these objects by handsome contribution to the Funds.

For a long course of years, the Directors had reason to congratulate themselves upon the success of their exertions, and they believe that they have conferred an important boon on Scotland, and on the Public Service.

Without entering on details, they may state the fact, that of the numerous Pupils who have received their Education at the Scottish Naval and Military Academy, upwards of one thousand have obtained Commissions in the Service of her Majesty, and of the East India Company – some of whom have risen to high rank in these Services.

The conduct of the Pupils, as a body, has been such as to reflect credit on the Institution, and the Directors have pride and pleasure in pointing to the long list of those who have acquired honourable distinction in the Crimean Campaign; and, in the war which is now raging in India, honourable mention has been made of many cases of distinguished conduct and individual valour amongst the Pupils of the Academy serving under Sir Colin Campbell.

Under the patronage of your Royal Highness, and the many distinguished persons who have allowed themselves to be connected with the Academy Office-Bearers and Ordinary Directors, the Institution continued to prosper till the introduction of the new system of Competitive Examinations by the Horse Guards, and it was then hoped that the sound and practical course of Education pursued by the Pupils of the Scottish Naval and Military Academy would prove their passport for obtaining the necessary certificate of qualifications for Commissions.

These expectations, however, have been entirely disappointed. The Examinations alluded to have completely ignored all Professional Education, whilst the acquisition of knowledge the slow process inseparable from sound education has been unite superseded by a class of Seminaries, where, the mere exercise of memory, three months of close application will suffice to enable a Pupil to pass the prescribed ordeal.

The Directors of the Institution, under the patronage of your Royal Highness, could not lend themselves course so delusive and superficial, and the consequence has been such a diminution of the number of their Pupils, as has compelled the Directors to resolve to discontinue, at the close of the present Session, the Scottish Naval and Military Academy; and they have considered it to be their duty thus to express to your Royal Highness, as Patron of the Institution, the causes which have led them unwillingly to take this step.

I have the honour to remain, Your Royal Highness' most obedient humble Servant,

R.S. SETON, Lieutenant Colonel, late Madras Artillery, Vice Chairman. Edinburgh Royal Academy Buildings. 17th July 1858.

Endnotes

Chapter 1: John Orr's Early Life and the Peninsular War

1. Holmes, Richard (2000) *Sidetracks: Explorations of a Romantic Biography*. Pantheon Books, New York. p.136.
2. Orr, John. Letter to F. Ferguson WS, 23 August 1841. Family archive.
3. Commission. Family archive.
4. Ibid.
5. Orr. Note written in old age. Family archive.
6. Bell, Major General Sir George (1956) *Soldier's Glory*. Editor Brian Stuart. G. Bell and Sons, Limited, London. p.43.
7. Harding-Edgar, John (2018) *Next to Wellington: General Sir George Murray*. Helion & Company Limited, England. p.39.
8. Thornton, James (1985) *Your Most Obedient Servant: Cook to the Duke of Wellington*. Webb & Bower, Exeter. p.58.
9. Orr. *Peninsular War Diary*. Entries dated 12, 13, 14 September 1813. Family archive.
10. Throughout the book I use *Measuring Worth* for currency conversions. There is a note at the beginning of the book about this decision.
11. Harding-Edgar *Next to Wellington*. p.31.
12. Orr. Note. Family archive.
13. Bell *Soldiers Glory*. p 11.
14. Mackenzie, Lieutenant Donald (2005) *Merely a Memorandum: From Spain to Waterloo in Wellington's Army*. Editor Guy Hutton-Wilson. Librario Press, Moray, Scotland. p.72.
15. Muir, Rory (2105) *Wellington: The Path to Victory 1769–1814*. Yale University Press, Newhaven and London. p.474.

16. Hay, William (2017) *Reminiscences 1808–1815 under Wellington.* Helion & Company Limited, Warwick. p.22.
17. Mackenzie *Merely a Memorandum*, p.75.
18. Schofield, Victoria (2012) *The Highland Furies: The Black Watch 1739–1899*. Quercus, Great Britain. p.302.
19. Muir *Wellington: The Path to Victory 1769–1814*. p.486.
20. Hamilton MD, Alex, surgeon. Letter to the Forces. Edinburgh. 26 April 1825. Family archive.
21. Orr. Copy of letter to Charles Martyn. Agent at Craigs Court, London. 2 May 1825. Family archive.
22. Wellington to Charles Stuart, 32 October 1812. WD, Vol 6. p.141 as noted in Rory Muir *Wellington: The Path to Victory 1769–1814*. p.489.
23. Hay *Reminiscences*. p.57.
24. Mackenzie *Merely a Memorandum*. p.83.
25. Clayton, Anthony (2013) *The British Officer: Leading the Army from 1660 to the present*. Routledge, Oxfordshire. p.79.
26. Esdaile, Charles (2003) *The Peninsular War*. Penguin Books, England. p.444.

Chapter 2: Quatre Bras, Waterloo and After

1. Orr. Note. Family archive.
2. Anton, James (1841) *Retrospect of a Military Life*. W.H. Lizars, Edinburgh. p.165.
3. Ibid., p.169.
4. Ibid., p.180.
5. Gronow, Rees (1862) *Reminiscences*. Smith Elder, London. p.49.
6. Stanhope, Philip Henry (1889) *Notes of Conversations with the Duke of Wellington.*1831–1852. John Murray, London. p.69.
7. Foulkes, Nick (2007) *Dancing into Battle*. Phoenix, London. p.117.
8. Anton *Retrospect of a Military Life*. p.186.
9. Ibid., p.189.
10. Orr. Note. Family archive.
11. Groves, Lieutenant Colonel Percy (1893) *Illustrated Histories of the Scottish Regiment: Book 1 The Black Watch*. W. & A.K. Johnston, Edinburgh. p.13.

12. Anton *Retrospect of a Military Life*. p.201.
13. Schofield *The Highland Furies: The Black Watch 1739–1899*. p.352.
14. Wellington's despatches to Earl of Bathurst. Waterloo. 19 June 1815.
15. Anton *Retrospect of a Military Life*. p.204
16. Fletcher, Ian, Editor (2007) *The Waterloo Campaign 1815: An Eyewitness History*. Folio Society, London. p.91.
17. Barlow, Captain George Ulrich (2018). *A Light Infantryman with Wellington*. Letters edited by Gareth Glover. Helion & Company, Warwick. p.263.
18. Anton *Retrospect of a Military Life*. p.207.
19. Buttery, David (2013) *Waterloo Battlefield Guide*. Pen & Sword, Yorkshire. p.84.
20. Duke of Wellington's despatch to Lord Bathurst.18 June 1815.
21. Cotton, Sergeant Major Edward (1913) *A Voice from Waterloo*. J.H. Briand, Brussels. p.64.
22. Anton *Retrospect of a Military Life*. p.211.
23. Macready, Edward quoted by Tim Clayton (2014) *Waterloo: Four days that changed Europe's Destiny*. Little Brown, London. p.411.
24. Certified copy of the letter from St Denis hospital. Family archive.
25. *The Greenock Advertiser*, 8 December 1879.
26. Crumplin, Michael and Gareth Glover (2019) *Waterloo After the Glory: Hospital Sketches and Reports of the Wounded After the Battle*. Helion & Company, Warwick. p.73.
27. Schofield *The Highland Furies*. p.360.
28. www.britishbattles.com/waterloo/waterloo-june-1815.htm.
29. Wauchope, Major General A.G. (1908) *The Black Watch* William Blackwood & Sons, Edinburgh & London. p.52.
30. Certified copy of the letter from Saint-Denis hospital. Family archive.
31. Anton *Retrospect of a Military Life*. p.248.
32. Chronology of the 42nd Royal Highlanders in family archive.
33. Letter from the committee conducting the Waterloo Subscription. 80 Cornhill, London. 22 April 1816.
34. Hoares's Bank, *Manuscript of the Month*. June 2015.
35. Hayward, John (1938–2019). Note for Spink & Co.
36. Southampton University. *Wellington and the Battle of Waterloo*. Online course 2015.

37. Anonymous owner. Information supplied by Martyn Downer. myfamilysilver.com.
38. TNA. Public Record Office. WO 25/770.
39. Clayton *The British Officer*. p.92.
40. Ibid.
41. Letter from Marquis of Lothian to John Orr. March 1817. Family archive.
42. Orr. Draft letter to the Duke of York. 28 April 1817. Family archive.
43. TNA. Public Record Office. WO 25/770. List of Full and Half Pay. John received 18 July 1822 £33 15s. On 22 October £34 10s. On 5 February 1823 £34 10s and on 7 April £34 2s 6d.
44. This post-nuptial agreement is a large and long document written on parchment, which is now difficult to read. Signed 3 December 1825, Glasgow. General Register of Sassines. National Records of Scotland.
45. Bundles of papers in the family archive.
46. Letter from Greenwood & Co, 8 July 1825. Family archive.
47. Bogle, Margaret Maule. Letter dated 11 June 1826. Gibraltar. Family archive.
48. TNA. Public Record Office. WO 25/770.
49. Bogle, Margaret to Jane Orr. Letter. 21 July 1830. Written in Gibraltar. Family archive.
50. Dalton, Charles FRGS (1904) *The Waterloo Roll Call*. Eyre and Spottiswoode, London. p.160.
51. Commission. Family archive.
52. Letter from Horse Guards to Colonel Macdonald. 16 July 1831. Family archive.

Chapter 3: Becoming Superintendent of the Scottish Naval & Military Academy

1. *Caledonian Mercury*, 28 July 1832.
2. *The Scotsman*, 4 August 1824.
3. *The Scots Magazine*, 1 August 1824. p.216
4. *The Scotsman*, 23 October 1824.
5. *Report of The Ordinary Directors of the Scottish Military and Naval Academy*, containing an essay by Lord Kerr, (Edinburgh: printed by M. Anderson, 1830). Copy in NLS.

6. *Caledonian Mercury*, 23 July 1825.
7. *Rules and Regulations of the Scottish Naval & Military Academy.* 1834. Oliver & Boyd.
8. *The Scotsman*, 24 August 1825.
9. *Caledonian Mercury,* 13 October 1925.
10. Ibid., 12 May 1832.
11. Report of The Ordinary Directors of the Scottish Naval & Military Academy, 1830.
12. Table 1. Appendix 1. Approximate number of students enrolling each year.
13. *Caledonian Mercury*, 28 May 1832. Major Downes. Second Letter.
14. Ibid., 12 May 1831.
15. *The Scotsman*, 8 October 1831.
16. Ibid., 21 March 1832.
17. *Caledonian Mercury*, 12 May 1832.
18. Report of the Ordinary Directors of the Scottish Military & Naval Academy 1830. p.10
19. Ibid., p.8.
20. *The Edinburgh Evening Courant*, 23 November 1829.
21. *Caledonian Mercury*, 28 July 1832.

Chapter 4: How the SNMA was run after John became Superintendent

1. *Blackwood's Magazine. Noctes Ambrosianae.* Vol 1. 1843 Part of one of the famous spoof dialogues between the Ettrick Shepherd (poet James Hogg) and Christopher North. Christopher North was the pseudonym of John Wilson who was a Scottish advocate and Professor of Moral Philosophy at the University of Edinburgh.
2. *Rules and Regulations of the Scottish Naval and Military Academy* (1834). Oliver & Boyd, Edinburgh.
3. *The Gentleman's Magazine* Vol XX. P 540.(1843) William Pickering, John Bowyer Nichols, London. pp.174–175.
4. *United Services Magazine* part II (1843) Henryurn, London. p.639.
5. Orr. Letter to Robert Kerr. 22 July 1843. Family archive.
6. *Caledonian Mercury*, 30 July 1835.

7. *Aberdeen Press & Journal*, August 27 1851.
8. Map showing the position of the Royal Academy Buildings on Lothian Road. Detail from the plan of the City of Edinburgh by W. & A.K. Johnston. Drawn by Alfred Lancefield, 1851. NLS.
9. Drawing of the Royal Academy Buildings in 1863 when it was in use as a Veterinary College run by John Gamgee. The SNMA had left in 1862. Ruth D'Arcy Thompson. *The Remarkable Gamgees*. (The Ramsay Head Press, Edinburgh. 1974).
10. *A Historical Perspective* (1830) Ordnance Gazetteer of Scotland, published by Thomas C. Jack Grange Publishing Works. 1882–1885. Plans attached to the Directors' Report.
11. *Caledonian Mercury*, 27 July 1833.
12. Roland, George (1832) *An Introduction Course of Modern Gymnastic Exercises*. Oliver & Boyd,_Edinburgh.
13. *Caledonian Mercury*, 27 March 1834.
14. *Oxford Dictionary of National Biography*. Vol 3. Edited by H.C.G. Matthew and Brian Harrison (2004) Oxford University Press, Oxford.
15. Yule, Sir Henry and A.C. Burnell (2015). *Hobson-Jobson*. Oxford University Press, New York.
16. Gilmour, Sir David (2018) *The British in India: Three Centuries of Ambition and Experience*. Allen Lane, an imprint of Penguin Books, Great Britain. p.417.
17. Sanghera, Sathnam (2021) *Empireland*. Penguin Random House, Great Britain. p.3.
18. Yule, Sir Henry (1851) *Fortifications for Officers of the Army and Students of Military History*. William Blackwood & Sons, Edinburgh.
19. *The Edinburgh Evening Courant*, 9 September 1851.
20. *Oxford Dictionary of National Biography*. Vol 60 Edited by H.C.G. Matthew and Brian Harrison (2004). Oxford University Press, Oxford. p.976.
21. Ibid. Clements Markham. *Manuscript History of the Royal Geographical Society*. p.461.
22. Panton, Joseph (2018) *Strength in Battle: The Memoirs of Joseph Panton*. Edited by Hugh Anderson. Australian Scholarly Publishing, North Melbourne. p.6.
23. Panton, Joseph, p.8.

Chapter 5: Orr Family Life

1. Panton *Strength in Battle*. p.11.
2. *Caledonian Mercury*, 15 July 1824.
3. These are all small seaside villages in Fife, across the Firth of Forth from Edinburgh.
4. Orr. Letter to Mrs Tomkinson. 28 July 1843. Family archive.
5. Orr. Letter to Colonel Hardy. 2 February 1840. Family archive.
6. Cockburn, Henry (1932) *Some Letters of Lord Cockburn*. Edited by Lord Cockburn. Grant & Murray, Edinburgh. p.67.
7. Warriston Cemetery.
8. Orr. Letter to Mr Wickham. 26 October 1842. Family archive.
9. NLS. OS Town Plan Edinburgh 1853. Sheet 34.
10. *The Funeral in Scots*. Dr. Dauvit Horsbroch. Centre for Scots Leid, Perth. The Scots Language Resource Centre.
11. Orr. Letter to Sir Thomas Whitehead. 28 November 1841. Family archive.
12. Panton *Strength in Battle*. p.6.
13. Ibid., p.12.
14. Grant, James (1883) *Old and New Edinburgh*. Cassell, Peter & Galpin & Company, London, Paris & New York.
15. *Caledonian Mercury*, 27 July 1848.
16. Orr. Letter to Edward Bligh. 7 August 1846. Family archive.
17. John Orr's passport. Family archive.

Chapter 6: Daily Life at the Academy

1. Scottish Naval & Military Academy flyer 1837.
2. Rules & Regulations of the Scottish Naval & Military Academy. p.3.
3. Howie J.C. (Volumes never published. Bound 1890) *Old Edinburgh Characters and Costumes* Vol1. Edinburgh City Archives.
4. Panton *Strength in Battle*. p.9.
5. Orr. Letter to Mrs Blair. 4 August 1843. Family archive.
6. Orr. Letter to Colonel Hardy. 1840. (Letter not dated.) Family archive.
7. Rough, Harold E. Jr. Editor. (2018) *British Army 1815–1914*. Routledge, New York. Introduction. p. iv.

8. Orr. Letter to Mrs Bousfield. 20 August 1842. Family archive.
9. Music list for the prize-giving of July 1847. Family archive.
10. *Caledonian Mercury*, 30 July 1846.
11. Ibid., 4 July 1839.
12. Ibid., 4 July 1844.
13. *The Scotsman*, 19 June 1852.
14. *The Edinburgh Evening Courant*, 19 June 1852.
15. Nenadic. S. (2014) 'Designs in the Nineteenth-century Scottish Fancy Textile Industry'. *Journal of Design History*. Vol 2 pp. 115–131. The University of Edinburgh. Edinburgh Research Explorer.
16. Kinglake, Alexander William (1885–1900) *Oxford Dictionary of National Biography* Vol 40.
17. *Illustrated London News*, 13 July 1861. Charles Nasmyth's Obituary.
18. *Caledonian Mercury*, 24 July 1854.
19. *Edinburgh News and Literary Chronicle*, 3 March 1854.
20. *Biographical Dictionary of Eminent Scotsmen*. Vol 3 (1875) Editor Robert Chambers, Blackie & Son. Glasgow. p.203.
21. *Illustrated London News*, 13 July 1861.

Chapter 7: John's Roll Book

1. Holmes, Richard (2017) *The Long Pursuit*. William Collins, London. p.80.
2. *Caledonian Mercury*, 23 July 1856.
3. *The London Gazette*, 5 May 1857.
4. National Army Museum. The first distribution of the VC by Queen Victoria, Hyde Park 26 June 1857. https://collection.nam.ac.uk/NAM. 1968-06-292-1.
5. Table 3 in Appendix 1.
6. Mount, Sir Ferdinand (2016) *The Tears of the Rajas*. Simon & Schuster UK Ltd, London. p.27.
7. Beames, John (1984) *Memoirs of a Bengal Civilian*. Eland Publishing Limited, London. p.74.
8. P.E. Razzell (1963) 'Social origins of officers in the Indian and British Home Army, 1758–1962', *British Journal of Sociology*, XIV. p.253. As quoted by Sir Hew Strachan in *Wellington's Legacy*, p.110.

9. Strachan, Sir Hew (1984) *Wellington's Legacy: The Reform of the British Army 1830–54*. Manchester University Press, Manchester, p.110.
10. Hood, General Sir Thomas Edward (1906) *A Varied Life*. John Murray, London. p.4.
11. Clayton R. Koppes (1976) 'Captain Maham, General Gordon and the Origins of the Term "Middle East"'. *Middle Eastern Studies*. Vol 12. No. 1 (Jan 1976). p.95.
12. *Oxford Dictionary of National Biography*. 1885–1900. Vol 32. Entry by George Clement Boase.

Chapter 8: Pleasures and Pains of Student Boarders

1. Orr. Letter to Major General Sir Thomas Whitehead. 22 October 1841. Family archive.
2. Orr. Letter to Mrs Bousfield. 20 August 1842. Family archive.
3. Orr. Letter to Mrs Montgomery. Ayr, 4 July 1840. Family archive.
4. Orr. Letter to Mr Godson. 11 August 1841. Family archive.
5. Orr. Letter to James Pedder 20 January 1840. Family archive.
6. Orr. Letter to Sir Thomas Whitehead.27 November 1841. Family archive.
7. Orr. Letter to Reverend W. Watson 21 April 1843. Family archive.
8. Orr. Letter to Reverend W. Watson. 30 April 1842. Family archive.
9. Orr. Letter to Reverend M. Tritton. 9 July 1843. Family archive.
10. Smyth, Brigadier Sir John (1961) *Sandhurst*. Weidenfeld and Nicolson, London. p.59.
11. Orr. Letter to Anthony Wilkinson. 31 March 1847. Family archive.
12. Orr. Letter to Reverend Vansittart. 11 August 1840. Family archive.
13. www.limerick.ie Notice of Captain Vansittart death. 22 May 1902.
14. Orr. Letter to J. Hamilton Rowan. 11 August 1840. Family archive.
15. Orr. Letter to Anthony Wilkinson 31 March 1847. Family archive.
16. Orr. Letter to Edward Bligh. 31 March 1847. Family archive.
17. Orr. Letter to J. Wickham. April 1842. Family archive.
18. Orr. Letter to J. Wickham. 5 June 1842. Family archive.
19. Orr. Letter to J. Wickham. 27 July. 1842. Family archive.
20. Panton *Strength in Battle*. p.15.
21. Ibid., p.23.

22. *Caledonian Mercury*, 27 July 1840.
23. Ibid., 26 July 1847.
24. Orr. Letter to Colonel Hardy. 10 September 1840. Family archive.

Chapter 9: Future Lives of Four of John's Boarders

1. Scurr, Ruth (June 2021) Reviewing *Goya* by James A. Tomlinson. TLS. p.18.
2. Quotations from a series of letters from John Orr to Mrs Tomkinson from 12 August 1841 until 5 August 1843. Family archive.
3. Orr. Letter to Mrs Tomkinson 12 May 1843. Family archive.
4. Orr. Letter to Edward Tomkinson. 28 July 1843. Family archive.
5. Duberly, Fanny. Edited by Christine Kelly (2007) *Mrs Duberly's War: Journal & Letters from the Crimea, 1854–6*, Oxford University Press, Oxford.
6. Ibid., p.23.
7. Ibid., p.24.
8. Ibid., p.47.
9. Photograph. Royal Collection Enterprises.
10. Woodham-Smith, Cecil (1973) *The Reason Why*. Penguin, London. p.252.
11. Stephens, Iain (1977) *Unmade Journey*. Stacey International, London 1977. p.14.
12. *The Times of India*, 2 December 2018.
13. *Business Standard*, 13 December 2018.
14. *Encyclopedia of Nineteenth Century Photography*, Editor John Hannay, New York London: Taylor& Francis (Routledge), 2008. p.1353.
15. Exhibition. Photo London 2018. Somerset House. Exhibited by Bernard Quaritch Ltd. London.
16. DiGiulio, Katherine (1994) *Natural Variations: Photographs of Colonel Stuart-Wortley.* California www.getty.edu. p.8.
17. Ibid.
18. Wilson, William *Los Angeles Times*, 14 May 1994.
19. *Australian Dictionary of National Biography*.
20. Panton *Strength in Battle*. p.9.
21. Ibid., p.25.
22. Ibid., p.28.

Chapter 10: The Directors' and John's Failure to Prevent the Academy's Decline

1. *Caledonian Mercury*, 22 July 1850.
2. Keay, John (2010) *India: A History from the Earliest Civilisations to the Boom of the Twenty-First Century*. Harper Press, London. p.428.
3. Gilmour, Sir David (2018) *The British in India.* Allen Lane, Great Britain. p.274.
4. Ibid., p.253.
5. Bailey, Peter A. (2009) *Researching Ancestors in the East India Company Armies*. Families in British India Society. Athenaeum Press, Great Britain. p.12.
6. Rough *The British Army 1815–1914. British Army in 1850.* Lt. Col. H. Moyse-Bartlett. p.59.
7. Harries-Jenkins, Gwyn (1977) *Army in Victorian Society*. Routledge & Kegan Paul, London. p.122.
8. Strachan, Sir Hew (1985) 'The British Army, 1815–1856'. *Journal of the Society for Army Historical Research*. Vol 63. No.254. (Summer 1985) p.68.
9. Strachan, Sir Hew (1980) 'The early Victorian army and the nineteenth-century revolution in government'. *English Historical Review*, 95. p.799.
10. Macdonald, Sir John. *The Times*, 24 October 1840. As quoted by Sir Hew Strachan (1984) *Wellington's Legacy*. p.111.
11. Memorandum about the Army Examination is in Appendix 5.
12. Royal Military Academy Sandhurst. In 1947 the RMC was renamed the Royal Military Academy Sandhurst when it was amalgamated with the RMA.
13. Tudor Burne, Owen. Hand-written note in the archive at RMC, Sandhurst. 3 May 1855.
14. House of Commons (1855) Report of the Select Committee on Sandhurst Royal Military College. [hereinafter Sandhurst Select Committee. 1855.] Note 1657.
15. Strachan, Sir Hew (1984) *Wellington's Legacy*. Quoting P.P 1854–5, XII, 311, pp. x, 27, 107–115, 172.
16. Sandhurst Select Committee. Notes 520 and 521.
17. Strachan *Wellington's Legacy*. p.130.
18. SNMA Prospectus dated 1843. Family archive.

19. *Caledonian Mercury*, 20 July 1849.
20. *The Scotsman*, 27 October 1849.
21. *Fife Herald*, 4 April 1850.
22. House of Commons' Select Committee Report Sandhurst. para 153. p.28.
23. Arkley, Patrick. Secretary of the Edinburgh Academy. *Public Exhibition Day. Prize List*. 28 July 1847.
24. *Caledonian Mercury*, 30 July 1846.
25. Ibid., 26 July 1847.
26. Ibid., 23 July 1849.
27. *The Witness*, 10 July 1858.
28. The Prince Consort, Prince Albert, was Patron to the SNMA.

Chapter 11: The Scottish Institute and John's Retirement

1. *The Scotsman*, 8 September 1858. Notice published by The Scottish Institute.
2. *Inverness Courier*, 9 September 1858.
3. Smyth *Sandhurst*. p.75.
4. *The Scotsman*, 25 July 1860.
5. *Daily Review*, 23 July 1863.
6. *The Edinburgh Evening Courant*, 23 July 1864.
7. *Caledonian Mercury*, 5 October 1865.
8. Grant, James (1883) *Old & New Edinburgh*. Vol II. Cassell & Company Limited, London, Paris, New York & Melbourne. p.138.

Chapter 12: John's Old Age and Death

1. *Greenock Advertiser*, 8 December 1879. Obituary of John Orr.
2. Duvall, E. and N.E. Duvall (2013) 'The first medical students in Edinburgh'. Article. Not published.
3. University of Edinburgh matriculation record. Supplied by Professor Roger Jeffery. The term 'The Seven' was initiated by Sophia Jex-Blake the leader of the group of women who were wanting to become doctors.
4. *The Guardian*, 6 July 2019.

5. Orr. Draft or copy of a letter to Right Honourable Secretary of War. 16 May 1874.
6. Colonel Aitchison, Scots Fusilier Guards. (1827–1911) He had not been at the SNMA, but his brother Alexander Allan Aitchison had been a pupil at the Academy in 1848–49 and had died in 1860.
7. List of donations in the family archive.
8. J.A.S. Freeland died of tuberculosis on 3 May 1880 aged 29 when he was aboard his own yacht, *The Gulnare*, in the Bay of Naples. He died a wealthy man, leaving funds in both Scotland and England.
9. *Glasgow Evening Post*, 15 October 1879.
10. Testimonial to Captain John Orr. Family archive.
11. Veitch, William Undertaker 13 Shandwick Place. 21 January 1880.
12. Smith, Michael. (2009) 'The Church of Scotland and the Funeral Industry in Nineteenth-century Edinburgh'. *The Scottish Historical Review* Vol 88. No. 225, Part 1. pp.108–133.
13. Veitch, William Undertaker.
14. *Greenock Telegraph and Clyde Shipping Gazette*, 8 December 1879.

In Retrospect

1. Holmes, Richard. British Council website. https://literature.britishcouncil.org/writer.richards-holmes.

Bibliography

Primary sources

Allan, Stuart and Allan Carswell (2004) *The Thin Red Line. War, Empire and Visions of Scotland*. National Museums of Scotland. Edinburgh.

Anonymous, An Experienced Officer. (1849) *Complete Guide to the Junior and Senior Departments of the Royal Military College, Sandhurst.* C. H. Law. London.

Anton, James. *Retrospect of a Military Life*. (1991) Ken Trotman Limited, Cambridge.

Barlow, Captain George Ulrich (2018) *A Light Infantryman with Wellington*. Letters. Edited by Gareth Glover. Helion & Company. Warwick.

Beames, John (2003) *Memories of a Bengal Civilian*. Eland Publishing Limited. London.

Bruce, Anthony (1980) *The Purchase System in the British Army 1660–1871*. Royal Historical Society. London.

Buttery, David (2015) *Waterloo Battlefield Guide*. Pen & Sword Books. Yorkshire.

Chambers, Robert (1875) *Biographical Dictionary of Eminent Scotsmen*. Vol 3 Chambers.

Clayton, Anthony (2007) *The British Officer: Leading the Army from 1660 to the present*. Pearson Education Limited. United Kingdom.

Clayton, Tim (2014) *Waterloo: Four days that Changed Europe's Destiny.* Little Brown. London.

Cockburn, Lord Henry (1932) *Some Letters of Lord Cockburn*. Edited by Lord Cockburn. Grant & Murray. Edinburgh.

Cooke, Lieutenant John (2000) *A True Soldier Gentleman: The Memoirs of Lieutenant John Cooke*. Editor Eileen Hathway. Shinglepicker Publications. Dorset.

Cotton, Sergeant Major Edward (1913) *A Voice from Waterloo*. Kiessling & Co. Brussels.

Crane, David (2016) *Witnessing Waterloo*. William Collins. London.

Crumplin, Michael and Gareth Glover (2019) *Waterloo After the Glory: Hospital Sketches and Reports of the Wounded after the Battle*. Helion & Company. England.

Dalton, Charles FRGS (1904) *The Waterloo Roll Call*. Eyre and Spottiswoode, London.

Esdaile, Charles (2003) *The Peninsular War*. Penguin Books. London.

Fletcher, Ian. Editor (2007) *The Waterloo Campaign 1815*. The Folio Society. London.

Foulkes, Nick (2007) *Dancing into Battle*. Phoenix. London.

Gilmour, Sir David (2018) *The British in India: Three Centuries of Ambition and Experience*. Allen Lane. UK.

Grange, Thomas Jack (1882–1883) *A Historical Perspective: Ordnance Gazetteer of Scotland.* Publishing Works.

Grant, James (1880) *Old and New Edinburgh* Vol II. Cassell, Peter, Galpin & Co. London, Paris, New York & Melbourne.

Gronow, Rees Howell (1862) *Reminiscences of Captain Gronow.* Smith Elder and Company. London.

Gordon, Thomas Edward (2018) *A Varied Life.* Forgotten Books. London

Groves, Lieutenant Colonel Percy (1893) *Illustrated Histories of the Scottish Regiments Book 1. The Black Watch (Royal Highlanders)*. W. & A. K. Johnston. Edinburgh and London.

Harding-Edgar, John (2018) *Next to Wellington: General Sir George Murray*. Helion & Co. Ltd England.

Hay, William (2017) *Reminiscences 1808–1815 under Wellington: The Peninsular and Waterloo. Memoirs of William Hay*. Helion & Co. Ltd. England.

Holmes, Richard (2016) *This Long Pursuit*. William Collins. London.

— (2000) *Sidetracks: Explorations of a Romantic Biographer*. Pantheon Books. New York.

Hood, General Sir Thomas Edward (1906) *A Varied Life*. John Murray. London.

Jeffery, Roger. Editor (2019) *India in Edinburgh: 1750s to the Present.* Social Science Press. India.

Keay, John (2010) *India: A History*. Harper Press. London.

Kelly, Christine, Editor (2008) *Mrs Duberly's War: Journal & Letters from the Crimea, 1854–6*. Oxford University Press. Oxford.

Kincaid, Captain Sir John (2014) *Tales from the Rifle Brigade*. Pen & Sword. Yorkshire.

Lynch, Michael (1991) *Scotland: A New History*. Century. London.

Mackenzie, Lieutenant Duncan. *Merely a Memorandum: From Spain to Waterloo in Wellington's Army*. Compiled and edited by Guy Hutton-Wilson (2005) Librario Publishing Ltd. Moray, Scotland.

Mount, Sir Ferdinand (2016) *The Tears of the Rajas*. Simon & Schuster. Great Britain.

Moyse-Bartlett, H. (1874) *The British Army in 1850*. Journal of the Society for Army Historical Research. Vol 52.

Muir, Rory (2015) *The Path to Victory 1769–1814*. Yale University Press. Newhaven and London.

Panton, Joseph, *Strength in Battle: The Memoirs of Joseph Panton* (2018) Edited by Hugh Anderson. Australian Scholarly Publishing. North Melbourne.

Roland, George (1832) *An Introduction Course of Modern Gymnastic Exercises*. Oliver & Boyd. Edinburgh.

Rough, Harold E. Jr. Editor (2018) *The British Army 1815–1914*. Routledge. Abingdon, Oxfordshire & New York.

Sanghera, Sathnam (2021) *Empireland*. Penguin Random House, UK.

Schofield, Victoria (2012) *The Highland Furies: The Black Watch 1739–1899*. Vol I. Quercus. London.

Smyth, Brigadier Sir John (1961) *Sandhurst*. Weidenfeld & Nicolson. London.

Stanhope, Peter Henry (1889) *Notes on Conversations with the Duke of Wellington 1831–1852*. John Murray. London.

Stephens, Iain (1977) *Unmade Journey*. Stacey International. London.

Strachan, Sir Hew (1984) *Wellington's Legacy: The Reform of the British Army 1830–54*. Manchester University Press. Manchester.

Thompson, Ruth D'Arcy (1974) *The Remarkable Gamgees*. Ramsay Head Press. Edinburgh.

Thornton, James (1985) *Your Most Obedient Servant: Cook to the Duke of Wellington*. Webb & Bower. Exeter.

Wauchope, Major General A.G. (1908) *The Black Watch*. William Blackwood & Sons. Edinburgh & London.

Woodham-Smith, Cecil (1973) *The Reason Why*. Penguin. England.

Yule, Amy Francis (1903) *A Memoir of Colonel Sir Henry Yule*. John Murray. London.

Yule, Sir Henry and A.C. Burnell (2013) *Hobson-Jobson. The Definitive Glossary of British India*. Oxford University Press. Oxford.

Secondary sources

Baxter, Ian A. (2009) *Baxter's Guide. Biographical sources in the India Office Records*. Families in British India Society in association with The British Library. 3rd edition.

Bell, Sir George (1956) *Soldier's Glory*. Editor Brian Stuart. G. Bell & Sons, Limited. London.

Cosh, Mary (2003) *Edinburgh in the Golden Age*. John Donald Publishers, Edinburgh.

Dalrymple, William. *Return of the King: The Battle for Afghanistan* (2014) Bloomsbury Publishing. London.

Devine, T.M. and **McCarthy,** Angela (2017) Editors. *The Scottish Experience in Asia, c. 1700 to the Present.* Palgrave Macmillan. Switzerland.

Dudgeon, R.C. (1872) *History of the Edinburgh, or Queen's Regiment Light Infantry Militia*. William Blackwood and Sons. Edinburgh.

Fletcher, Ian. Editor (2007) *The Peninsular War 1812–1814: An Eyewitness History* (2007) Folio Society. London.

Fry, Michael (2009) *A History of Edinburgh*. Macmillan. London.

Holmes, Richard (2003) *Wellington. The Iron Duke*. Harper Collins. London.

— (2002) *Redcoat: The British Soldier in the Age of Horse and Musket*. Harper Collins. London.

— (2006) *Sahib: The British Soldier in India.* Harper Perennial. London.

— (2011) *Soldiers: Army Lives and Loyalties from Recoats to Dusty Warriors.* Harper Press. London

Kay, John (1838) *Kay's Original Portraits and Caricature Etchings.* Vol 2. Part. 2 (1842) Adam and Charles Black. Edinburgh.

Knowles, Lieutenant Robert. (2004) *The War in the Peninsular: Some letters of a Lancashire Officer*. Spellmount Limited. Kent.

McGowan, Dr John (2013) *A New Civic Order: The Contribution of the City of Edinburgh Police 1805–1812*. Turlough Publishers. Edinburgh.

Mahon, Lieutenant Colonel the Honourable William (2017) *Waterloo Messenger: Life of Henry Percy*. Pen & Sword. Yorkshire.

Mitchell, Ann (1998) *No More Corncrakes*. Scottish Cultural Press.

Murgatroyd, Sarah (2002) *The Dig Tree*. Text Publishing. Melbourne 2002.

Oman, Sir Charles (2005) *A History of the Peninsular War. Vol 5: October 1811 to August 1812*. Greenhill Books. London.

Otley, C.B. (1973) *The Educational Background of British Army Officers. Sociology*. Vol 7.

Parker, John. *The Black Watch* (2006) Headline Book Publishing. London.

Mockler-Ferryman, Major A.F. (1900) *Annals of Sandhurst*. William Heinemann. London.

Reid, Stuart (2010) *Wellington's Highland Warriors*. Frontline Books. Yorkshire.

Robinson, Andrew (2019) *India: A Short History*. Thames & Hudson Limited. London.

Royle, Trevor (2010) *Crimea: The Great Crimean War 1854–1856*. Abacus. London.

Simpson, James. (1816) *Visit to Flanders*. William Blackwood. Edinburgh.

Snow, Peter (2010) *To War with Wellington*. John Murray. London.

Snow, Peter and Snow, Dan (2017) *The Battle of Waterloo*. National Army Museum. London.

Speirs, Edward M., Jeremy A. Craig; Matthew J. Strickland, Editors. (2014) *A Military History of Scotland*. Edinburgh University Press. Edinburgh.

Stanhope, Lieutenant Colonel The Honourable James (2010) *Eyewitness to the Peninsular War and the Battle of Waterloo*. Pen & Sword. Yorkshire.

Thomas, Hugh (1961) *The Story of Sandhurst*. Hutchinson. London.

Thompson, Mark S. (2020) *Wellington's Favourite Engineer: John Fox Burgoyne.* Helion & Co. Ltd. England.

Urban, Mark (2004) *Rifles: Six Years with Wellington's Legendary Sharpshooters*. Faber & Faber. London.

Youngson, A.J. (1966) *The Making of Classical Edinburgh*. Edinburgh University Press. Edinburgh.

Index